# 'BYSTANDERS' TO THE HOLOCAUST

# Books of Related Interest

# 'BYSTANDERS'
## to the
# HOLOCAUST:
## A Re-evaluation

*Editors*

## DAVID CESARANI
## PAUL A. LEVINE

**FRANK CASS**
LONDON • PORTLAND, OR

First published in 2002 in Great Britain by
FRANK CASS PUBLISHERS
Crown House, 47 Chase Side, Southgate, London N14 5BP, England

and in the United States of America by
FRANK CASS PUBLISHERS
c/o ISBS, 5824 N.E. Hassalo Street
Portland, Oregon 97213-3644

Website: www.frankcass.com

British Library Cataloguing in Publication Data

'Bystanders' to the Holocaust : a re-evaluation
1. Holocaust, Jewish (1939-1945) – Foreign public opinion, American
2. Holocaust, Jewish (1939–1945) – Foreign public opinion, British
3. Holocaust, Jewish (1939–1945) – Foreign public opinion, Swiss
4. Holocaust, Jewish (1939–1945) – Foreign public opinion, Swedish
5. Holocaust, Jewish (1939-1945) – Government policy – United States
6. Holocaust, Jewish (1939-1945) – Government Policy – Great Britain
7. Holocaust, Jewish (1939-1945) – Government policy – Switzerland
8. Holocaust, Jewish (1939-1945) – Government Policy – Sweden
I.Cesarani, David II.Levine, Paul A.
940.5'318

ISBN 0 7146 5270 9 (cloth)
ISBN 0 7146 8243 8 (paper)

Library of Congress Cataloging-in-Publication Data:

Bystanders to the Holocaust : a re-evaluation / edited by David Cesarani,
Paul A. Levine.
p. cm.
Includes index.
ISBN 0-7146-5270-9 — ISBN 0-7146-8243-8 (pbk.)
1. Holocaust, Jewish (1939–1945)—Moral and ethical aspects. 2.
Holocaust, Jewish (1939-1945)—Social aspects. 3. Holocaust, Jewish
(1939–1945) – Historiography. 4. World War,
1939-1945 – Collaborationists. 5. World War, 1939-1945 – Jews – Rescue.
I. Cesarani, David. II. Levine, Paul A.
D804.3 .B95 2001
940.53'18—dc21

2001006178

This group of studies first appeared in
'"Bystanders" to the Holocaust: A Re-evaluation'
a special issue of The Journal of Holocaust Education, Vol.9, Nos.2 and 3
(Autumn/Winter 2000) published by Frank Cass and Co. Ltd.

Printed in Great Britain by Antony Rowe Ltd., Chippenham, Wiltshire

# Contents

# List of Illustrations

# Acknowledgements

The editors would like to thank Mia Löwengart, Programme Coordinator at the Programme for Holocaust and Genocide Studies at the University of Uppsala, for her essential contribution to the colloquium on 'bystanders' and this publication, and Dr Jo Reilly, Parkes Centre for the Study of Jewish/non-Jewish Relations, University of Southampton, and co-editor of the *Journal of Holocaust Education*. The Institute for Contemporary History, London, supported the colloquium at an early stage. The following took part in the colloquium and the editors wish to acknowledge their stimulating input: Professor Kristian Gerner, Professor Dalia Ofer, Dr Gulie Ne'eman Arad, Stéphane Bruchfeld, and Kjell Grede, who presented his extraordinary film *Good Evening, Mr Wallenberg*. Professor Harald Runblom, Director of the Centre for Multiethnic Research and the Uppsala Programme for Holocaust and Genocide Studies, participated in the colloquium and his continuing support for the 'bystanders' project and wise counsel have been invaluable. Graham Hart, our editor at Frank Cass Publishers, shepherded the volume into production and offered much helpful advice. Frank Cass himself takes a personal interest in the publications which bear his name, many of which would never see the light of day without his commitment to education about the Holocaust.

# Introduction

## DAVID CESARANI and
## PAUL A. LEVINE

### I

Despite the commencement of a new millennium and predictions, even aspirations, that the bloody history of the twentieth century would be laid to rest at the stroke of midnight on 31 December 1999, there has been no let up in the volume of scholarship, popular history, novels, films, drama, poetry, artwork, museums, memorials – or controversies centring on the persecution and mass murder of the Jews between 1933 and 1945, universally known as the Holocaust.[1] One strand in this proliferation has concerned the behaviour of the so-called 'bystanders'. But who were they? According to Deborah Lipstadt 'those we have always viewed as bystanders to the Holocaust' include 'neutral governments and agencies, Jews living in relative safety, occupied countries, ordinary Germans, and above all, the Allied governments'.[2]

These two distinct groups were not always considered in the same breath. For a long while, the attitudes and actions of the German people and those under German domination during the war years were treated separately from the conduct of the democracies in the 1930s, or the responses of the neutral states and the Allies in the 1940s. The behaviour of the latter group was commonly subsumed under such headings as 'allied responses' or 'attempts at rescue'. The term 'bystanders' was not commonly used. However, in an influential historiographical study published in 1987, Michael Marrus gathered a discussion of the responses of the Allies, the neutral powers, the Vatican, and the Jews of the 'free world' under the title 'Bystanders'. In a book published five years later, Raul Hilberg used 'Bystanders' to label a series of chapters covering the nations in Hitler's Europe, 'Helpers, Gainers, and Onlookers', those who sought to alert the world to the fate of the Jews, Jewish rescuers, the Allies, neutral countries, and the churches. Hilberg's book, entitled *Perpetrators, Victims, Bystanders*, reflected (and to some extent anticipated) the impact of new research that was changing the perspective on all these subjects, and eroding the distinctions between them. Almost without it being noticed he decisively established a previously diverse subject matter in one of three monolithic blocs.[3] By the end of the decade Lipstadt articulated the received wisdom that these groups had 'always' been viewed as 'bystanders'.

The erosion of pre-existing conceptual partitions was accelerated by the flood of revelations about the depth of economic collusion between the neutrals and the Nazi war machine, their readiness to profit from genocide, and the extent of Allied knowledge of the mass murder of the Jews as compared to the paucity of their response. Lipstadt notes that 'Many of these bystanders have spent fifty years protesting their innocence. But historians have repeatedly demonstrated – and the recent stories reaffirm – that they were not innocent and virtually no one, including the American public, was ignorant.'[4] However, the unprecedented clustering of the United States and Britain in the company of Nazi collaborators or the populations of occupied Europe did not go unnoticed or unchallenged. At the close of the 1990s a substantial 'backlash' developed that challenged the historical basis for such conclusions and proposed that political motives were responsible for casting the Allies as little better than accomplices of the Nazis.[5] Such exchanges have polarised rather than clarified the terms of debate and done little to advance historical understanding.

This volume grew out of an international colloquium convened in Uppsala, Sweden in September 1999 expressly to discuss the current state of 'bystander' historiography. The 'Uppsala Colloquium on the Bystander in Holocaust History' was organised by the recently formed Uppsala Programme for Holocaust and Genocide Studies in cooperation with the Parkes Centre for the Study of Jewish/non-Jewish Relations at the University of

Southampton. The establishment of a Programme for Holocaust and Genocide Studies at the University of Uppsala, where the colloquium took place, was itself an expression of the new-found interest in Sweden for scholarly inquiry into the role which that country played during the Holocaust. Though it was recognised that the 'bystander' in Holocaust history comprises a broad spectrum of historical actors, the colloquium chose to concentrate on the response of nations or other political entities (i.e. the Yishuv – the Jewish community of Palestine) which because of their democratic character might have been expected to respond to the genocide differently from nations or agencies without a participatory and representative political framework. The colloquium thus set the stage for a necessary re-evaluation of the liberal, democratic 'bystander' in Holocaust history.

Much has been written on the relations between Germans and Jews in the Third Reich, how Hitler's collaborator-states behaved towards the Jews, and how the peoples and institutions of Nazi-occupied Europe responded to the discrimination, despoliation, deportation, and mass murder visited on their Jewish populations, but this book will not add to that vast literature. Rather, one of its objectives is to restore the distinction between radically different kinds of 'bystander' and to show that an analysis of the indifference or empathy displayed towards the Jews in areas under Nazi control or influence has little bearing on what happened in the democratic countries that were neutral or at war with Germany. Another intention of the contributors is to restore nuance to our appreciation of how governments, agencies, and individuals reacted to the Nazi assault on the Jews. The essays presented here insist on contextualising attitudes and practical steps, restoring (for better or worse in terms of how historical actors behaved) the element of informed choice to political leaders, civil servants, non-governmental agencies, and members of the public. They were not marionettes of some historical force that destined them to be 'bystanders', but human beings acting alone or in concert, and making fateful decisions of their own volition.

No discussion of the 'bystander' phenomenon can ignore its contemporaneity: the growth of interest in the subject is as much about the present as it is about the past. It results from the implication of former Allied and neutral states in aspects of the Final Solution and its aftermath, and the discovery that this past complicity has practical, contemporary ramifications. Moreover, the reckoning with erstwhile evils has become irretrievably intertwined with perceptions of how to handle current ones. The response of the democracies and the neutral states between 1933 and 1945 to the crisis of the Jews has an acute, even painful immediacy. Here we confront the role of politicians, civil servants, the media, opinion makers, and a variety of politically active groups in a constellation that is similar to the one we inhabit today. It seems that the world's response to the persecution and murder of the Jews may be a working through of anxieties about how democracies and the various individuals and groups that constitute them respond to the continuing abuse of human rights, ethnic cleansing, and genocide. If this is true, then it is clearly necessary to develop a more nuanced, historicised understanding of rescue activities, or the lack of them, in the 1930s and 1940s.

## II

It is worth recalling that in the first two decades after the war the question of how 'bystander' groups responded to the Nazi persecution of the Jews was hardly an issue. For the most part, victory temporarily erased the memory of bitter wartime disputes. Within certain government circles in the USA and amongst some campaigners in Britain during the war there had been fury over Allied reactions to information about the maltreatment and mass murder of European Jews. The terms and tone of the post-war debate were prefigured in late 1943, when some officials in the Treasury Department of the US government, outraged at the way officials in the State Department had consistently thwarted any effort by the USA to help the Jews, produced a report entitled 'Report to the Secretary on the Acquiescence of This Government in the Murder of the Jews'. The shocking contents of the report led to the establishment of the only government agency tasked to help

Jews in wartime Europe, the US 'War Refugee Board'.[6] But many years would pass before the implications of wartime action or inaction regarding the Jews would be held up to public scrutiny.

As several authors in this collection note, the Allies and the neutral powers in Europe felt that they had good reason for being satisfied with their conduct in the face of Nazi barbarism. The British and the Americans had expended much blood and treasure to defeat Nazism: as a result of this hard-won victory the remnant of Europe's Jews were saved and, as they saw it, this called for self-congratulation rather than self-reproach. A similar mood of contentment was evident in the democratic neutral states. According to the official narrative propounded by the political, military, and economic elites in Switzerland and Sweden, these countries had preserved their neutrality and territorial integrity despite considerable pressure, fended off the threat of German invasion, and within feasible limits succoured the victims of Nazi persecution and the ravages of war. These potent and deeply entrenched narratives went largely unchallenged. On the other hand, many Jews, including former refugees, survivors, and those lucky ones who were citizens of countries that had avoided Hitler's grasp, had a less rosy view and memory of events. But amidst the general triumphalism their interpretation was unappealing, unwanted and unheeded. In any case, Jewish communities around the world were so shattered by the genocide and preoccupied with rebuilding Jewish life that they could barely see beyond present needs. The virtuous record of the Allies and the neutrals only began to face challenges in the 1960s.[7]

The trial of Adolf Eichmann in Jerusalem in 1961 for the first time presented the Jewish narrative of the Nazi years uncluttered by other issues and focused on the origins, implementation, and victims' experience of the 'Final Solution'. Eichmann's role in organising the forced emigration of Jews from Austria and Germany in 1938–9 drew attention to the refugee policies of other countries, while amongst the mass of documentary evidence and testimony there were examples of how, during the genocide, desperate and largely unanswered pleas for help reached the free world. Eichmann himself expatiated on contacts which the Nazis, offering Jews in return for ransom and political advantage, had initiated with representatives of the Allies and neutral powers. This apparently 'new' information piqued the interest of American and British journalists who were intrigued by the role of their governments. Subsequently, Hannah Arendt's book on the trial raised the question of how the Jewish leadership had reacted to the Nazi menace and Rolf Hochhut's play *The Representative* pointed an accusing finger at the Vatican.[8] Arthur Morse's impassioned book *While Six Million Died: A Chronicle of American Apathy*, based on a series of newspaper articles, inaugurated the inquest on the policy of the US government and indirectly triggered parallel inquiries into the conduct of American Jews. When archives holding the relevant documents for refugee and immigration matters in the 1930s were opened to scrutiny in Britain in the 1970s, the same process began there – albeit in a lower key.[9]

By the late 1980s, the main arguments about Allied conduct had assumed a settled form. A. J. Sherman, Henry Feingold, David Wyman, Alan Kraut and Richard Breitman had subjected the refugee policies of Britain and America in the 1930s to scrutiny based on access to the relevant government records and had drawn up a 'balance sheet' of achievements and failures. In a key part of these studies the historians tried to assess how far immigration and refugee policy (inasmuch as it existed) had been determined by anti-Jewish attitudes amongst officials and politicians. They asked whether prejudice distorted their assessment of events in Germany as compared to the context of international relations at the time, notably the pursuit of appeasement. They also factored into the decision-making process the effects of domestic issues such as unemployment, popular antisemitism or pro-refugee feeling, and pressure from right-wing pro-Nazi movements.[10]

In a series of influential studies based on new documentary sources, Walter Laqueur, Martin Gilbert, David Wyman, and Bernard Wasserstein led the way in exploring and revealing how much the Allies knew about the mass murder of the Jews, when this information became available to them, and how they reacted. These scholars paid particular attention to the individual and collective formulation of policy towards Jews seeking to escape from Nazi and Axis-ruled Europe, the question of whether Auschwitz-Birkenau could have been bombed, the creation of governmental relief agencies (notably the US War Refugees Board), and the response to specific offers by Nazi and Axis leaders to ransom or release Jews.[11] Meanwhile, Israeli historians produced the first in-depth and archive-based studies on the response of the Jewish community in Palestine. American Jewry, in particular, was subjected to a searching assessment, with largely scathing results. The fruits of this research were often shocking both to society at large and the vested interests on either side of the debate. Surviving historical actors or their self-appointed champions responded vigorously to what they saw as conclusions that either vindicated or threatened their reputations: each new study provoked newspaper discussion and often stimulated television documentaries which further popularised the issues.[12]

Wyman's argument about the role of Franklin D. Roosevelt, Gilbert's verdict on the bombing of Auschwitz, and claims about the Jewish leadership in the USA and Palestine occasioned particular dispute that rumbled on in popular histories, learned books and journal articles into the 1990s.[13] However, as Tony Kushner notes in his contribution to this volume, the exchanges became increasingly polarised and sterile. The titles of two opposed interpretations help to tell the story: Monty Penkower, *The Jews Were Expendable: Free World Diplomacy and the Holocaust* (1988) versus William D Rubinstein, *The Myth of Rescue: Why the democracies could not have saved more Jews from the Nazis* (1997).

In one camp were those like Penkower who attributed Allied policy to an unpleasant blend of antisemitism and expediency; in the other, as represented by Rubinstein, were those who saw nothing for which the Allies should repine. In his contribution to this book, Tony Kushner observes of this polarisation that, 'Given the centrality of the Holocaust in contemporary philosophical and theoretical debates about the nature of humankind in the modern age and beyond, this is a dangerous if understandable development.

For rather than nuancing our understanding of the complexity of human responses during the Holocaust, the bystander category is in danger of aiding the tendency to see the subject in Manichean terms, as a symbol of mass evil alongside much less prevalent absolute good (with the emphasis put on the latter to enable hope for the future).' One indication of how widely this dichotomy has become diffused is the teaching pack produced by the Imperial War Museum, London, for use with secondary school groups, drawing on its Holocaust Exhibition. The relevant section is entitled: 'The Allies: liberators or bystanders?'[14]

Clearly, this is not just another ivory tower debate. For understandable reasons both versions play to present-day needs in society and politics. In the first case, the demonisation of Allied leaders and publics serves to distance us from their negative beliefs and actions (or inaction) while, in the second, we are encouraged to sink into the complacent certainty that no more could have been done to help the Jews than was the case. In either instance, we are not encouraged to apply the lessons of the past to what governments and publics think and do about refugees, asylum seekers, and cases of genocide or the mass abuse of human rights in other countries today. Either we have nothing to learn from the past because the historical actors were so nefarious that we cannot possibly be like them; or they were so decent we need only follow their example – and do very little because no more can be done. In view of the central place which the Nazi era occupies in modern culture and its role as a point of reference for so much political and moral debate, not to mention the associated controversies about 'bystanders', it is more important than ever to return to the concept with a new and critical eye.

## III

As we have seen, in the mid 1990s the role ascribed to the 'bystanders' was largely confined to action or inaction when confronted by the destruction of the Jewish population in occupied Europe and the response of governments and the public in the Allied and neutral states. Bystanders in the Nazi zone were divided into rescuers and those who were indifferent to the fate of the Jews or malevolently inclined towards them. Donald Niewyk and Francis Nicosia, co-editors of *The Columbia Guide to the Holocaust*, summarise the dichotomy as follows: 'Bystanders, Europeans who witnessed the persecution of Jews, Gypsies, and the handicapped found themselves willy-nilly before a choice: they could act by helping to rescue the victims or by joining in persecuting them, or they could do nothing.'[15] Those outside were likewise differentiated between rescue activists and the rest. Debate was polarised between those who argued that rescue was possible, who accordingly held governments and leaders responsible for sins of omission, and those who did not.[16] The eruption of the 'Nazi gold' issue from 1995 to 1999 suddenly and dramatically altered the basis of this compartmentalisation.

The transformation began with the hearings of the US Senate Banking Committee, presided over by Senator Alfonse d'Amato in 1996–97, which publicised the accusations made against Swiss banks by Holocaust survivors. D'Amato provided an unprecedented platform for frail and elderly Jews whose murdered relatives had made deposits in these institutions prior to the war but whose heirs were prevented from retrieving the assets due to the duplicity or insensitivity of the banks when adjudicating claims. In 1997, investigators pursuing the Swiss hit upon a new line of attack when they realised that the Third Reich had sold to the Swiss national bank and commercial banks gold looted from the treasuries of conquered states and from the Jews. This was not news to historians, but there was global indignation that Switzerland had profited from the Nazi trade in plundered gold and astonishment when it was learned that international efforts to restitute the gold that had begun in 1945 were still continuing.[17]

Thanks to the inherent nature of the issue and the effect of media globalisation, the revelations about the Swiss banks and the Nazi gold trade became the subject of worldwide comment. The current stance of Swiss bankers on the subject of 'dormant accounts' as well as the fate of the surviving 'Nazi gold' was the focus of intense international lobbying and rapidly climbed the political agenda in dozens of countries. In response to the pressure of world opinion an international conference embracing 40 states and major international agencies was held in London in December 1998 to clarify the situation and resolve what should be done with the remaining Nazi-era bullion still held by the authorities who had taken charge of it five decades earlier. Within a short time the net of complicity in the Nazi gold trade had widened to take in Sweden, Portugal, and Turkey. The obverse of the sale of gold to these countries was the purchase from them of raw materials and commodities necessary for the German war effort. Suddenly, the previous stance of the neutral countries did not look so neutral or morally correct. A flood of official reports drawing on declassified intelligence data showed that despite pleas and pressure from the Allies, they had helped to launder stolen gold, some of it originating from murdered Jews, and supplied the wherewithal to enable Germany to continue its war effort.[18]

The revelations about 'Nazi gold' led to consideration of the Nazis' economic war against the Jews and the systematic despoliation of a huge range of assets including mortgages, debts owed to Jews, insurance policies, bank accounts, equities, property, businesses, partnerships, cash, precious metals and diamonds, and art works. This vast plunder, on a scale barely understood before the 1990s, was documented and described in a series of reports, articles, and books that flowed from the word processors of government archivists, investigators and historians acting on behalf of class actions in US courts and official inquiries, independent scholars, and journalists.[19]

What seemed most shocking was the ethos of 'business as normal' that prevailed in Nazi-occupied countries and in the neutral states. The Nazis would not have been able to capitalise on these purloined assets unless there existed an internal market for stolen goods in occupied Europe. Their plundering of Jewish-owned businesses and property in the Reich and in occupied countries, euphemistically dubbed 'aryanisation', involved surveying and registering an array of enterprises and then expropriating them for direct exploitation by Germans or selling them off to local people. The dispossession of the Jews, like mass murder, required extensive local collaboration. This practice, as much as participation in genocide, helped cement the Germans with their associates. It distributed culpability much more widely than previously thought and transformed the notion of the 'bystander' within the Nazi domains.[20]

The Nazis' asset stripping and looting activity also required a vast laundering operation abroad. As investigation after investigation showed how this function was performed by the neutral states, their status as 'bystanders' was increasingly called into question. Research showed that they were no longer responsible merely for 'sins of omission'; they were guilty of 'sins of commission', too – in the very literal sense of taking a considerable profit from exchanging gold, currency, and commodities with the Third Reich.[21] Finally, investigators discovered that banks in Britain, the USA, and British-run Palestine were not above quietly appropriating the assets of Jewish refugees or less fortunate depositors who perished at the hands of the Nazis. Their actions and their reluctance to restitute frozen or confiscated assets to claimants after the war drew them into the sordid web of those who benefited from persecution and genocide.[22]

Much of the evidence that the neutrals and the Allies had benefited to a greater or lesser degree from the genocide and despoliation of the Jews came from recently declassified intelligence material in the US National Archives and the British Public Records Office.[23] The end of the Cold War and the desensitisation of many historical intelligence issues had facilitated the opening of these previously closed archives, but as the campaign against the Swiss banks and the uproar over 'Nazi gold' gained from access to newly disclosed files, the demand for even more releases gathered momentum. The on-going release of Second World War intelligence material had an unforeseen consequence. Reports by operatives of the American Office of Strategic Services and the decrypts of German signals obtained by British intelligence at the Government Code and Cypher School at Bletchley Park revitalised the debate of the 1970s and 1980s about what and when the Allies knew about the mass murder of the Jews and the whys and wherefores of the decision whether or not to bomb Auschwitz-Birkenau.[24] Following this torrent of revelations, the democracies and the 'free world' were no longer so distanced from the Nazi murder-machine and the question of rescue was suddenly less academic than it had once seemed.[25]

There is another contemporary dimension in which to place the current fascination with the Allies and the neutrals. As Deborah Lipstadt notes, 'Stories about the bystanders are, in some fashion *about* us.' To Lipstadt this means specifically the manner in which American Jews have reread the past in the light of current preoccupations. 'American refugee/rescue policy reminded Jews of both the consequences of powerlessness and why the Jews needed that power now.' The condemnation of the US government of the 1940s and the then Jewish leadership also reflected a generational revolt in the Jewish community. 'Young Jewish activists working on behalf of Soviet Jews proclaimed that they would not repeat their parents' mistakes.'[26] Lipstadt reinforces Peter Novick's contention that the construction of America as a 'bystander' is a relatively recent development actuated as much by social and political trends as by scholarly research.[27]

Parallel forces may have been at work in the wider world. Tony Kushner argues here that 'The moral concern about bystanders comes out of the rather complacent assumption that few of us will become perpetrators, and an equal optimism that we won't become victims, while at the same time we are aware that in an age of almost instant global communications, we are all co-presents witnessing, even if only through the media, the genocides, ethnic cleansing and other manifestations of extreme racism that besmirch the contemporary world.' Kushner is frustrated that given this degree of interest the subject should be treated in such unhelpful, polar terms. Yet he acknowledges that it is precisely the desire to identify that leads to the elision of subtlety: 'Put bluntly, we like our bystanders to be as bifurcated as the categories of victim and perpetrator.' He fears that unless the 'moral ambiguity' of the 'bystanders' is brought to the fore, ordinary people will 'find it hard if not impossible to make connections to the Holocaust other than in fascination at its sheer horror or by taking glib inspiration from the two dimensional representation of its canonised non-Jewish heroes such as Oskar Schindler and Raoul Wallenberg.'[28] Glib inspiration may be preferable to dull apathy in the face of genocide or human-rights abuses, but Kushner is surely correct to warn that the simplification of choices during the Nazi era into good versus evil can demoralise those who are faced with an apparent choice between what is good and unrealistic as against what is mediocre but works; in other words a choice between greater or lesser evils.

The current preoccupation with personal choice and its centrality to individual identity may also have contributed to the interest in 'bystanders' in the Allied and neutral countries. Since the end of the Cold War the majority of the world's population is living in more or less democratic countries in which consumerism reigns and people are constantly invited to make choices. Global popular culture dramatises choice as the expression of individuality, steadily corroding traditional solidarities while the motive to act out of duty or collective loyalty is remorselessly supplanted by the pursuit of pure self-interest.[29] It is hardly surprising then that individual heroic figures who embody both choice and virtue are immensely seductive. Individuals or collectivities acting out of shared religious fervour or class solidarity appear as fanatics or dinosaurs. Resistance fighters and the rescuers of Jews in Nazi Europe retain an allure because their actions highlight ethical decisions on an individual basis, but they are inevitably perceived at one remove from most of us who live in democratic societies.

Those who enjoy conditions of free information, choice, and action identify readily with historical actors who they believe, correctly or otherwise, to have been similarly blessed. This sense of identification with recipients of news about the Nazi genocide has been fuelled by the collapsing together of past and present events. Barbie Zelizer convincingly argues that use of imagery from the Nazi years as a trope for representing contemporary atrocities has blurred perceptions and responses; viewers of contemporary events in the Balkans, Rwanda, or Chechnya were 'seeing' the past and reacting to it as much as they were responding to the present.[30] Since democratic action and information, especially visual information, are so tightly interwoven in postmodern society, there is a powerful tendency to project a similar nexus backwards in time. Because we react to what we see today, we expect those who 'saw' things in the past also to have reacted. To react is to chose, and as choice is described as a key to individual identity, a subject of perennial interest, we may be seeing at work another aspect of the contemporary fascination with 'bystander' history.

# IV

The essays which follow attempt to shed light on a cluster of related issues all of which revolve around the choices that were conceivable and practicable in their historical context. David Cesarani, Tony Kushner, and Paul Levine make the case for a more shaded and contextualised account of those involved in making or challenging policy towards persecuted Jews and Jewish refugees. They take a comparative approach within their essays and their studies stand in relation to one another. Raya Cohen and Meredith Hindley in like manner seek to contextualise the activity of Jewish rescue workers and humanitarian relief agencies, breaking out of the interpretative dichotomy of rescue versus betrayal, humanitarianism versus antisemitism. In all these case studies the temporal and geopolitical framework is crucial: what was known at the time and what could have been done in any particular location? The weight of precedent was just as important to the making of choices as were current perceptions. Sven Nordlund and Karin Kvist show that in the late 1930s and 1940s, Sweden's policy towards aliens was rooted in the attitudes and legislation of the preceding 15 years. But although tainted by racism and antisemitism, it was flexible enough to adapt to changing needs and circumstances. The flexibility of policy makers in Sweden calls into question the notion that neutrality is something rigid. The concept of neutrality is most closely associated with Switzerland and it is here subjected to searching critique by

Jacques Picard. Finally, to remind us of the human dimension of rescue, Sune Persson tells the story of Count Folke Bernadotte, his courageous team of Swedish officers and men, and their mission to bring victims of the concentration camps to safety on the 'White Busses' in the closing months of the war.

David Cesarani argues that previous research into 'rescuers', their motives, and conduct in Nazi Europe offers few clues to understanding what motivated and guided rescue activists in the democracies in the 1930s and 1940s. Would-be rescuers in the free world faced specific (and familiar) obstacles to recognising that there was a humanitarian crisis which their governments were not dealing with adequately. Having exposed the rationalisations for official passivity, these activists had to find ways either to modify the outlook of responsible politicians and officials or take matters into their own hands. They could mount public campaigns to achieve the former, an option that was fanciful in Germany or occupied Europe, but the outcome was uncertain and slow to achieve. Alternatively, they could defy the authority of their legitimate rulers and bring Jews out of Europe by working around the laws governing immigration or, later, send aid to them in defiance of the regulations that forbade economic ties with the enemy.[31] However, if they flouted the law individuals and institutions boasting close relations with the authorities put at risk their hard-won status and access to power. In the summer of 1939, with their resources stretched to breaking point, Anglo-Jewish refugee organisations were so fearful of breaches of the immigration regulations that they preferred a total suspension of emigration rather than risk a chaotic influx of Austrian and German Jews without the proper papers or the means to maintain themselves.[32] It is notable that Nicholas Winton, a rescuer who shredded the red tape in his efforts to get endangered children out of Prague, was not associated with any major communal or relief organisation and therefore had less to lose.

Jewish activists in Switzerland during the war felt similarly constrained. Raya Cohen shows that the beleaguered delegates of the Jewish Agency, the World Jewish Congress, and the Zionist youth movements were painfully aware of the disaster unfolding

across the frontier but lacked the resources to act alone. Their
parent bodies in the distant USA and Palestine, distracted by
domestic issues, did not share their envoys' appreciation of the
crisis and starved them of funds. In any case, under the Allied rules
governing trading with the enemy, the delegates were not
permitted to transmit funds or even foodstuffs into Nazi-occupied
Europe. Alfred Silberschein was actually punished by his
superiors in the Hechalutz organisation for devising ways to send
food and money to Zionist youth in Poland. His comrades could
not understand the pressures he was under and even today,
amongst the few survivors, there remains an acute feeling of
betrayal. This resentment against the official Jewish agencies has
been incorporated into much of the historiography, but Cohen
notes that the 'betrayal' is often mistakenly attributed to the
craven attitude of Jewish leaders.[33]

Contrary to the expectations of those under Nazi domination, the
Jewish delegates in Switzerland had limited freedom of action.
Their tragic situation is clarified when it is compared to other relief
workers. This reveals that the isolation and helplessness of the
Jewish envoys was far from unique and was not the product of
irrational fears about their status in the eyes of gentiles. By analysing
the dilemmas facing humanitarian relief workers during the war,
Meredith Hindley shows that Jews were not alone in facing
appalling choices. Nor were Jewish relief efforts the victim of
entrenched prejudice.

Hindley argues that there were several parallel catastrophes in
Europe between 1941 and 1945, among them famine and genocide.
These crises were a result of the new type of warfare being waged
on all sides. In Eastern Europe and the Balkans the Nazis
remorselessly stripped their conquered territories of all resources,
leaving the local population with little on which to survive. At the
same time, they implemented murderous policies towards the Jews.
Meanwhile, the Allies imposed an economic blockade against the
Third Reich and its conquests with the intention of depriving its
people and war machine of subsistence. The blockade, combined
with German depredations, was only too effective. When food

shortages loomed in France in 1940, and when famine threatened Greece the following year, relief agencies requested permission to send aid. In the absence of any developed body of international law on the treatment of civilians, these agencies could only make a moral case backed up by the pleas of governments-in-exile and public campaigns. Such tactics were effective in rather special, favourable circumstances. Most of the time, however, arguments for relief bounced off the implacable bureaucrats and military personnel ensconced in Whitehall and the US State Department. The same unyielding treatment meted out to Jewish supplicants in 1942–43 was dished out to the non-Jewish relief agencies.[34]

Filled with expectations that their comrades would send help, Jews in the Polish and Slovakian ghettos could not understand the poverty of the response. They ascribed the worst motives to those whom they were convinced had let them down, not realising that Jewish activists were imprisoned in a military and political logic that held sway precisely because it was eminently reasonable and founded on a democratic consensus, rather than the outcome of prejudice amongst a few officials.

Even so, within these constraints, a few exceptional individuals in Britain, the USA, Switzerland, and Sweden did continue to harry government officials or try to shift the terms of the argument for relief and rescue. Some, like Eleanor Rathbone, were prominent parliamentarians while others, such as the Swede Gösta Engzell, were civil servants. Searching for a nuanced explanation of their activism, David Cesarani finds little in common amongst those in Britain except a cosmopolitan outlook and a familiarity with European society. Yet this was sufficient in the conditions of the 1940s to enable them to challenge the received wisdom about the conduct of the war and how best to relieve the plight of the Jews. Surprisingly, there is no evidence that rescue activists had to like Jews to be moved by their plight, and there are even cases in which they combined strenuous efforts to help them with an abiding dislike of Jewish people and Judaism.[35]

The fact that self-confessed 'antisemites' such as Harold Nicolson MP could also agitate for rescue suggests a need to challenge the familiar dichotomy of antisemites versus the 'good guys'. In his essay, Tony Kushner strives to move the terms of analysis away from this polarity and to introduce the element of ambivalence into personal and political decision-making. Britain saw itself as a liberal, democratic country in the 1930s, opposed to all that Hitlerism stood for. Yet the government, the press, and a large section of the population believed that it was necessary to restrict the scale of Jewish immigration for fear of causing antisemitism. This was not just because of high unemployment or other objective factors: the Jewishness of the refugees was perceived as an obstacle to the successful assimilation of large numbers into what was fondly believed to be an ethnically and culturally homogeneous society. Conversely, spasms of generosity, such as the period from mid-1938 to mid-1939, were not the result of a sudden conversion to philo-semitism. They were a response to the new conjunction of international forces which included the aftermath of the Munich agreement, the closing of Palestine to Jewish refugees, and repugnance engendered by the Nazi pogrom of 9–10 November 1938. In a detailed examination of two key political players in the 1940s, Ernest Bevin and Herbert Morrison, Kushner exposes the fallacy of the tenaciously-held conviction that liberalism equates with pro-refugee and pro-Jewish policy.[36]

Paul Levine's study of Gösta Engzell, Under Secretary at the Foreign Ministry of Sweden (the *UD*), points in the same direction and shows the importance of comparative studies. Like Britain, Sweden was a liberal democratic country in which information about events in Europe circulated freely. Despite abundant proof that Jews were the subjects of intense racial persecution in Germany in the late 1930s, Engzell saw no cause to relax Sweden's restrictive immigration regulations. Indeed, at the time of the Evian conference, in July 1938, he specifically warned about the consequences that might arise from the pressure to expel Jews from other countries. The same spectre haunted officials in Whitehall and buttressed their determination to maintain rigid immigration controls.[37]

Sweden, much like Switzerland and Britain, introduced visa controls during 1938 with the express purpose of screening out would-be Jewish refugees. Even transmigrants or those with skills that would enable them to move on were deterred from entering the country. While 'political refugees' were welcomed, 'racial persecutees' were deemed a separate category: precisely because they were Jewish they were denied political sanctuary.[38] These tough immigration rules were rigorously upheld throughout the first years of the war even though Engzell and his colleagues could see the horror raining down on Polish and Russian Jews. They were equally unmoved by information about the deportation of Jews from western Europe. But when the Final Solution reached their borders and touched Jews from their own Scandinavian cultural sphere, they were jolted into action.[39]

Levine argues that Engzell was moved to change course by important, confidential sources of information about the massacre of the Jews. When the Jewish communities of Norway and then Denmark were threatened with transportation to Poland, in late 1942 and late 1943 respectively, he did not need to be convinced of the need to save them. Moreover, having instructed his officials to assist Jews in kindred Scandinavian countries, he extended their remit to those Jews in other countries, notably Hungary, who had even a tenuous connection with Sweden.[40] Engzell's new approach displayed some elements of pragmatism: although the outcome of the war was still in the balance and Germany remained the dominant power on the European continent and capable of threatening Sweden, some in *UD* anticipated that this might not last. Nevertheless, his motive seems to have been primarily humanitarian. The extraordinary character of his transformation is indicated by a comparison between policy in Sweden and in Switzerland at this time. In July 1942, confronted by information that Nazi policy towards the Jews all over Europe had turned towards mass murder and so threatened to trigger a refugee influx on the scale of 1938, the head of the Swiss Federal Police, Heinrich Rothmund, ordered that Jews fleeing racial persecution should be turned away at the borders. While Sweden allowed the number of Jewish refugees on its territory to double and supported those that reached safety, the Swiss made supreme efforts to prevent any increase and loaded the burden for supporting them onto the small Swiss–Jewish population.[41]

Both Sweden and Switzerland made choices about the meaning and content of neutrality. Jacques Picard, a member of the Independent Commission of Experts on Switzerland in the Second World War, demonstrates that neutrality cannot be taken as a monolithic geopolitical and legal concept. Switzerland's interpretation of neutrality was pragmatic and flexible. To understand how the country situated itself in relation to Nazi Germany, Picard begins with a detailed exposition of Nazi economic thinking and geopolitical ambitions. This governed the relationship with the Swiss, although it was not wholly one-sided. Both the Germans and the Swiss were seared by the experience of German hyperinflation in the 1920s and then the Depression and were determined to find ways to avoid similar financial disasters. The Nazis set out to free Germany from economic instability and vulnerability to currency markets by instituting a policy of self-sufficiency or autarky. This concept blended their nationalism with respectable economic doctrines and actually echoed the policy of the last Weimar governments, an approach that was well regarded in Swiss financial circles. State control and rigid currency exchange policy enabled the Nazis to pursue rearmament, but the 'clearing system' which they created and the principle of reciprocity on which they based trade suited Switzerland. Swiss banks bore the wounds inflicted by German economic disorder and welcomed the new, stable system underwritten by export credits.

However, even as they adapted to the economic regimen of the Third Reich, Swiss experts could see that it was gearing for war. The blitzkrieg waged by Hitler extended Germany's economic hegemony and brought in vast amounts of plunder. The despoliation of the Jews helped finance the Reich's military machine: racial war funded conventional war. But the Nazis needed contacts with foreign suppliers and buyers and a conduit through which to exchange gold for hard currency or goods and commodities. Switzerland knowingly provided that medium, but did the country have a choice? After the war the officially sanctioned narrative claimed that a mixture of military preparedness and shrewd use of economic instruments kept the Germans at bay. Yet, as Picard shows, Switzerland constantly trimmed its neutrality to fit the circumstances. In 1939–40 senior Swiss officers discussed joint military action with France. When the army was demobilised in 1940 and the rump withdrawn to the Alpine 'redoubt' this was not to threaten an endless last-stand, but actually to clear the way for raising the tempo of economic cooperation with Germany. Manpower released from the army went into factories located, moreover, in industrial areas in the lowlands that would have been given up if the 'redoubt' was a serious option. Thus, instead of planning to resist occupation, the Swiss intended to persuade the Germans that it was not necessary. Within a short time, the Swiss economy was absorbed into the German war effort. And since the Swiss were considered 'aryans', this arrangement was a perfect fit from the German point of view.[42]

Picard argues that the Swiss shared this racialised perception. The objection to an influx of Jewish refugees was not due to a fear of pressure on resources, but rather a desire to protect the homogeneity of their society against a specific group long perceived as alien and undesirable. Yet the Swiss also thought of themselves as a liberal, tolerant people: they wanted to limit the number of Jews precisely in order to prevent the emergence of a 'Jewish Question'.[43] It seems that this stance was not so very different from the posture of the British or the Swedes in the 1930s.

Indeed, the contributions by Sven Nordlund and Karin Kvist show the value of the comparative approach. Examining the debate over immigration policy in the 1930s, Nordlund shows that it was rooted in a law passed in 1927 that combined a desire to conserve the Nordic race with protection of the native labour market. A subsequent Aliens Act of 1937 specifically directed immigrant workers into areas that would not threaten natives. One way of doing this was to encourage them to set up new businesses and become self-employed. This policy fell heavily on Jews attempting to migrate to Sweden. Although Nordlund maintains that they were the victims of a generalised xenophobia and protectionism rather than antisemitism, he also observes that East European Jews stood markedly less chance than others of obtaining business licences. The authorities would only issue such permits after receiving testimonials and statements from businessmen and even neighbours. These were frequently laced with anti-Jewish prejudice. Some Jews saw a possibility of setting up in the import/export trade with Germany, only to find that they were the vicitms of pressure from German enterprises not to deal with Jews. Nordlund reveals that Swedish businessmen frequently informed on Jews to the Germans and abetted the 'aryanisation' process in their own country by eliminating Jews from firms trading with Germany. Ironically, labour shortages in Sweden in the middle of the war led to a loosening of the strict controls on Jewish immigrants and a widening of job opportunities. But the authorities remained cool towards their presence and did little to assist the restitution of Jewish property in Germany or deal with Jewish assets marooned in Sweden.[44]

The degree to which neutral Sweden adapted to Nazi attitudes and methods is further explored by Karin Kvist. Her study of the previously neglected records of the government's Foreigner's Bureau reveals that from 1938 to 1942, officials in the Bureau formulated and imposed a policy that was designed to reduce Jewish immigration to a trickle. They deliberately defined a 'political refugee' who could claim asylum in such a way as to eliminate Jews escaping racial persecution. Those German Jews who did manage to enter Sweden were monitored closely and enumerated on a regular basis according to explicitly racial criteria. In 1942, it appeared as if the imported Nazi racial categorisation might be extended to Sweden's Jewish citizens. Fortuitously, the arrival of 1,000 Norwegian Jewish refugees, who were anyway viewed with greater favour, came at a time of labour shortages and the Bureau relaxed its surveillance. Within a year the Swedish state had adopted a helpful attitude towards Jewish refugees and the Bureau was actually dissolved.[45]

The transformed perception in Sweden of the Jewish victims of Nazi racial policy found its most stirring expression in the rescue missions of Raoul Wallenberg and Count Folke Bernadotte. While

Wallenberg's humanitarian enterprise is well known, if widely misunderstood, Bernadotte's is less familiar and is clouded by controversy. Between March and May 1945, on the instructions of the Swedish Foreign Ministry, Bernadotte marshalled and led a fleet of 75 vehicles with 250 military and medical personnel via Denmark deep into German territory to pluck Scandinavian and French nationals from the concentration camps of Theresienstadt and Ravensbrük. The mission was preceded by complex negotiations with Himmler and other SS officials and some parts of it, such as the intention to rescue Jews, may have been masked in written and oral communications. As a result, a conviction developed that the buses had been tasked to pick up only non-Jews. Persson elevates Bernadotte from the mire of conflicting accounts and concludes that 11,000 Jews were brought to safety in Sweden on buses that ran a gauntlet of strafing by RAF fighter-bombers ranging over Northern Germany. One Swedish officer was killed and another seriously injured in these attacks.[46]

By this stage of the war all the neutral states had joined with the Allies in the task of rescuing Jews. The choice to help was easy now that the Third Reich was nearly defeated, but their role in the last chaotic months of the Third Reich and the 'liberation' contributed to establishing the memory of each as a 'rescuer nation'. For decades afterwards, the Allied struggle against Nazism and Fascism, like the neutral countries' preservation of their neutrality, straitjacketed the narrative of responses to Jewish suffering in the 1930s and during the war. Having ended up on the side of the angels, virtuosity was read back into history. Challenges to this triumphalism were met with outrage, causing scholarship and public debate to polarise until one monolithic account was mirrored by another. In both instances the dimension of volition was lost and actions were ascribed to predetermined motives. What these essays show is that governments, societies and individuals were actually fissured in any number of ways, with policy and political actors constantly shifting as circumstances and perceptions changed. In hindsight many wrong or dubious decisions were made, but unless we accept that these outcomes were not foreordained, we cannot appreciate the right decisions. What makes the rescue activists so remarkable is that they were not programmed by philo-semitism or moral rectitude to do what they did. They were human beings, watching events, analysing them, and responding as they saw fit. A few chose not to stand idly by. The miracle of humanity is that there are such humanitarians.

NOTES

1.  For diverse reflections on this phenomena, which themselves added to the controversy, see Tim Cole, *Images of the Holocaust* (London: Duckworth, 1999); Peter Novick, *The Holocaust In American Life* (New York: Houghton Mifflin, 1999); Norman G. Finkelstein, *The Holocaust Industry* (London: Verso, 2000). For more balanced meditations, see Peter Hayes (ed.), *Lessons and Legacies*, Vol.3: *Memory, Memorialization, and Denial* (Evanston, Ill.: Northwestern University Press, 1999).
2.  Deborah Lipstadt, 'The Failure to Rescue and Contemporary American Jewish Historiography of the Holocaust: Judging From a Distance', in Michael J Neufeld and Michael Berenbaum (eds.), *The Bombing of Auschwitz* (New York: St Martin's, 2000), p.228.
3.  Yisrael Gutman and Efraim Zuroff (eds.), *Rescue Attempts During the Holocaust* (Jerusalem: Yad Vashem, 1977), devotes less than 100 out of 600 pages of text to British and American responses. In the proceedings of the Yad Vashem conference on *The Historiography of the Holocaust Period*, held in March 1983, although there are several contributions on reactions and responses to the mass murder of the Jews and the activity of rescuers, the term 'bystanders' is hardly used and is never applied to the British or the Americans: Yisrael Gutman and Gideon Grief (eds.), *The Historiography of the Holocaust Period* (Jerusalem: Yad Vashem, 1988). Compare this to Michael Marrus, *The Holocaust in History* (London: Penguin, 1987), pp.156–83, and Raul Hilberg, *Perpetrators, Victims, Bystanders: The Jewish Catastrophe 1933–1945* (New York: HarperCollins, 1992), pp.xi–xii and the fuller discussion pp.195–268. The respective chapters in Donald Niewyk and Francis Nicosia (eds.), *The Columbia Guide to the Holocaust* (New York: Columbia University Press, 2000) maintain the distinction between 'The Behaviour of Bystanders' in Europe and 'The Question of Rescue' encompassing the Allied powers and the neutrals. Most encyclopaedias of the Holocaust do not have a discrete entry on 'bystanders'.
4.  Deborah Lipstadt, 'The Failure to Rescue and Contemporary American Jewish Historiography of the Holocaust', p.228
5.  William D. Rubinstein, *The Myth of Rescue: Why the democracies could not have saved more Jews from the Nazis* (London: Routledge, 1997), pp.1–14; Novick, *The Holocaust In American Life*, pp.12–13, 57–9, 245–6.
6.  For the text of the Report, whose title was changed to the more neutral 'Report to the Secretary' before its final delivery to the President, see Michael Berenbaum (ed.), *Witness to the Holocaust* (New York: Harper Collins, 1997), pp.284–94.
7.  See the following contributions by Tony Kushner, Jacques Picard, Raya Cohen, and Sven Nordlund.
8.  Hannah Arendt, *Eichmann in Jerusalem* (New York: Viking, 1963); Rolf Hochhuth *The Representative* (London: Oberon Books, 1998 edn.). The play was also known as *The Deputy*.
9.  For a comprehensive and critical account of these developments see Tony Kushner, *The Holocaust and the Liberal Imagination* (Oxford: Blackwell, 1994), pp.11–18.

10. Arthur Morse, *While Six Million Died: A Chronicle of American Apathy* (New York: Random House, 1968); Henry Feingold, *The Politics of Rescue: The Roosevelt Administration and the Holocaust 1938–1945* (New Brunswick, NJ: Rutgers University Press, 1970); David Wyman, *Paper Walls: America and the Refugee Crisis, 1938–1941* (Amhurst: University of Massachusetts, 1968); A.J. Sherman, *Island Refuge: Britain and the Refugees from the Third Reich, 1933–1939* (London: Paul Elek, 1973); Richard Kreitman and Alan Kraut, *American Refugee Policy and European Jewry,1933–1945* (Bloomington: Indiana University Press, 1987). See also Irving Abella and Harold Troper, *None Is Too Many: Canada and the Jews of Europe, 1933–1948* (Toronto: Lester and Orpen Denys, 1983).
11. Walter Laqueur, *The Terrible Secret: Suppression of the Truth about Hitler's Final Solution* (Boston: Little Brown, 1980); Martin Gilbert, *Auschwitz and the Allies* (London: Michael Joseph, 1981); David Wyman, *The Abandonment of the Jews: America and the Holocaust, 1941–1945* (New York: Pantheon, 1984); Bernard Wasserstein, *Britain and the Jews of Europe, 1939–1945* (Oxford: Oxford University Press, 1988). See also Monty Penkower, *The Jews Were Expendable: Free World Diplomacy and the Holocaust* (Detroit: Wayne State University Press, 1988).
12. Dalia Ofer, *Escaping the Holocaust: Illegal Immigration to the Land of Israel, 1939–1944* (New York: Oxford University Press, 1990), and Dina Porat, *The Blue and the Yellow Stars of David: The Zionist Leadership in Palestine and the Holocaust, 1939–1945* (Cambridge, Mass.: Harvard University Press, 1990). Both had appeared earlier in Hebrew. Aaron Berman, *Nazism, the Jews and American Zionism, 1933–1948* (Detroit: Wayne State University Press, 1990). Such was the furore over the claims about the role of America's Jewish leadership that a quasi-official inquiry was set up to investigate: Seymour Finger, *American Jewry during the Holocaust* (New York: Homes and Meyer, 1984).
13. See Lucy Dawidowicz, 'Indicting American Jews' (1983) and 'Could America have Rescued Europe's Jews' (1985), in Neal Kozody (ed.), *What is the Use of Jewish History* (New York: Schocken, 1992), pp.179–201, 157–78; Henry Feingold, *Bearing Witness: How America and Its Jews Responded to the Holocaust* (Syracuse, NY: Syracuse University Press, 1995); Verne Newton (ed.), *FDR and the Holocaust* (New York: St Martin's, 1996); Shabtai Teveth, *Ben Gurion and the Holocaust* (New Tork: Harcourt Brace, 1996); Louise London, *Whitehall and the Jews, 1933–1948: British Immigration Policy, Jewish Refugees and the Holocaust* (Cambridge: Cambridge University Press, 2000); Rubinstein, *The Myth of Rescue*; Neufeld and Berenbaum (eds.), *The Bombing of Auschwitz*.
14. See pp.60–61 below; Paul Salmons, *Reflections* (London: Imperial War Museum, 2000), pp.170–78.
15. Niewyk and Nicosia (eds.), *The Columbia Guide to the Holocaust*, p.109.
16. Niewyk and Nicosia (eds.), *The Columbia Guide to the Holocaust*, pp.119–20.
17. Arthur Smith, *Hitler's Gold: The Story of the Nazi War Loot* (Oxford: Berg, 1989); Jacques Picard, *Switzerland and the Assets of the Missing Victims of the Nazis* (Zurich: Bank Julius Baer, 1993); Peter Hug and Marc Perrenoud, *Assets in Switzerland of Victims of Nazism and the Compensation Agreements with East Bloc Countries* (Berne: Swiss Confederation Federal Department for Foreign Affairs Task Force, October 1996); *Riksbankens Guldaffärer med Nazityskland: rapport till Riksbanken av den särskilt tillsatta arkivutredningen* (Stockholm: Government Offices, 1997) with English summary.
18. William Slaney (ed.), *US and Allied Efforts to Recover and Restore Gold and Other Assets Stolen or Hidden by Germans During World War II* (Washington: State Department, May 1997); Historians in Library and Records Department of the Foreign and Commonwealth Office [Historians LRD], *Nazi Gold: Information from the British Archives*, 2nd edn. (London: FCO, Jan. 1997).
19. Tom Bower, *Blood Money* (London: Pan Books, 1997); Adam Lebor, *Hitler's Secret Bankers* (London: Pocket Books, 1997); Gregg J. Rickman, *Swiss Banks and Jewish Souls* (New

Brunswick: Transaction Publishers, 1999); Jean Ziegler, trans. John Brownjohn, *The Swiss, The Gold, and the Dead* (New York: Harcourt Brace, 1998); George Carpozi, *Nazi Gold* (Far Hills, NJ: New Horizon Press, 1999); Itamar Levin, trans. Natasha Dornberg, *The Last Deposit: Swiss Banks and Holocaust Victims' Accounts* (Westport, Conn.; Praeger, 1999); Hector Feliciano, *The Lost Museum: The Nazi Conspiracy to Steal the World's Greatest Works of Art* (New York: Basic Books, 1997); Elizabeth Simpson (ed.), *The Spoils of War* (New York: Harry N. Abrams, 1997); Peter Harclerode and Brendan Pittaway, *The Lost Masters: The Looting of Europe's Treasure Houses* (London: Gollancz, 1999).

20. See for example: Frank Bajhor, *Arisierung in Hamburg: Die Verdraengung der jüdischen Unternehmer 1933–45* (Hamburg: Christians, 1997); Yitzhak Arad, 'Plunder of Jewish Property in the Nazi-Occupied Areas of the Soviet Union', in David Silberklang (ed.), *Yad Vashem Studies*, Vol.29 (Jerusalem: Yad Vashem, 2001), pp.109–48; Martin Dean, 'Jewish Property Seized in the Occupied Soviet Union in 1941 and 1942: The Record of the *Reichshauptkasse Beutestelle*', *Holocaust and Genocide Studies* [HGS], Vol.14, No.1 (2000), pp.83–101; Martin Dean, 'The Plundering of Jewish Property in Europe: Five Recent Publications Documenting Property Seizure and Restitution in Germany, Belgium, Norway and Belarus', *HGS*, Vol.15, No.1 (2000/1), pp.86–97; Harold James, *The Deutsche Bank and the Nazi Economic War Against the Jews: The Expropriation of Jewish-Owned Property* (Cambridge: Cambridge University Press, 2001).

21. From this now bulky literature, see the flawed but provocative study by Gerard Aalders and Cees Wiebes, *The Art of Cloaking Ownership: The Case of Sweden. The Secret Collaboration and Protection of the German War Industry by Neutrals* (Amsterdam: Amsterdam University Press, 1996); The Commission on Jewish Assets in Sweden at the Time of the Second World War, *Sweden and Jewish Assets. Final Report* (Stockholm: The Government Office, 1999); Georg Kreis (ed.), *Switzerland and the Second World War* (London and Portland, OR: Frank Cass, 2000).

22. Holocaust Educational Trust, *'Ex-Enemy Jews': The Fate of the Assets in Britain of Holocaust Victims and Survivors* (London: Holocaust Educational Trust, Sept. 1997); Historians LRD, *British Policy Towards Enemy Property During and After the Second World War* (London: FCO, April 1998).

23. Richard J. Aldrich, *The Hidden Hand: Britain, America and Cold War Secret Intelligence* (London: John Murray, 2001), pp.6–7.

24. Richard Breitman, *Offical Secrets: What the Nazis Planned, What the British and the Americans Knew* (London: Allen Lane, 1998). See also Bernard Wasserstein, *Britain and the Jews of Europe 1939–1945*, 2nd edn. (Leicester: Leicester University Press, 1999), pp.ix–x.

25. The notion of the 'free', i.e. non-Nazi dominated world, requires some qualification since it included the USSR, and fascist/authoritarian states in Europe and South America.

26. Lipstadt, 'The Failure to Rescue and Contemporary American Jewish Historiography of the Holocaust', pp.232–4.

27. Novick, *The Holocaust In American Life*, p.12.

28. See below, pp.60, 61.

29. A social commentator who spotted this trend early on and summed it up better than most who followed was Michael Ignatieff, *The Needs of Strangers* (London: Chatto and Windus, 1984), pp.135–42.

30. Barbie Zelizer, *Remembering to Forget: Holocaust Memory Through the Camera's Eye* (Chicago: University of Chicago Press, 1998), esp. pp.171–201; Barbie Zelizer (ed.), *Visual Culture and the Holocaust* (London: Athlone Press, 2001), pp.202–38. See also Jeffrey Shandler, *While America Watches: Televising the Holocaust* (New York: Oxford University Press, 1999).

31. See below, pp.28–56.

32. London, *Whitehall and the Jews*, p.141.

33. See below, pp.146–70.

34. See below, pp.33–48.
35. See below, pp.77–103.
36. See below, pp.57–76.
37. London, *Whitehall and the Jews*, pp.87–91.
38. See below, Karin Kvist, p.203 and Sven Nordlund, p.279.
39. See below, pp.217–22.
40. See below, pp.224–9.
41. Independent Commission of Experts Switzerland – Second World War, *Switzerland and Refugees in the Nazi Era* (Bern: Independent Commission of Experts, 1999), pp.85–99.
42. See below, pp.103–45.
43. See below, pp.132–4.
44. See below, pp.171–98.
45. See below, Karin Kvist, pp.199–211.
46. See below, pp.237–68.

# Mad Dogs and Englishmen: Towards a Taxonomy of Rescuers in a 'Bystander' Country – Britain 1933–45

## DAVID CESARANI

### I

In recent years historians and scholars from a variety of other disciplines have begun to look at those people who rescued, or attempted to rescue, Jews from the Nazis and their accomplices. Eva Fogelman's 1995 study, *Conscience and Courage*, lists no less than 80 books, chapters and articles (the majority published since 1970) dealing with rescue stories and over 100 monographs and articles analysing aspects of the subject.[1] However, most of these studies have focused on the activity of rescuers in Nazi Germany or adjacent countries, or those based in Nazi-occupied countries in wartime Europe. Comparatively little notice has been taken of refugee activists and rescuers who operated from so-called bystander countries that were geographically removed from the Third Reich.[2]

Yet on closer examination it appears that the substantial literature about the covert missions of those living under the Nazis sheds little light on the activity of refugee workers and rescuers in 'bystander' countries. The evaluative criteria used by Eva Fogelman in *Conscience and Courage*, the most systematic inquiry into the conduct and motivation of rescuers living under Nazi rule, are frequently inapplicable in these cases. Fogelman's approach may even lead one to underestimate the difficulties and dilemmas of rescue work carried out in more benign circumstances.

In *The Holocaust and the Liberal Imagination* Tony Kushner demonstrates how the ethos of liberal democracy militated against an appreciation of specific Jewish suffering and the need for targeted aid. It could actually frustrate those who were aware of the Jewish predicament and eager to assist its victims. The vagaries of official refugee-policy were not attributable solely to antisemitism, ignorance, or indifference: 'The failings of Britain and the United States with regard to the Jewish crisis during the Nazi era may ... be explained by the failure of the state and society to solve the contradictions and ambiguities of liberalism.' Kushner suggests that Jews received succour from 'exceptional individuals' who were willing and able to defy the received wisdom of the time. These individuals were 'essentially outsiders'.[3]

Whereas Eva Fogelman's paragons risked their lives for the sake of established ideologies and accepted notions of civilised behaviour, Kushner's heroes are rebels against convention, received wisdom, and models of public action.[4] This is not the only thing that differentiates the two kinds of rescuers. In Nazi-occupied Europe, government had lost much or all of its legitimacy: someone who became aware that Jews were in danger did not feel compelled to operate within legal constraints when it came to helping them. The main deterrence was fear of detection and the risk of a terrible punishment. The same was true for anti-Nazis living within the Third Reich. By contrast, the refugee activists and potential rescuers who lived in free, democratic societies did not face such terror – but the modus operandi and spirit of democracy could be no less paralysing.

In these countries citizens expected their legitimate government to deal with major domestic emergencies and international crises. Individuals or groups who were alerted to tragedies abroad were able to organise assistance, but the most significant ways to alleviate the crisis – such as the modification of immigration controls to facilitate the entry of refugees – remained the prerogative of government. Policy could only be changed by political action, which had to be channelled through elected representatives and the official bureaucracy. Consequently, a would-be activist not only had to become aware of the crisis personally, they also had to figure out that their elected representatives and the legitimate agencies were not as well informed, or knew but were uncaring, or were not acting effectively by way of a remedy. Once they had realised this they faced the problem of what to do.

Political action in a democracy tends to be long-drawn-out, time consuming, wearying, frustrating, and often forlorn. Yet citizens in a democratic state habitually turn to government in times of crisis. It takes a particular kind of initiative to act independently of the authorities, especially if this involves circumventing or subverting established, statutory procedures. The position of the dissident refugee-worker or potential rescuer was made difficult precisely *because* they had the good fortune to reside in states that remained unoccupied and where government retained its authority.

As Tony Kushner has observed, only a few exceptional individuals seemed capable of surmounting this dilemma.[5] However, his explanation for their action is circular: they defied convention because they were unconventional. One thing that set these 'outsiders' apart from their fellows was precisely their active concern for refugees and the plight of the Jews. But where did this concern come from? And what liberated it from the tyranny of conventional ideas? Here Eva Fogelman's dissection of rescuers may be helpful, albeit applied in a different setting. She argues that for rescuers a 'heightened sense of empathy overrode Nazi propaganda and their own instinct for self-preservation. They saw these victims of Nazi persecution as people, different from themselves, but still part of the same human community.' This did not come automatically: it required a trigger, a 'transforming encounter', potent enough to overcome misinformation about the Jews, and to differentiate their fate amidst the general confusion of wartime and pervasive war-related suffering.[6]

The next step was to take action on the basis of this awareness. Such action required a suitable, non-suicidal opportunity. The rescuer needed to be rational and calculating, but above all they had to have a 'willingness to take responsibility, a personal sense of competency, and empathy'. They had to break with the idea that others (including official agencies) would do something, and they required a belief that an individual could make a difference. They had to be confident of their own abilities and, just as important, to be placed in a situation in which they could offer practical aid: 'without resources, support and stamina one could not act'. In addition to a host of practical skills, rescuers had to be very good at coping with fear and stress.[7]

Fogelman notes that when they were not insulated from fear by naivety or emotional immaturity, rescuers were sustained by a range of beliefs – religious or ideological – and/or rage against the Nazis. Some were driven by the conviction that all mankind was a single fraternity. Others were animated by varieties of Christian faith. Many simply felt compassionate towards fellow humans who were in a pitiable condition. She also located 'judeophiles' who were motivated by a love of Jews as a group with distinctive characteristics that they held dear, or by a veneration of Jews as the bearers of a great religious message. A few were 'concerned professionals' such as diplomats, doctors, nurses, or social workers who saw the Nazis violating professional codes of conduct; or they perceived Jews simply as 'clients in trouble, patients in need'. These people were supremely confident and felt that since they lived by a 'higher law' – their vocation or code of practice – they had a right and a duty to defy the Nazis. Often they were activated by 'humanitarian ideals'.[8]

Ultimately, Eva Fogelman, by profession a social psychologist and psychiatrist, concludes that rescuers were made by events in childhood. She suggests that they were raised in nurturing, loving homes in which an altruistic parent or guardian provided a model of righteousness. Frequently a childhood loss had sensitised them to the plight of victims in society. These individuals were subsequently raised to be independently minded, competent, disciplined and caring. Above all, at home they learned the values of tolerance, were encouraged to assist others and acquired the 'habit of helping'.[9]

Let us now apply these criteria to 12 non-Jewish refugee activists and rescuers working in Britain between 1933 and 1945, 11 men and one woman, of different ages, from a broad spectrum of backgrounds. This selection is not intended to be representative of the many thousands of men and women who sat on refugee committees, raised money, took in Jewish families or children, wrote to newspapers or their MPs, or attended mass meetings demanding a more sympathetic treatment of the refugee question.[10] Instead, it represents activists who took a leading role in the public sphere: by joining parliamentary debates, by publishing newspaper articles and books on the refugee question that were intended to influence public opinion in their favour, and by organising and running groups that brought aid to refugees.

This group merits examination for several reasons. It is not covered by existing studies of rescuers for the simple reason that in Nazi Germany and in German occupied countries there was no public opinion for such people to shape and lead. Nor was there a public sphere or a civil society in which they could organise and inspire groups of helpers. Furthermore, since many were involved in political life or had access to the political realm, their activity sheds light on the openings and obstacles presented to activists in liberal democracies. These campaigners were exemplars and motivators: without them to break the mould it is arguable whether larger numbers of the public would have found a voice, the inspiration to act, or the possibility of doing something useful.

For those of us who are concerned with the past because of the light it sheds on the present there is an urgency about understanding the motives and conduct of refugee activists in free, pluralistic, and democratic societies – as against the hidden enterprise of those living under dictatorships or operating in enemy-occupied lands. In most parts of the world (with a few abysmal exceptions) totalitarianism has withered away; but war, civil conflict, the forced displacement of populations, the mass abuse of human rights, and genocide has not. The awareness of catastrophe and the response to it now occurs in open societies. Therefore, when approaching this subject, we have more to learn from reactions to the crisis of 1933–45 in Britain, the USA, and the other free democracies, than from responses to Nazi persecution in areas under Nazi control. I will now give brief biographies of these 12 key activists, covering their social background, education, politics, religious beliefs, and track record on Jewish issues. I will then try to identify what it was that made them aware of the Jewish emergency and their motives for acting in response to it.

## II

Josiah Wedgwood (1872–1943) was born to wealth and privilege. He was heir to one the families associated with the birth of the modern industrial and consumer society in eighteenth-century England. Although his forebears had been Puritans who fought with Cromwell, he was raised in the Church of England and was educated at Clifton School. Wedgwood visited Germany in 1885 and fell in love with German culture. Nevertheless, he opted for active service in the Great War and encountered the Zion Mule Corps, a Jewish unit raised by Zeev Jabotinsky, in Gallipoli. During the war the novelist Dorothy Richardson introduced him to Zionism and he met Chaim Weizmann, the Zionist leader, in 1916. He became a Gentile Zionist and for the rest of his life he fought for the Jewish National Home. Wedgwood was elected to Parliament as a Liberal in 1906 and in 1918 he was sent to Russia on a military–diplomatic mission to locate Alexander Kerensky, the moderate revolutionary leader who had been deposed by the Bolsheviks. He was despatched to Hungary a year later and met Bela Kun, the Jewish-born leader of the short-lived Hungarian Soviet Republic. The bloody, antisemitic reaction against Kun's regime appalled him. Wedgwood drifted leftward throughout his unorthodox political career. In 1918, he became an Independent Radical, before aligning with the Independent Labour Party and, finally, the Labour Party. Throughout the 1920s he was a critic of the government's immigration policy and a champion of the rights of immigrant 'aliens'.[11]

Wedgwood was one of the first MPs to put a parliamentary question (PQ) to the Home Secretary about the plight of Jewish refugees and to ask that controls on immigration be relaxed on their behalf. In 1933 and 1937 he called on the government to use the charter of the League of Nations to protect Jews in that part of

Silesia which was under the League's supervision. After the
*Anschluss* in 1938, he proposed a measure to temporarily suspend the
Aliens Restriction (Amendment) Act which set out the very limited
conditions for admission to the UK. He also suggested making
changes to the Nationality Act to enable the naturalisation of
Austrian Jews seeking to enter Britain. The following month in
Parliament he advocated a relaxation of immigration restrictions
arguing that such an influx would boost Britain's declining
population. In February 1939, Wedgwood called for government aid
to be provided for refugees who reached other countries,
particularly those stuck in the Balkans. A year later he tried to obtain
government funding for the Central Committee for Refugees.
During April to December 1940, he was a ferocious critic of the
government's policy of interning 'enemy aliens'. In the following
year he took up the case of the 2,000 mainly Jewish refugees who
had been deported to Australia on the SS *Dunera*.[12]

Wedgwood worked closely with a number of refugee activists in
Parliament, including Eleanor Rathbone MP, Victor Cazalet MP, and
Lord Noel Buxton. He wrote hundreds of letters on behalf of Jews
seeking admission to the UK and personally guaranteed over 200.
According to his niece and biographer C.V. Wedgwood, 'He signed
so many that the Home Office finally refused to take any more from
him and he had to marshal his friends to help.' He accommodated a
large number in his own house.[13]

Eleanor Rathbone (1872–1946), one of Wedgwood's staunchest
allies, was born into a wealthy family that had been active in
Liverpool's commerce and politics for six generations. The family
had been Quakers, but her father was a Unitarian and her mother
was an Anglican. As a child, Eleanor gravitated towards the Society
of Friends. She was educated privately and attended Somerville
College, Oxford. In Liverpool she followed the family tradition of
Liberal politics and engaged in social work. She became a feminist
and a leader of the women's suffrage movement. After serving on
Liverpool City Council for over 20 years she was elected to
Parliament as an MP for the Combined English Universities.
Rathbone was devoted to the rights and welfare of women around

the world, especially India, and travelled extensively to investigate their situation. She was involved with the League of Nations Union and in 1929 visited Germany. Her interest in women's affairs took her to Palestine in 1934 and she was immediately enamoured of the Zionist movement, which appeared to her as a force for women's emancipation in the Middle East. From then on she was a committed Gentile Zionist.[14]

Her awareness of Jewish troubles preceded this conversion. In April 1933, in a parliamentary debate on Germany, she counselled that Britain should take a hard line with the new National Socialist government. She also asked in a PQ whether the immigration regulations would be modified to assist émigrés and exiles. She witnessed the plight of refugees during several trips to the Balkans, Czechoslovakia, and Spain with the Duchess of Atholl (another refugee campaigner) in 1937. Rathbone unremittingly asked PQs on refugee matters, wrote letters on behalf of refugees who were experiencing problems with the British authorities, helped raise money for refugee aid bodies, pressed officials for visas to help get political opponents of Nazism out of the Third Reich, gave countless speeches and published numerous articles on the refugee problem. This took up so much of her time that she remarked, 'I sometimes think I have become the MP for refugees.'[15]

In November 1938, Rathbone co-founded the All-Party Parliamentary Committee on Refugees. Early in the following year she made a personal visit to refugee camps in Czechoslovakia and subsequently used her parliamentary platform to demand aid for their luckless inhabitants. In the last parliamentary debate before the outbreak of war she pleaded for the admission of more refugees to Britain. During July–August 1940, Rathbone savaged the government's internment policy. She went to one of the worst camps, at Huyton racecourse, near Liverpool, to see conditions for herself. In a powerful speech delivered in the pouring rain she gave hope to a crowd of soaking internees by assuring them that 'you are not forgotten'. Thanks to her pressure, two advisory committees (serving the Home Secretary and the Refugee Department of the Foreign Office) were set up to monitor internment and speed the release of internees.[16]

During 1941, Rathbone made contact with refugee intellectuals and anti-Nazi exiles such as Sebastian Haffner, Heinrich Fraenkel, and Arthur Koestler. She arranged for Haffner and Fraenkel to address MPs at the House of Commons. In November 1941, she presented the American Ambassador with Koestler's ingenious plan to rescue refugees from Vichy France. The plan foundered as a result of bureaucratic delays and America's entry into the war.[17] Thanks to Koestler, in October 1942 Rathbone received from the Polish underground courier Jan Karski first-hand information about the mass murder of the Jews in Europe. Karski was in London on a mission for the Polish Government-in-exile but he had a private assignment to pass on details about conditions in the Warsaw Ghetto and about Belzec death camp. Rathbone was one of the few influential people to take him seriously at first hearing.[18]

Karski's mission and other evidence helped prompt the government to issue an inter-allied statement on 17 December 1942 condemning the genocide against the Jews and promising retribution against those responsible. However, public outrage drained away without discernible action. In order to maintain awareness of the Nazis' extermination programme and lobby the government to both protest and initiate rescue measures, in March 1943 Rathbone formed the National Committee for Rescue from Nazi Terror. She berated the meagre results of the Bermuda conference, convened in April 1943 in response to the earlier wave of public sympathy for the Jews. At the same time as using the committee to keep Jewish suffering to the fore she joined Wedgwood in demanding that the government make concessions to the Zionist movement and, in particular, allow increased immigration to Palestine. Her inability to budge the government on any of these issues engendered hatred for the Home Secretary Herbert Morrison and a permanent sense of guilt. Physical and mental exhaustion as a result of her efforts may have contributed to her untimely death in 1946.[19]

Victor Cazalet MP (1896–1941) served on Rathbone's Refugees Committee and took over as chairman around 1941. Cazalet was born into a well-to-do family of Huguenot origin. His mother, who had a strong influence over his development, was a Christian

Scientist and he emulated her faith. He was educated at Eton and after strenuous war-service went to Oxford.[20] Cazalet travelled to the anti-Bolshevik areas of Russia on military duties in 1919 and in common with most officers of the British intervention force helping the 'White' forces he expressed uncomplimentary opinions of the Jewish population which he encountered. Believing that Jews in the United States were responsible for anti-White feeling he complained that 'If we could get rid of Jewish influence in America, we should hit the root of the problem.'[21]

After military service Cazalet was drawn into social-work circles and became involved in the boys' club movement in the East End of London, home to half of the capital's Jewish inhabitants. He travelled incessantly. He visited the Baltic States (where his family had business) and Poland in 1922, and toured the Middle East, including Palestine, in 1924. His grandfather had been an early proponent of the restoration of the Jews to Palestine and after this trip Cazalet became a vigorous champion of modern Zionism. He entered Parliament as a Conservative in 1924. During a trip to the USA in 1925 he met Henry Ford and was mildly critical of the American tycoon's antisemitism. 'Ford', he wrote, 'has one bugbear – International Jewish financiers.'[22]

In August 1933, Cazalet went to Germany. He was reportedly astonished by the vehement antisemitism he came across in Hitler's entourage but after a visit to Dachau concentration camp he described it as 'quite well run and no undue misery or discomfort'. He returned to Germany in 1936 and toured a 'labour camp' which he later compared favourably to similar establishments in the USSR. Such views chimed with his general foreign policy outlook. Throughout the late 1930s Cazalet was seen as an appeaser of Germany because he loyally supported Prime Minister Stanley Baldwin and his successor, Neville Chamberlain. Cazalet actually expressed unease about British policy towards the dictatorships, but due to a feud with Winston Churchill, the most outspoken opponent of the government, he refused to align with the anti-appeasers.[23]

In April 1938, Cazalet journeyed to Vienna where he witnessed the dire condition of the city's Jews. He was galvanised by this experience. In July he addressed the House of Commons about the refugees, he wrote pro-refugee articles, and he joined Rathbone's committee. By the end of the year he commented that 'All my time seems to be taken up with refugees.' He spoke out against internment in August 1940, and later linked the suffering of Jews in Polish ghettos to the situation of Jews in Palestine. In his last speech to the House of Commons, in May 1943, he attacked the results of the Bermuda Conference. Contrasting what had been achieved in Bermuda with what was happening in Europe he bitterly told fellow MPs that 'The Jews are being exterminated today.' He died in a plane crash later that year.[24]

Cazalet shared an interest in Zionism, social work and East End boys' clubs with Wyndham Deedes (1883–1956), a most unusual ex-soldier. Deedes was born into an old gentry family. His father was a professional soldier who died young, leaving his wife and offspring in straitened circumstances. Wyndham attended Eton, but left early to join the army and fought against the Boers in South Africa. Although the rest of his education was self-acquired he was a natural autodidact and acquired fluency in a number of languages including German and Turkish. En route to a posting in Malta he went on a 'grand tour' of Italy, the Balkans and Hungary. From 1910 to 1914 he was seconded to the Ottoman army and served in Tripoli, Tunisia and Smyrna. Deedes was nominally an Anglican, but was commonly referred to as 'a deeply religious man' with a profound sense of Christian duty. One who knew him described his 'almost prophetic sense of justice'. Deedes toyed with social work but remained in the military and served throughout the Near and Middle East. In 1918 he was appointed to the military government of Palestine where he created and ran the British mandate civil service. He left Palestine in 1923 and engaged in social work in Bethnal Green, where he lived with his mother until his retirement in 1946.[25]

Deedes remained a passionate Gentile Zionist after he returned to England from Palestine. With his friend and former colleague Norman Bentwich he made several trips to Eastern Europe on behalf of the Zionist movement. He gave his name to the Council for

German Jewry (CGJ) formed in 1933, but paid special attention to the plight of 'non-Aryan Christians'. He was the joint director of emigration and training for the CGJ, in which connection he travelled to Germany with Bentwich in May 1936, to consult with German Jewish leaders. While there he delivered a letter from the Archbishop of Canterbury to Rudolf Hess, criticising Nazi policy towards the Jews. He himself remonstrated with Hess, the Deputy Führer, over the treatment of Jews. Deedes later helped to found a scheme to bring vulnerable children out of Nazi Germany and became chairman of the non-denominational Children's Inter-Aid. In November 1938, he was a moving force behind the organisation of the *Kindertransport* programme, which led to the evacuation of nearly 10,000 unaccompanied Jewish and non-Jewish children to Britain. He later undertook an exhausting fund-raising tour of South Africa to raise money to help the refugees. During the war he told the Association for the Jewish National Home that 'The Nazi attempt at the extermination of the Jews in Europe moved him to the depths of his soul; and justice for the Jews was his test of the sincerity about the new order for which the western democracies professed to be fighting.'[26]

Deedes was joined in his refugee work by Noel Buxton (1885–1946), scion of a rich brewing family of long-standing Quaker affiliations. Buxton was educated at Harrow and Cambridge, and worked briefly at the family brewery in Spitalfields in the East End of London, before entering politics in 1905 in the Liberal interest. He travelled widely and became a Balkan expert with an abiding interest in the Armenians. He served on the Whitechapel Board of Guardians and represented one of the most heavily Jewish districts of London on the London County Council. He was also involved in social work centred on Toynbee Hall, a cynosure of Jewish immigrant life. Buxton was a Liberal MP in 1905–6 and again from 1910 to 1918. In 1919 he joined the Labour Party, was re-elected to Parliament in 1922 and held ministerial office from 1929 to 1930, when he left the Commons. Buxton visited Berlin a number of times in the 1920s and in 1933, when he had an interview with Hitler. The Führer screamed at him after receiving some adverse comments about Nazi policy towards political opponents. Even so, Buxton revisited Germany in 1935 and 1937 and was known as an appeaser.[27]

Noel Buxton was closely associated with the League of Nations between the wars and became heavily engaged in the refugee problem. He was instrumental in the formation of the Save the Children Fund. During a 1934 visit to Paris he was shocked to see the barracks and slums where refugees lived. Through his role in Save the Children he played an important part in the formation of the Refugee Children's Movement which oversaw the *Kindertransports*. He took in several child refugees himself.[28]

Buxton's sister-in-law Dorothy (an activist in her own right) co-authored an influential book on the refugee question with the Nobel laureate Norman Angell (1872–1967), our next campaigner. Angell's parents were conventionally middle class and politically Conservative, but he was one of nature's rebels. At the age of 17, after a few years spent at a *lycée* in France, he emigrated to America where he held various jobs and had numerous adventures before he finally chanced on his vocation as a journalist and writer. From 1898 to 1904 he lived in Paris and covered the Dreyfus case for the Harmsworth press (which included the mass circulation *Daily Mail*). In 1912 he published *The Grand Illusion*, a cogent argument against war that became a global bestseller. After the Great War he was a proponent of the League of Nations and a founder of the Royal Institute for International Affairs. He was briefly a Labour MP and was awarded the Nobel Peace Prize in 1931.

In book after book the hugely well-travelled Angell critically dissected nationalism and xenophobia. In 1939 he published *You and the Refugee* with Dorothy Buxton. It was 'a plea for accepting virtually as many of the refugees from the Hitlerian persecution as could be got out of the countries he was overrunning. The book too was an attempt to destroy ... the illusion that a foreigner taking a job in Britain necessarily threw a Briton out of work.' *You and the Refugee* quickly went through two editions. Angell himself took a Viennese family into his home as housekeepers and tried to help others who were interned. He moved to the United States in 1940, but in 1944 wrote a pamphlet *Have we room for the refugees?* for the National Committee for Rescue from Nazi Terror.[29]

The Dreyfus affair which Angell helped to publicise had a great impact on the young Harold Nicolson (1886–1968), then attending Wellington School. Nicolson's father was a diplomat, so Harold had a highly cosmopolitan upbringing, including long spells in Budapest and Tangiers. He lived for six months in Germany before going to Balliol College, Oxford. In 1907 he entered the diplomatic service, rose swiftly, and played an important back-room part at the Versailles Peace Conference. In 1919 he accompanied General Smuts on a diplomatic mission to Bela Kun's regime in Hungary. Despite his sympathy for Dreyfus, Nicolson disliked Jews intensely and described the Hungarian Foreign Minister as 'a little oily Jew'. During a stay in Berlin in 1927–8 he often remarked on the prominence and 'vulgarity' of German Jews. According to his friend and biographer, James Lees-Milne, 'Try as he might he could not bring himself to like Jews ... His attitude towards them was irrational.' Aside from considering Jews 'touchy and insensitive', Lees-Milne considered that 'his attitude was old fashioned prejudice. He found them vulgar.' More than that, he found them physically repulsive and could not bear to share a swimming pool with Jews or blacks: 'they poison the water' he confided to his diary.[30]

Nicolson was a prolific writer and in 1930 left the foreign service to enter politics and earn his keep as a journalist. He gravitated towards the dissident Labour minister Sir Oswald Mosley, joined Mosley's New Party, and edited his paper *Action* during 1931. After the New Party was humiliated in the 1931 General Election, Nicolson accompanied Mosley to Rome and Berlin where Sir Oswald decided to relaunch himself as a full-blown fascist. Nicolson was one of the last of the intellectuals in Mosley's circle to break with the leader over his increasingly open antisemitism and fascism, waiting until April 1932 to sever his ties with him.[31]

Two years later he heard from German émigrés in Sweden first-hand reports about Nazi brutality. Yet they did not markedly affect his view of the Third Reich. In January 1936, he played host to Charles Lindbergh and his family during their trip to England, remarking neutrally in his diary on Lindbergh's admiration for Germany. By the next time they met, in May 1938, things had changed. Lindbergh was even more closely identified with Nazi Germany and racial thinking, and Nicolson, who was now better informed about such matters, felt uncomfortable with his guest's embrace of 'Nazi theology'. During a trip to the Balkans on behalf of the Foreign Office that year, he witnessed more of the hardships facing Jewish refugees. Later, Sir Robert Clive, who had been based at the British Embassy in Berlin, briefed him about the extent of the persecution of German Jews.[32]

Following his dalliance with Mosley, in 1935 Nicolson was elected to Parliament for National Labour. As an MP he sat on Rathbone's Refugees Committee and took up numerous refugee cases. During the war he tried to help Arthur Koestler's wife, who was trapped in Vichy France. He was horrified by the news that Jews were being slaughtered en masse and despaired at the lack of any significant response. In December 1942, he wrote 'It is a horrible thing that we are so saturated with horrors that this Black Hole on a gigantic scale scarcely concerns us.' Even so, his private attitude towards Jews remained disdainful. Just a few days after he heard Eden's parliamentary statement on the extermination of Europe's Jewish population he reported to his son that a Jewish officer had been stationed in the grounds of his home at Sissinghurst, but 'recalling how but three days before I had stood in tribute to the martyred Jews of Poland, I was most polite to Captain Rubinstein'. In March 1943, he joined the Committee for Rescue From Nazi Terror and was active on a number of fronts. In October 1943, he visited refugee camps in Sweden holding Jews who had just been spirited out of Denmark. He was a member of a major deputation to the Foreign Secretary in January 1944 that requested more aid for the Jews. Yet he never ceased to be 'Jew conscious'. In his diary entry for the day peace in Europe was declared, he described the street scene and picked out 'a Jewess in a paper cap'.[33]

David Astor, like Nicolson, had worked with Arthur Koestler on refugee and rescue projects and been influenced by Koestler's searing experience of persecution and flight. Although Astor came from one of the wealthiest families in the world, his biographers consider him an 'outsider' and he identified instinctively with victims and underdogs. Astor, who was born in 1912, grew up in a magnificent country house and was educated at Eton and Balliol, but his parents' American roots and their eccentric ways set them apart from English society. Furthermore, David Astor rebelled against his mother's Christian Science faith and from his late teens chose to live outside the family circle. Astor was phenomenally well connected, well travelled, and cosmopolitan. Through his parents, Waldorf and Nancy Astor, both Tory MPs, he met the movers and shakers of British foreign policy. He lived in Heidelberg in 1931 and while at Balliol became a close friend of Adam von Trott zu Stolz. In 1939 he acted as a broker between Trott, now an anti-Nazi member of the German Foreign Office, and British government officials.[34]

David Astor's parents were regarded as arch-appeasers of Nazi Germany. His mother was antisemitic and according to her brother-in-law, counted among her pet hates 'Socialism, Roman Catholics, psychiatry, the Jews, the Latins, the *Observer*'.[35] David Astor rejected all that his parents represented, gravitating towards socialism, engaging in psychoanalysis, embracing anti-Fascism, and befriending Jews. In early 1941, while still in the Marines, he began to take a role in *The Observer* newspaper which his father had bought from Lord Northcliffe in 1911. He introduced into its pages numerous refugee and émigré writers including Sebastian Haffner, Isaac Deutscher, and Arthur Koestler. In November 1941 he invited Koestler to contribute an article publicising the precarious situation of Jewish refugees and anti-Fascist exiles in Vichy France. The article was intended to bolster the campaign to get the USA to adopt Koestler's scheme for refugees to be admitted to internment camps on US territory. Astor accompanied Rathbone to a meeting with the American Ambassador to lobby for the plan. During Spring and Summer 1944, he sat with Koestler on a committee gathered around Chaim Weizmann that tried to persuade the government to take energetic measures to save the Jews of Hungary. Astor became a great admirer of Weizmann and a life-long Zionist.[36]

To return to the pre-war years, the next example of leadership is Herbert Henson, the Bishop of Durham. Born into an ecclesiastical family in 1863, Henson described his own father as a 'bigot'. He was educated privately, graduated from Oxford, and was elected to All Souls. After his ordination he was appointed head of Oxford House, the university settlement in Bethnal Green in the East End of London. His arrival at this centre of social work staffed by Oxford volunteers coincided with the onset of mass Jewish immigration from Eastern Europe. Henson rose steadily through the church hierarchy. He was made Bishop of Hertford in 1887, but only in the face of opposition from Anglo-Catholics who suspected his orthodoxy. In 1920 he was consecrated as Bishop of Durham, the third most important seat in the Church of England after Canterbury and York. Henson was unusually interested in the situation of Christians in the international arena and threw himself into controversies about the treatment of rubber workers in Peru and missionary activity in Kenya. For an Anglican Bishop he was well travelled.[37]

Although he was a 'liberal churchman', Henson held many conventional views about Jews and Judaism. He criticised Unitarianism because it shared similar doctrines to those which led Jews to 'reject' Christ. He condemned marriage between Jews and Christians because the partners would not be able to pray together or share the same 'standard of essential morality'. When Freud died at around the same time as the sexologist Havelock Ellis he commented that 'the latter was driven into exile by Hitler's fanatical anti-semitism. Neither of the two men was a buttress of morality, as morality is understood among Christians.' He considered the Jews an 'amazingly inscrutable people [who] can neither unite among themselves nor recognise their true friends'.[38]

But Henson developed an early distaste for Fascism and Nazism, which he regarded as secularising and blasphemous movements. Reflecting on the events of 1938, and the conflict between the Church and the Nazi Party in the Third Reich, he compared Hitler to Diocletian and Julian the Apostate. He had earlier, in 1935, achieved unexpected notoriety as a champion of Jewish rights after he spoke out in the Anglican Church Assembly against the treatment of Jewish academics at Heidelberg University. Immediately after reports of the speech appeared in the press he was plied with information by Jews campaigning against Nazism, and after giving more considered thought to the matter he wrote a protest letter to *The Times* on the eve of Heideberg's 550th anniversary celebration. He also contributed the introduction to *The Yellow Spot*, a 1936 book attacking Nazi racial policy. The November 1938 pogrom (*Kristallnacht*) aroused in him 'sentiments of disgust and detestation'. On 12 November he succeeded in getting his Dioscesan Conference to adopt a powerful resolution: 'That this conference of clergy and laity desires to express the disgust and horror with which it has heard of the recent anti-semitic outrages in Germany, and requests the Bishop of Durham to communicate this Resolution to the Chief Rabbi, and to assure him of the deep sympathy with the Jewish people which this Conference feels and shares with the general body of British citizens.' In an accompanying, personal letter to Chief Rabbi Dr J. H. Hertz he referred to the 'abominable oppression' in Germany.[39]

Revd James Parkes (1896–1981) was even more of an unorthodox churchman. He was born and educated in Guernsey where his father was a horticulturist; his mother died when he was young. Parkes served in the Great War, suffering the effects of poison gas, and attended Oxford from 1919–23. He joined the Student Christian Movement in 1921 and began a career as a student activist, interrupted briefly by his ordination and ministry in Hampstead. From 1923 to 1935 he lived in Prague and Geneva, where he ran the International Student Service.[40]

Parkes travelled widely in Europe, often to Germany. He became involved in general relief and refugee work in the early 1920s and learnt at first hand about the anti-Jewish violence in universities throughout Central Europe. In July 1928 he arranged a conference on the matter and turned himself into an expert on the 'Jewish problem'. This led to his 1930 book *The Jew and his Neighbour*, one of the first analyses of antisemitism by a Christian thinker. Through this work he came into contact with Jewish intellectuals and community leaders, notably the Sieff-Marks family that owned Marks and Spencer. From 1935 Israel Sieff made it possible for Parkes to research and write a string of path-breaking books on Jewish history,

Christian–Jewish relations, and antisemitism. In 1934–35, Parkes collected information on the 'Protocols of the Elders of Zion' for a famous trial in Bern. Despite intimidation by local Nazis he gave crucial evidence about the authenticity of the document that contributed decisively to the judgment that it was a farrago.[41]

In 1933 Parkes began organising support for students fleeing Germany and toured the US to raise money for their upkeep. This inaugurated a continuous involvement in Jewish refugee work, which from 1937–38 onwards was increasingly channelled into support for Zionism. In 1939 he intervened to 'rescue' Jewish boys brought from Prague to England by missionaries who intended to convert them to Christianity. During the war he was instrumental in the formation of the Council of Christians and Jews which was intended to publicise the suffering of Jews in Europe and combat antisemitism in Britain. Parkes often worked with Eleanor Rathbone and was a member of the National Committee for Rescue from Nazi Terror.[42]

Some of the Jewish children Parkes sought to retrieve from the hands of Christian conversionists had been brought to the UK by Nicholas Winton. Winton was born in 1909 into a well-to-do family. In an interview he recalled: 'My parents were Jewish but completely non-religious. I had no connection with the Jewish community in England because I was baptised and brought up as a Christian.' Educated at University College School in London and Stowe, Winton trained and worked as a banker in France and Germany before joining the London stock exchange. Nevertheless, he described himself as 'left-wing'. In December 1938 he went on holiday to Prague and was shown around the refugee camps by a friend who was working with the British Committee for Refugees from Czechoslovakia which had been set up to help Czechs displaced from the Sudetenland. This experience spurred him to action and he returned to Britain determined to find people who would take in or sponsor the children of refugees. Winton was an energetic and ingenious fund-raiser, and he was ably assisted by Quaker and Unitarian groups. He circulated photographs of the children and published a regular appeal in Sir Edward Hulton's *Picture Post*, a hugely popular illustrated magazine whose proprietor had backed many progressive, anti-Fascist, and refugee causes.[43]

Between January and September 1939, Winton and a co-worker in Prague, Trevor Chadwick, a Latin teacher, arranged 8 transports carrying 669 Jewish children to the UK. Winton quickly lost patience with the red tape at either end. Fearing that time to save the youngsters was running out, on occasion he flagrantly ignored the visa and immigration regulations. About 100 of the children were sponsored by the conversionist Barbican Mission, but Winton later commented 'I knew, the Chief Rabbi knew, and the Barbican Mission knew that these children were going to be turned into Christians. That didn't worry me in the slightest. What is better: a converted Jew or a dead Jew?' But Winton acknowledged that 'the Chief Rabbi and others didn't see it like that.' He served in the RAF during the war and afterwards returned to business although he remained involved in a variety of charitable causes.[44] In 1999, Yad Vashem, the Holocaust memorial authority in Jerusalem, recognised Winton as a Righteous Gentile.

Frank Foley (1884–1958) stands alongside Winton as one of the handful of British Righteous Gentiles. Foley was born in rural Somerset, the son of an upwardly mobile railway engineer. His mother was a Roman Catholic who initially sent Foley to a Catholic school. From 18 to 21 years he attended a Catholic seminary in France and studied philosophy in Germany. He became a teacher shortly before the outbreak of the Great War, whereupon he entered military service. After being wounded he was transferred to military intelligence. He served in the British Control Commission in Germany in 1918–19 and then joined the Secret Intelligence Service. Working under the guise of a Passport Control Officer (PCO), Foley moved to Berlin and lived there until his recall in 1939. His Berlin home was in a Jewish district and he acquired many Jewish friends, including Wilfred Israel, a rich Anglo-German Jew who emerged as a central figure in refugee work between 1933 and 1940. Israel and several of Foley's other Jewish contacts supplied him with intelligence. After 1933 there was in effect a quid pro quo by which he helped Jews with emigration matters in return for their assistance with his intelligence gathering.[45]

Foley used his official position as a PCO to provide entry visas to the UK for persons recommended to him by his Jewish intelligence contacts such as Israel and Hubert Pollack. His liberal interpretation of the regulations covering visas for 'capitalists', the rules for guarantees, and the transfer arrangements for emigrants intending to migrate to Palestine helped to facilitate the emigration of dozens of Jews who would not otherwise have qualified. In 1938 he urgently requested and obtained 1,000 immigration visas for young people aiming for Palestine. On occasions he personally delivered visas to Jewish men being held in prison or concentration camps, notably those who had assisted his spying operation. He wrote several stark reports for the Foreign Office on the plight of German Jews and in 1938 successfully urged that more resources be given to the visa departments. During *Kristallnacht* he hid Rabbi Leo Baeck, one of the leaders of the German Jewish community, and other prominent Jews in his home and allowed Baeck to brief journalists about the pogrom while staying there. In 1939 Foley returned to London leaving behind 80 visas which he had passed on to Jewish friends. During the internment crisis he wrote comfort letters to internees who he had helped to leave Germany, but made no other known interventions on behalf of Jews. Foley had a 'good war' and held senior positions in military intelligence. He died in 1958.[46]


# III

What, then, can we deduce if we analyse this cast of characters according to an adapted version of Fogelman's taxonomy? They were all well travelled and several were highly cosmopolitan by background, such as Cazalet and Astor, or by choice, such as Parkes. Wedgwood, Nicolson, Astor, Parkes, Foley, and Winton had spent substantial periods in Germany or Central Europe. Deedes had been stationed in North Africa and Turkey for several years. Even Bishop Henson had seen a bit of the world and had an interest in international affairs. So their awareness of the crisis afflicting the Jews was assisted by direct personal experience of conditions in Europe pre-1914 or inter-war. In several cases an encounter with refugees triggered action. For Angell and Nicolson the Dreyfus Affair was an important moment in their lives.

Each of these activists was by nature a 'doer', some maniacally so. They all possessed a strong sense of personal responsibility. For Rathbone, Deedes, Nicolson, and Astor it took the form of torturous guilt-feelings that allowed them little rest or relaxation.[47] Their feeling of social obligation was frequently expressed through social work. Henson, Buxton, Deeds, and Cazalet were all active social workers and, significantly, had all spent some time in this role in the Jewish districts of East London. Thanks to their wealth, or profession, or position in society they had the opportunity to act in a meaningful way or galvanise others. It helped that they were all immensely well networked. It is no accident that most of them knew each other even before 1933. Wedgwood, Rathbone, Cazalet, Nicolson, Buxton, and Henson were all in Parliament at the same time; Astor's parents were both MPs. But what turned awareness into action? What led them to exploit their contacts on behalf of a pariah group? David Astor's parents knew and saw as much as he did, but showed no concern for refugee issues. Nancy and Waldorf Astor may have been disinclined to make a fuss about refugees because they were appeasers, but Cazalet and Buxton were in their camp and both became passionate about the fate of the Jews.

Ideology may have had some role to play. Wedgwood, Rathbone, Angell, and Buxton were rooted in late Victorian liberalism. They believed in progress and the possibility that individuals could change the world for the better. They also believed that Britain was a progressive force in international relations and had a duty to use its influence for the benefit of the downtrodden. Buxton and Angell were internationalists who placed high hopes on the League of Nations. Winton was left wing, a typical member of the 'pink generation'. On the other hand, Cazalet was a Tory patriot, Nicolson was Tory inclined to the point of Fascism, and Bishop Henson was a vehement opponent of socialism.[48]

While considering the importance of political positioning and ideology, it may be instructive to draw on the provocative thesis recently advanced by Norman Geras in *The Contract of Mutual*

*Indifference. Political Philosophy After the Holocaust.* Here Geras adds a
new twist to the critique of liberalism advanced by Tony Kushner
and others, arguing that 'A liberal culture underwrites moral
indifference.' Geras points out that classic liberal thought is about
negatives: accepting anything that is not harmful to others and not
interfering in their affairs unless they do something that is. At times
of persecution and genocide, however, Geras maintains that 'A legal
and moral culture of rights and obligations largely structured
around the notion that one should refrain from harming others, but
that helping them is a matter of individual inclination, is plainly
inadequate.' The zero-sum social and economic system of liberal
capitalism reifies and reinforces this theory: 'it has been the norm for
the wealth and comfort of some to be obtained through the hardship
of others, and to stand alongside these. It is a whole mode of
collective existence.' It does not encourage compassion. Victorian
English liberalism was, therefore, no necessary guarantee of
progressive attitudes in the foreign arena.[49]

Nor is religion a more definitive factor. Henson was a bishop and
Parkes was ordained, but men of their outlook were rare birds in
the Anglican church. Parkes' personal theology was highly
unconventional. Foley was a 'devout Roman Catholic'. Deedes was
described as 'a Christian friend of the Jews' and Wedgwood (who
was violently anti-Catholic) routinely explained his philo-Zionism
in terms of the biblical heritage Jews shared with 'Anglo-Saxons'
(though he also said of the English and the Jews, 'We both are
moneylenders and unpopular... wanderers among strange peoples...
traders...'). Cazalet declared in New York in 1941 that 'it is because
I am a Christian and an Englishman that I claim the right and
privilege to speak for the Jews. My contention has always been that
the Jewish problem is a Christian problem.'[50] However, the faith in
Christian Science that gave Cazalet a sense of purpose did not stop
Nancy Astor being a crude Jew-hater, and Astor abandoned it
completely. Buxton was a typical Victorian Quaker, but Angell was
a typical Victorian atheist. Frank Foley told Benno Cohn that 'he was
acting as a Christian and that he wanted to show us how little the
Christians who were then in power in Germany had to do with real

Christianity.'[51] Winton, by contrast, was cynical about religion.

Fogelman identifies philo-semitism, a by-product of certain forms of Christian faith, as a motivation for rescuers. Some historians, notably W.D. Rubinstein and Hillary Rubinstein, even attribute the allegedly benign attitude of governments and populations in the English-speaking democracies to philo-semitism.[52] Gentile Zionism is certainly a theme running through the careers of these rescuers, but not consistently so. Wedgwood, Rathbone, Deedes, Cazalet, Parkes, and Astor were zealously pro-Zionist as well as pro-Jewish. But Bishop Henson, Norman Angell, and Noel Buxton said nothing in favour of Judaism or in support of Zionism. While he respected Judaism, Henson believed that Jews had a radically different moral system to Christianity: the two could not be mixed. Winton cared so little for Jews qua Jews that he did not care if Jewish children were stripped of their identity.

The identification with Jews could take other forms. Astor adored Jews because they were warm, expressive, and represented cosmopolitan culture, typified by psychoanalysis. But Henson, by contrast, despised Freud and thought Jews were 'inscrutable'. Cazelet went through a phase of seeing Jews in negative, stereotypical terms. Nicolson was so far from being a philo-semite that he confessed to feeling a 'physical aversion' to Jews and never changed his mind. Most perplexing in this taxonomy is evidence such as this that indifference or even hostility towards Judaism or dislike of Jews was actually no barrier to helping them. Other factors – a religious belief in the unity of mankind, an ideology such as internationalism, or simple human compassion – must have overridden it.

Age and generation played an influential part in these responses, as did self-identity, sexuality and gender. Despite his wealth and privilege, Astor felt like an outsider in his family and in British society as a whole. Parkes was an isolated figure within the Church of England and Henson was something of a maverick, too. Nicolson was a homosexual and the same was probably true to a greater or lesser degree for Rathbone, Deedes, and Cazelet. This may have encouraged an identification with persecuted outsiders and engendered an appreciation of tolerant societies in which diversity, of all types, was regarded as non-threatening. Indeed, it is highly significant that all these activists were willing to accept difference, even if they did not like that which set the Other apart. Wedgwood was a great English patriot, but he combined Englishness with a sense of diversity in his appeals for more immigration: immigrants, he argued, strengthened the Anglo-Saxons! Deedes spoke powerfully against assimilation because 'it is a sign of intolerance, and an act of impoverishment'. He articulated a way of thinking that anticipated contemporary multi-culturalism.[53]

Nicolson believed that gender was an element in Rathbone's concern for unfortunate others. She had 'feminine qualities of identification, of fanaticism, and of persistence'.[54] Women are unfortunately under-represented in this sample: one could add Rathbone's companion Katherine the Duchess of Atholl, the novelist and PEN (international writers' club) organiser Storm Jameson, Bertha Bracy, who ran the Quaker refugee operation, Greta Burkill, who worked with great effect to find jobs and places for Jewish academics, Dorothy Hardisty, the head of the Refugee Children's Movement from 1939 to 1948, and the Gentile Zionist Blanche Dugdale. But was gender decisive? Rathbone undoubtedly identified with other women, of all ethnic backgrounds and beliefs, but it was Nick Winton who set out to rescue children from Prague.[55]

The notion that their empathy for the plight of others was rooted in a similar kind of childhood or childhood experience is equally unhelpful. The individuals assembled here could not have had more diverse experiences of infancy and growing up.

In conclusion, the only experiences that seem to unite this band of refugee activists and rescuers are those of cosmopolitanism and a sense of personal responsibility. They were all well travelled and had experienced different cultures and societies. It was this, I think, that gave them the security to advocate help for people who were commonly dismissed as 'aliens' and 'foreigners'. They were schooled in a practical form of internationalism and were used to activity that routinely crossed international as well as cultural boundaries. Familiarity with Germany and central Europe may also have been terribly important. To them events in the 1930s and 1940s were not taking place in a 'far away land of which we know little'. They did not have to imagine the terror in order to empathise with the victims or feel rage against the perpetrators. For them it had become very real and personal and, hence, it was impossible for them to ignore it or to remain idle.

## NOTES

I would like to acknowledge the generous assistance of Professor Tony Kushner who read an earlier draft of this chapter. His research on refugee issues in Britain is a fundamental starting point for any work on this subject.

1. See Eva Fogelman, *Conscience and Courage: Rescuers of Jews during the Holocaust* (London: Cassell, 1993), pp.363–76. The first major, international conference on the subject was held in 1974, at Yad Vashem, Jerusalem.
2. For remarks on the absence of work on the democracies, see Tony Kushner, *The Holocaust and the Liberal Imagination* (Oxford: Blackwell, 1994), pp.11–18. For examples of recent general studies in this area see A.J. Sherman, *Island Refuge: Britain and Refugees from the Third Reich 1933–39* (London and Portland, OR: Frank Cass, 1994 edn.); Bernard Wasserstein, *Britain and the Jews of Europe 1939–1945* (Leicester: Leicester University Press, 1999 edn.); Louise London, *Whitehall and the Jews 1933–1948* (Cambridge: Cambridge University Press, 2000); Gerhard Hirschfeld, '"A High Tradition of Eagerness..."': British Non-Jewish Organisations in Support of Refugees' in W. Mosse (ed.), *Second Chance. Two Centuries of German-Speaking Jews in the UK* (Tübingen: J.C.B. Mohr, 1991), pp.599–610; David Wyman, *Paper Walls: America and the Refugee Crisis, 1938–1941* (New York: Pantheon, 1967) and idem, *The Abandonment of the Jews: America and the Holocaust* (New York: Schocken, 1984); Richard Breitman and Alan Kraut, *American Refugee Policy and European Jewry* (Bloomington: Indiana University Press, 1987); Vicki Caron, *Uneasy Asylum: France and the Jewish Refugee Crisis, 1933–1942* (Stanford: Stanford University Press, 1999); Paul Levine, *From Indifference to Activism: Swedish Diplomacy and the Holocaust, 1938–1944* (Uppsala: Uppsala University Press, 1996); Jacques Picard, *Die Schweiz und die Juden 1933–1945* (Zurich: Chronos, 1994); Irving Abella and Harold Troper, *None Is Too Many: Canada and the Jews of Europe* (Toronto: Lester and Orpen Dennys, 1983).
3. Kushner, *The Holocaust and the Liberal Imagination*, pp.45–6, 273.
4. Fogelman, *Conscience and Courage*, pp.41–66, 163–97.
5. Kushner, *The Holocaust and the Liberal Imagination*, p.48.
6. Fogelman, *Conscience and Courage*, pp.41–55.
7. Ibid., pp.57–60, 69–71, 80–82.
8. Ibid., pp.85–7, 163–5, 182–97.
9. Ibid., pp.253–66.

10. Yvonne Kapp and Margaret Mynatt, *British Policy and the Refugees, 1933–1941* (London and Portland, OR: Frank Cass, 1997; originally published in 1941), p.37 provides a reminder of the groundswell of pro-refugee sympathy and positive action. See also Hirschfeld, '"A High Tradition of Eagerness..."' in Mosse (ed.), *Second Chance*, pp.599–610 and for a local study, Tony Kushner and Katherine Knox, *Refugees in an Age of Genocide* (London and Portland, OR: Frank Cass, 1999), pp.145–54, 164–8.

11. See, *passim*, J.B. Stein, *Our Great Solicitor: Josiah C. Wedgwood and the Jews* (Selinsgrove: Susquehanna University Press, USA, 1992) and C.V. Wedgwood, *The Last of the Radicals: Josiah Wedgwood MP* (London: Cape, 1951). On post-1918 anti-alienism and Wedgwood's outspoken opposition to government policy, see David Cesarani, 'Anti-Alienism in England after the First World War', *Immigrants and Minorities*, Vol.6, No.1 (March 1987), pp.5–29.

12. Stein, *Our Great Solicitor*, pp.98–9, 101–3, 105–6, 107–8, 110, 113–14; Wedgwood, *The Last of the Radicals*, pp.216–17, 230.

13. Wedgwood, *The Last of the Radicals*, p.217.

14. For biographical details, see Mary Stocks, *Eleanor Rathbone: A Biography* (London: Gollancz, 1949); Johanna Alberti, *Eleanor Rathbone* (London: Sage, 1996).

15. Stocks, *Eleanor Rathbone*, pp.224–6, 238, 241–4.

16. Ibid., pp.260–61, 282–8; Alberti, *Eleanor Rathbone*, pp.134–5, 175.

17. Stocks, *Eleanor Rathbone*, p.299; David Cesarani, *Arthur Koestler: The Homeless Mind* (London: Heinemann, 1998), pp.184–5. In 1942, Rathbone also helped get a visa for Koestler's estranged wife who was stuck in Marseille. Ibid., p.202.

18. Cesarani, *Arthur Koestler*, pp.202–3; E. Thomas Wood and Stanislaw M. Jankowski, *Karski: How One Man Tried to Stop the Holocaust* (New York: John Wiley, 1994), pp.178–80.

19. Stocks, *Eleanor Rathbone*, pp.300–301, 318–23; Kushner, *The Holocaust and the Liberal Imagination*, pp.179, 181–7. See also the documentation provided in William D. Rubinstein, *The Myth of Rescue* (London: Routledge, 1997), pp.128–40.

20. See Robert Rhodes James, *Victor Cazalet: A Portrait* (London: Hamish Hamilton, 1976), chapter 1.

21. Ibid., p.55.

22. Ibid., on Ford, p.108; on Palestine, pp.174–8, 193–7.

23. Ibid., pp.156, 182–3.

24. Ibid., pp.202, 204–5, 224–6, 240, 251, 284.

25. For details of his early life, see John Presland, *Deedes Bey: A Study of Sir Wyndham Deedes 1883–1923* (London: Macmillan, 1942); for his religious beliefs see the various contributions to Eliahu Elath, Norman Bentwich, Doris May (eds.), *Memories of Sir Wyndham Deedes* (London: Gollancz, 1958), pp.20, 26, 33, 48, 53, 56, 59, 73.

26. Contribution by Bentwich in Elath, Bentwich, May (eds.), *Memories of Sir Wyndham Deedes*, pp.74–7.

27. See Mosa Anderson, *Noel Buxton: A Life* (London: Allen Unwin, 1952).

28. Ibid., pp.80–81, 110–11, 120, 134.

29. Norman Angell, *After All: The Autobiography of Norman Angell* (London: Hamish Hamilton, 1951), especially pp.96–100, 262–4, 280, 295 and 330–31.

30. James Lees–Milne, *Harold Nicolson: A Biography*, Vol.1, *1886–1929* (London: Chatto and Windus, 1980), especially pp.7, 120–21, 322–4.

31. James Lees-Milne, *Harold Nicolson: A Biography*, Vol.2, *1930–1968* (London: Chatto and Windus, 1981), especially pp.7–8, 15–18, 20–25.

32. Nigel Nicolson (ed.), *Harold Nicolson: Diaries and Letters 1930–39* (London: Collins, 1966), 8 September 1936 (p.272) and 22 May 1938 (p.343); Lees-Milne, *Harold Nicolson: A Biography*, Vol.2, pp.71–2, 105, 118. Cf. A. Scott Berg, *Lindbergh* (London: Macmillan, 1999), pp.360–62, 371–2, 373.

33. Lees-Milne, *Harold Nicolson: A Biography*, Vol.2, pp.157, 164; Nigel Nicolson (ed.), *Harold Nicolson: Diaries and Letters 1939–45* (London: Collins, 1967), 9 December 1942 (p.266), letter to Ben Nicolson, 20 December 1942 (p.268), 11 January 1944 (p.344), 7 May 1945 (p.456); Cesarani, *Arthur Koestler*, p.201.

34. Richard Cockett, *David Astor and the Observer* (London: Deutsch, 1991), pp.2–59.

35. Derek Wilson, *The Astors 1763–1992* (London: Weidenfeld and Nicolson, 1993), pp.228, 232, 257–8, 263–76, 342.

36. Cockett, *David Astor and the Observer*, pp.81–2; Cesarani, *Arthur Koestler*, pp.184–5, 212.

37. See entry by A.T.P. Williams in *Dictionary of National Biography* [DNB] (Oxford: Oxford University Press, 1971).

38. R.H. Henson, *Retrospect of an Unimportant Life*, Vol.2, *1920–1939* (Oxford: Oxford University Press, 1943), pp.313, 364; idem, *Retrospect of an Unimportant Life*, Vol.3, *1939–1945* (Oxford: Oxford University Press, 1950), pp.58, 257.

39. Henson, *Retrospect of an Unimportant Life*, Vol.3, pp.337, 354–5, 376, 379, 413–16.

40. James Parkes, *Voyages of Discovery* (London: Gollancz, 1969), pp.1–128. See chapters 8 and 12 for his eccentric personal and 'political' theology.

41. Idem, pp.84–7, 110–35, 126–35.

42. Idem, pp.104–6, 150, 174–5. On the CCJ see Kushner, *The Holocaust and the Liberal Imagination*, pp.165–8.

43. See Mark Jonathan Harris and Deborah Oppenheimer, *Into the Arms of Strangers: Stories of the Kindertransport* (London: Bloomsbury, 2000), pp.148–51. Barry Turner, *...And the Policeman Smiled* (London: Bloomsbury, 1990), pp.92–6; *Independent* (20 June 1998); 'Britain's Schindler', BBC Radio 4, transmitted June 1999, script by Tony Kushner.

44. Turner, *...And the Policeman Smiled*, pp.250–51. In a 1999 interview for a documentary film, Winton told a different story: 'There was one organisation over here, the Barbican Mission, which took quite a few children. I had no clue at the time that that particular organisation was there for converting Jews.' Harris and Oppenheimer, *Into the Arms of Strangers*, p.149.

45. Michael Smith, *Foley: The Spy Who Saved 10,000 Jews* (London: Hodder and Stoughton, 1999), *passim*, but especially pp.3–6, 7–15, 31, 51, 65. On Foley, Wilfred Israel and the intelligence nexus, see Naomi Shepherd, *A Refuge From Darkness: Wilfred Israel and the Rescue of the Jews* (New York: Pantheon, 1985), pp.90, 107–8, 129–31.

46. Smith, *Foley*, pp.65, 70–71, 76–82, 92–4, 133, 159, 164–5.

47. On Rathbone, in particular, see Stocks, *Eleanor Rathbone*, p.258.

48. On Henson's anti-socialism, see entry by A.T.P. Williams in *DNB*.

49. Norman Geras, *The Contract of Mutual Indifference: Political Philosophy after the Holocaust* (London: Verso, 1998), pp.58–9.

50. Wedgwood, *The Last of the Radicals*, p.181; Rhodes James, *Victor Cazalet*, pp.176–7.

51. Smith, *Foley*, pp.131–2.

52. See W.D. Rubinstein and H.L. Rubinstein, 'Philosemitism in Britain and in the English-Speaking World, 1840–1939: Patterns and Typology', *Jewish Journal of Sociology*, Vol.40, Nos.1/2 (1998), pp.5–46, esp.23–25.

53. Deedes in an address to the English Zionist Federation, November 1942, Bentwich in Elath, Bentwich, May (eds.), *Memories of Sir Wyndham Deedes*, p.73.

54. Cited in Stocks, *Eleanor Rathbone*, p.143.

55. On women activists, see Norman Rose (ed.,) *Baffy: The Diaries of Blanche Dugdale* (London: Valentine Mitchell, 1973); Katherine, Duchess of Atholl, *Memoirs* (London: Allen Unwin, 1960); Margaret Storm Jameson, *Autobiography of Storm Jameson: Journey from the North*, Vol.2 (London: Collins, 1970); Ray Cooper, *Refugee Scholars: Conversations with Tess Simpson* (Leeds; Moorland Books, 1992).

# 'Pissing in the Wind'? The Search for Nuance in the Study of Holocaust 'Bystanders'

## TONY KUSHNER

*I've been pissing in the wind*
*I chanced a foolish grin*
*and dribbled on my chin*
*Now the ground shifts beneath my feet*
*The faces that I greet never know my name*[1]

As we cross the threshold into a new millennium, interest in the Holocaust continues to escalate. At an artistic and cultural level, representations of the Holocaust, especially in film and literature, have never been so intense and pervasive. Equally remarkably, well over 50 years later the legal confrontation with the Holocaust through issues of compensation, return of property and war crimes trials has gathered critical momentum. Recent efforts by international and national governments, as well as by private bodies, have attempted, with greater or lesser success, to achieve justice in areas that were either superficially examined or totally ignored/dismissed at the end of the war.[2] More generally, the Holocaust is now commonly perceived in the western world as one of the defining moments of the twentieth century, raising the essential moral questions about human nature and the nature of modernity.

It is important to remember, however, that the concept of the Holocaust as a particular part of the Second World War, or more generally of the Nazi era, involving specifically the planned extermination of European Jewry, took many years to evolve, a process that was uneven and is still perhaps incomplete. One example of this gradual evolution has emerged from one of the recent attempts to achieve compensation not from a perpetrator nation, but a so-called bystander, Britain. Assets from the deposit accounts of continental Jews in British banks were confiscated by the government during the war, as these belonged to people who were now citizens of enemy nations or enemy-occupied countries. After the war, attempts by those who survived or by their relatives to claim back the money or property were for the large part turned down by the British government. Being Jewish was not enough to prove that one was a victim of the Nazis rather than an enemy alien. As one Treasury official put it, 'I do not know how you will distinguish between the Jew who has been persecuted because of his race or religion, and one who has been sent to a concentration camp for committing a criminal offence against the law of his country.'[3] Moreover, experiences of slave labour, hiding and the ghettos were not proof of having suffered persecution. The category of victim was limited to some of those who had died or survived the concentration camps, the definition of which was vague but undoubtedly heavily influenced by perceptions of the images of the liberated western camps such as Buchenwald and Belsen.[4]

In similar fashion in 1945 the Home Office allowed in, on a temporary basis after much campaigning, a very small number of child survivors, but it stipulated that they must not all be Jewish and that they should come from one or two named camps, particularly, again, Belsen.[5] In short, the immediate legacy of the images of 1945 and the subsequent war crimes trials was that of essentially undifferentiated Nazi atrocities. There was little interest in the victims and only a short-lived concern to confront and deal with the perpetrators of atrocities. In the new Cold War logic, the latter were soon transformed from the German nation as a whole into very specific parts of it. In essence, the higher echelons of the Nazi state structure were blamed, especially the 'criminal' SS, who could be labelled as exceptional monsters, mad(wo)men or sadists, unrelated to everyday folk like 'us'.[6] The concept of the bystander was all but lacking at this time, an absence of consideration eased by the American, British, Soviet, French and Polish involvement in the immediate post-1945 war crimes trials. The world was divided between the Nazis and those who had resisted them, even if this meant, particularly in the case of France, creating a national myth that has been so powerful it is still to be fully overcome.[7]

Perceptions some 50 years later have, however, changed remarkably. Rightly, much time and energy has been spent researching the motivations of the murderers, and the estimates of the number of those involved was growing ever larger well before the sensationalist work of Daniel Goldhagen. We may never ultimately know why so many ordinary people agreed to take part in the Final Solution, but it is clear that choice played a bigger role than was previously acknowledged. The detailed scholarship revealing the sheer scale of those involved and the greater freedom to say 'no' might have further undermined the idea that genocide was carried out by two dimensional, leather-clad, diabolic beasts. Nevertheless, the hugely popular success of Goldhagen's imagery of bloodthirsty Germans acting as 'willing executioners', in contrast to the relatively obscure work of Christopher Browning and his understated portrayal of mundane 'ordinary men' in a police battalion stumbling into mass murder, suggests that we still prefer our killers to be presented as evil sadists.[8] More strikingly, the victim has gone from total obscurity, or as an object simply there to represent the evils done by the perpetrator, to one of major interest, if still not centre stage. Survivor evidence was largely excluded from the post-war trials,[9] and in many different countries where they settled, treatment of the surviving Jews was shabby and even violent; they were often seen as an embarrassment and their stories were ignored or silenced.[10] Steven Spielberg's project founded in the 1990s, the Survivors of the Shoah Visual History Foundation, which aimed to interview as many survivors as possible, is one illustration of change,[11] although how to incorporate the voices of the victims, other than as rather tokenistic illustrations of what the Nazis did, remains an unsolved dilemma in historical writing on the Holocaust and in the growing number of museums devoted to the subject.[12] Considerations of gender, age, religious and political background, to name but a few, have started to be addressed, complicating the 'victim' category even when confined to consideration of the Jews. Nevertheless, 'victim' is now firmly established as the second part of the tripartite division of the principal actors of the Holocaust. The third, of course, is the 'bystander', as unquestioned on a popular level today as it was absent from consideration in 1945.

The recent Goldhagen-Browning debate about the importance or otherwise of antisemitism and/or Germanness in the motivation of the murderers, as much as the fraught controversies of the 1950s and 1960s about alleged Jewish passivity and collaboration, show the power of Holocaust scholarship to stir up deep-felt emotions regarding perpetrators and victims. But it is, perhaps, the area of the bystander which has caused the greatest soul-searching and anger in recent years. Indeed it must be suggested that it is the popular division of the Holocaust into the neat categories of perpetrator-victim-bystander[13] that is fundamental to why it is seen as raising all the crucial moral questions of our age.[14] There is no serious doubting of the horror and scale of the crime, now little questioning of the impact on the victims and, finally, few exceptions to a general awareness that little or nothing was done to stop it happening by those who stood by. The moral concern about bystanders comes out of the rather complacent assumption that few of us will become perpetrators, and an equal optimism that we will not become victims, while at the same time we are aware that in an age of almost instant global communications, we are all co-presents witnessing, even if only through the media, the genocides, ethnic cleansing and other manifestations of extreme racism that besmirch the contemporary world. However, whereas the ambiguities and contradictions of human nature make the study of bystanders so fascinating, significant and ultimately relevant to today, there seems to be little desire for this to be brought out in studies of the Holocaust.

Put bluntly, we like our bystanders to be as bifurcated as the categories of victim and perpetrator. Given the centrality of the Holocaust in contemporary philosophical and theoretical debates about the nature of humankind in the modern age and beyond, this is a dangerous if understandable development. For rather than nuancing our understanding of the complexity of human responses during the Holocaust, the bystander category is in danger of aiding the tendency to see the subject in Manichean terms, as a symbol of mass evil alongside much less prevalent absolute good (with the emphasis put on the latter to enable hope for the future). As Shoshana Felman has written in relation to literary critic Paul de Man and the heated reaction to his exposure as a collaborator in Belgium during the war:

> [he] was 'Nazi': in denouncing him as one of 'them', we believe we place ourselves in a different zone of ethics and of temporality; 'we', as opposed to 'they', are on the right side of history – a side untouched, untainted by the evil of the Holocaust.[15]

Even Zygmunt Bauman in his *Modernity and the Holocaust*, which throughout strips away the power of individual agency, concludes by praising those people who 'chose moral duty over the rationality of self-preservation ... Evil is not all-powerful. It can be resisted.'[16] The danger is that ordinary people today, with all their moral ambiguities, will find it hard if not impossible to make connections to the Holocaust, other than in fascination at its sheer horror or by taking glib inspiration from the two-dimensional representation of its canonised non-Jewish heroes such as Oskar Schindler and Raoul Wallenberg.[17] This article will illustrate this point further by examining in particular the recent representation, especially within the historiography, of Britain's responses and reactions to the plight of the Jews during the Nazi era.

During the war a group of dedicated campaigners, especially the MP Eleanor Rathbone, attempted to mobilise public opinion in Britain to force the government and international bodies to recognise and publicise the plight of European Jewry, and from there to take whatever action was possible to help and rescue the 'victims of Nazi terror'.[18] Although these campaigners were prolific, their work and writings were largely forgotten in the immediate post-war period. Outside a few Zionist circles for whom Britain was now 'enemy number one', there was no mention of the activists and the embarrassing issues they had raised in the war. Instead, a more comfortable mythology developed that nothing was known and that only with liberation of the camps did knowledge become available. Ironically, the liberation of the western camps, rather than prompting questions of what could have been done to stop them, was more often than not used to show the moral certainty of the British and American war effort. Images from the camps were 'proof positive' that it had indeed been a 'just war'.[19]

The contesting of this mythology has taken a long time to gather momentum and is still far from complete. Both the US Holocaust Museum in Washington and the Imperial War Museum Holocaust Exhibition in London start or end with the respective American and British soldiers liberating western concentration camps in the spring of 1945. Nevertheless, beyond these initial images they both have critiques of American/British responses to the Jewish plight during the Nazi era. There is still a problem, however, with the prism through which they confront the role of these particular bystanders, which in turn reflects a continuing problem in the historiography.[20] In both Britain and the US, the first books on responses to the Holocaust were crude, semi-journalistic and angry in tenor.[21] By the early 1960s, the comforting myth of ignorance had grown to create a reassuringly safe cocoon against self-reflection at the time when the concept of the Holocaust as a separate entity, largely through the Eichmann trial, was starting to emerge. Books such as those by Arthur Morse, and to a lesser extent David Wyman in the United States and Andrew Sharf in Britain, attempted to shatter the illusion that nothing was known or that nothing could have been done.[22] The tone of complacency gave way to one of accusation. Yet the tendency towards condemnation, shock and sensationalism, which was understandable as the emotional subject was 'rediscovered' during the 1960s, has still not disappeared. Indeed, the anger has been revived more recently with campaigns for legal redress evidenced by the successful lobbying of the Holocaust Education Trust in Britain and in the US by its much more powerful equivalents in the world of organised American Jewry. Moral outrage has been reinforced in the former case by the willingness of sections of the British media to give attention to material released from the Public Record Office, the details of which, particularly in relation to state knowledge of the Holocaust during the war, including within the intelligence world, have often already been reported.[23]

Nevertheless, in Britain through the 1970s and 1980s, more detailed scholarship emerged, but less intensively because of the slow release of government papers and the limited interest in the Holocaust across society and culture as a whole. The first serious work on Britain, tellingly by an American, was A.J. Sherman's *Island Refuge*, covering British refugee policy from 1933 to the outbreak of war. Using what was still a relatively limited range of government papers available in the public domain, Sherman provided a solid narrative of official responses to the Jewish refugee crisis. Yet even in Sherman's self-conscious desire to concentrate on description, it is significant that his conclusion is entitled 'A Balance Sheet'. Indeed, in his much-quoted final paragraph Sherman states that when 'Great Britain's refugee policy [of the 1930s is] compared with that of other countries it emerges ... as comparatively compassionate, even generous'.[24]

It is the 'balance sheet' approach that has continued to dominate the historiography since Sherman's book was published in 1973. Sherman in particular compared Britain to the US – for example, setting the failure of the Wagner-Rogers bill to bring 20,000 refugee children in 1939 against the success of the Kindertransports which brought 10,000 children to Britain before the outbreak of war. He therefore rejected the charge 'of indifference to the fate of refugees from the Nazi regime'.[25] Subsequently, little genuine national comparative work has been carried out either on the 1930s or the Second World War with regard to the liberal democracies. Instead the balance sheet metaphor has been applied within individual nation states in relation to what was done, and not done, for Jews persecuted by the Nazis. Returning to museum representation of the Holocaust in the Anglo-American world, anti-refugee sentiment, including that within the state structure, is included in the two national museums, but is done so in a self-conscious desire to show fairness alongside the help offered to the persecuted. Indeed, the Imperial War Museum convened an emergency meeting when finalising its text and display, to debate whether the exhibition was either too critical or too uncritical of British responses.[26]

On one level it can be argued that with the Imperial War Museum's narrative ending with the numbing images of British soldiers liberating Belsen and in view of the new exhibition's setting in London – that is, in the heart of the former empire that within the national mythology of Britain 'stood alone' and eventually defeated Nazism – a few examples of British Union of Fascist antisemitic anti-refugee propaganda and anti-refugee comments from newspapers are not likely to create a sense of an atmosphere of self-criticism for the visitor. At a more fundamental level, however, the balance-sheet approach, whilst understandable when a large bureaucratic institution confronts something as difficult as the Holocaust, is ultimately unhelpful either as an analytical tool or one designed to prompt self-reflection. Reviewing the literature in 1987, Michael Marrus stated that 'there is a strong tendency in historical writing on bystanders to the Holocaust to condemn, rather than to explain.' He adds that 'Historians have quite properly combed the seamy underside of Allied and Jewish policy, searching through records sometimes deliberately hidden from view. But they should take care in using such material, to give contemporaries a fair hearing.'[27] The key is to understand why they reacted and responded in the way they did, not avoiding the moral issues raised, but doing so by exploring the possibilities of choice that were available to contemporaries, inside and outside of government.

The early work on allied responses to the plight of the Jews was marred not just by its accusatory nature but by its lack of any wider sense of context. There was little awareness of either the dynamics of the bystander nation or the chronological development and confused nature of Nazi antisemitic policy. In contrast, the more detailed research that has taken place in the last 25 years has had greater success in dealing with questions of *realpolitik* – the other concerns of government departments and Jewish organisations in the Nazi era. Even more fruitful has been the longer term approach to government policies, especially involving immigrants and refugees – showing how they had evolved *before* the Nazi rise to power and the continuity or otherwise after 1933. The work of Louise London on Britain, Richard Breitman and Alan Kraut on the US, and Paul Levine on Sweden are excellent examples of contextualised, bureacratic history.[28] It is still the case, however, that far less progress has been made with understanding the cultural, societal and ideological underpinnings of either state or society's responses to the plight of the persecuted Jews in the liberal democratic and other bystander nations. In this respect, one of the greatest barriers to progress is the use or avoidance of the term 'antisemitism'.

Michael Marrus, in his survey of literature on bystanders, states that, 'Generally speaking, few historians believe antisemitism to have been decisive in blocking aid to the Jews' – a view from which he does not seem to dissent.[29] Bernard Wasserstein, in his follow up to Sherman's account of British government responses, taking the story through the Second World War, provides what is still the dominant analysis, blaming 'bureaucratic indifference' for the fact that there was 'little to celebrate in [his] account of British policy towards the Jews of Europe between 1939 and 1945'. Wasserstein, whilst not ignoring what he called 'the tinge of anti-Semitism in the words of some British officials and politicians' states bluntly that 'anti-Semitism does not by itself explain British conduct ... conscious anti-Semitism should not be regarded as an adequate explanation of official behaviour.'[30]

The problem here is one of context and definition. The list of self-identifying antisemites in twentieth-century Britain would hardly enter the hundreds.[31] What do we mean by antisemitism in a British or other liberal democratic context? The easiest answer is to concentrate on the extreme – for example, fascists such as Oswald Mosley who could be seen to be obsessed by the Jewish peril. Racism in Britain has been and continues to be blamed on such extremists, helping to avoid confrontation with a wider problem. Ultimately such Nazis and neo-Nazis can be seen to be merely imitating those on the diseased continent; indeed, as not really English at all.[32] But beyond the swastika-wearing fringe, how British society and culture deals with minorities such as Jews proves to be far more difficult to confront, leading to the paradoxical situation where politicians and others throughout the twentieth century have praised the tolerance and essential British decency towards foreigners whilst simultaneously doing their best to exclude them from entry lest they bring racism with them.[33]

Throughout the discourse of government officials reproduced by Sherman, Wasserstein and others, it is apparent that the Jewishness of the victims of Nazism as potential refugees to Britain, Palestine and elsewhere in the empire, or as other recipients of British support, mattered. But neither Sherman, who rejected the term 'indifference', nor Wasserstein, who embraced it, were comfortable analysing the implications of that contemporary bureaucratic confrontation with Jewishness. What I attempted to do in *The Holocaust and the Liberal Imagination* (1994) was to explore this question through the prism of the dominant ideology and culture of Britain and the US in the Nazi era and beyond. Antisemitism, or other forms of racism, has often been explained as owing to the absence or relative weakness of liberalism. But the situation in Britain, the US and many other liberal democracies during the 1930s and 1940s was more complex. Assimilation was still seen as the dominant solution to the so-called 'Jewish question' in liberal thinking. If antisemitism persisted in the modern, enlightened world, it was because Jews insisted on retaining their difference, or rather went beyond a religious identity that was perceived as being compatible with national belonging. The more different the Jews, the more dangerous – hence the hostility of British and many other officials to Jews from eastern Europe, one which often went alongside praising the much more integrated Jewish communities of western Europe.[34] In short, a fundamental ambivalence existed: genuine anguish at the violence of Nazi antisemitism but a failure to confront why it was happening and a tendency to blame the victims if not to support the severity of the punishment; belief in Britain as a genuinely tolerant society that prided itself on the help it had offered refugees in the past, but a fear of letting in other than carefully selected individual Jews, or individual groups of Jews, lest they bring antisemitism with them.[35]

Paul Levine has argued that very similar considerations were employed by leading civil servants in the Swedish Foreign Office until the middle of the Second World War. What is intriguing, however, is how the two countries followed at specific times very different policies towards the persecuted Jews. From 1933 to 1938, highly selective immigration policies dominated in both Britain and Sweden. In the former country, however, entry was opened up in the year before war, with some 40,000 Jews allowed entry only for a policy of almost total restrictionism to be adhered to during the conflict and the years that followed.[36]

How do we explain this relatively large number admitted in the last months of peace? Undoubtedly British guilt after Munich, especially after the moral integrity of appeasement was totally destroyed in the light of *Kristallnacht*,[37] alongside the closing of the doors to Palestine, explain why procedures were eased by the government. But other factors were at work enabling the movement to be defended along liberal grounds. First, almost all those allowed entry to Britain were on temporary visas – that way they would not create a permanent 'problem'. Second, they would be spread out and re-trained so as to normalise them – whether as trainee agricultural workers, domestic servants or nurses. It is no accident that Ernest Bevin, who, as Foreign Secretary in the 1940s was to exclude Jews from Britain, was very positive, as general secretary of the world's largest trade union during the 1930s, towards the entry of several thousand German Jewish youngsters who were to be trained in agricultural techniques in the British countryside, with the hope that they would practice their new skills in Palestine or elsewhere.[38]

Bevin is worth a little more attention in order to tease out further the problems of utilising the term 'antisemitism' in a British context. After the war, Bevin became a great hate figure in large parts of the Jewish world. His opposition to Jewish immigration to Palestine and insensitivity to Holocaust survivors helped lead to him being perceived as motivated 'by a personal hatred of Jews'. As Alan

Bullock, Bevin's biographer, comments, 'From this sprang the stereotype of him as the latest in the long series of persecutors of the Jews beginning with Titus and Haman and continuing down to Hitler and Himmler'. Subsequently, 'pop' psychology has been employed to explain Bevin's alleged hatred of Jews as coming out of his troubled childhood. His crudity and insensitivity are undoubted – he simply made no attempt to empathise with the horrors inflicted so recently on the Jewish people.[39]

What *is* remarkable about Bevin is that he stubbornly stuck to a classic liberal position on the Jews. Such a claim about Bevin in *The Holocaust and the Liberal Imagination* was called 'untenable' by one reviewer and 'far-fetched' by another. If 'liberal' is seen *per se* as an absolute good, then the surprise at the label attached to Bevin can be understood.[40] But what Bevin wanted was for the Jews to return to their various 'homelands' rather than attempting to escape their countries of citizenship, or former citizenship, and, he claimed, jumping to the 'head of the queue' to leave the continent of Europe. Jews, Bevin argued, should return 'home' from the DP camps and become once again good Germans and Poles and so on. In 1945 and 1946 as Foreign Secretary, he allowed a small number of young Jews to come to Britain as long as the men would go on the land and the women became nurses. He wanted them to become useful and to stop an 'undesirable concentration of them in towns'. When this failed to happen, unsurprisingly given their physical state, the Jewish survivors were kept out whilst at the same time the British government enabled hundreds of thousands of continental non-Jews, some of whom had been Nazi collaborators, to enter because they were seen as desirable, assimilable immigrants.[41]

Bevin's policies, however, followed on from those of his rival and fellow Labour cabinet minister, Herbert Morrison, Home Secretary from 1940 to the end of the Second World War. Both men were sincere anti-Nazis at home and abroad; Morrison on a personal level was surrounded by Jewish friends and work colleagues.[42] On the one hand, the label antisemite does not seem to help other than to provide a neat but ultimately superficial explanation of their policies. On the other, to reject the possibility that Jewishness had anything to do with official thinking avoids confronting the contemporary obsession with the subject.[43] Indeed, the almost total restrictionism against Jewish refugees from September 1939 to 1950 carried out by the British government has to be explained, and this can only be done successfully by analysing how liberal ambivalence, especially the idea that Jews bring antisemitism with them, was taken to its logical extreme, becoming in itself ingrained into bureaucratic mentality and practice.[44]

It is worth pausing briefly to ponder why such restrictionist thinking broke down in Sweden from mid-1942. Clearly the situations of Sweden and Britain cannot be directly compared at that point in time. As Paul Levine has illustrated, there were highly pragmatic reasons, such as the way the war was going, that explain why Sweden went from measures of tentative individual rescue of Jews up to 1942 to ones in 1943, and particularly in 1944, of mass rescue.[45] But what is fascinating is how a senior official such as Gösta Engzell, whose comments about foreign Jews and the causes of antisemitism could have come straight out of the mouths and writings of Herbert Morrison or Ernest Bevin, helped facilitate in the second half of the war the rescue of Jews, many of whom had the most limited or non-existent Swedish connections. To label Engzell an antisemite or, equally ludicrously, a philo-semite, misses the point.[46]

The reality is that most bystander responses were marked by a fundamental ambivalence to Jews and Jewish suffering. Not only is ambivalence difficult to pigeonhole, but it was fluid and dynamic, able to respond to different impulses and demands in an unpredictable manner. Thus, at the point at which British officials learned to deal with calls to aid Jews in the most universal way possible (that is, to win the war and to reject the idea that Jews particularly were being singled out for persecution), Swedish officials learned to give meaning to the concept of asylum and to overcome the negative tendencies of their ambivalent thinking. Yet the latter tendency had been true of Britain in the year before the war. The result was that tens of thousands of ordinary people were involved in refugee work in Britain during 1939. Not surprisingly, however, given the previous hostility, the treatment that refugees received on entering Britain was mixed. Not all could confront their own ambiguities about Jews, but it did not stop them demanding that the persecuted be allowed entry. Liberal ambivalence within the state and the public enabled both restrictionism and generous rescue policies to succeed within bystander nations at different times and different places.

The failure in much subsequent scholarship on Britain and the Holocaust since *The Holocaust and the Liberal Imagination* was published to confront the nature of liberalism and the importance of ambivalence is on one level disappointing but on another deeply revealing. Some reviewers have engaged in the central argument and quite rightly called for more detailed work to explore much further the nature of liberalism and its relation to nationalism and ethnic difference.[47] A more common response, however, has been to assume that this is yet another accusatory text that sees 'antisemitism' as the answer to why so little was done, or, paradoxically, to condemn the book for not reaching that conclusion. In any case, the desire for black or white explanations is telling. Ambivalent figures are not welcome, and there has been an increasing tendency to seek out the moral giants in the bystander worlds whose actions either confirm the weakness of those around them or confirm that ordinary mortals could have done little to help. In 1999 alone, Frank Foley, senior Passport Control Officer in the British embassy in Berlin, *and* Nicholas Winton, a businessman who helped bring refugee children to Britain from Czechoslovakia in 1939, were labelled 'Britain's Schindler'. In both cases, market research (accurate as it happens) revealed that this is what the public wanted to hear and read. Crudely constructed renderings of the work of Winton and Foley, as Anne Karpf suggests, 'function as the happy endings of the Holocaust that we impossibly crave'.[48]

Such tendencies, which seem to be growing in Holocaust commemoration, have many problems associated with them. First, they highlight the role of the major figure in the process, as is the case with Raoul Wallenberg, ignoring the very many ordinary people who enabled their actions to have their spectacular success.[49]

Second, they make saints or angels, both words used to describe Foley, out of these figures, often ignoring their more complex nature and their reasons for engaging in rescue and relief.[50] Third, they allow self-congratulation to become dominant – as illustrated in Britain in 1999 with the plaque unveiled in the House of Commons, 'in deep gratitude to the people and Parliament of the United Kingdom for saving the lives of 10,000 Jewish and other children who fled to this country from Nazi persecution on the Kindertransport 1938–1939'.[51] There is no mention, of course, of the parents who were excluded from this refugee movement. Was this generous in the circumstances or fundamentally inhumane? The question is unanswerable – no balance sheet approach can take away the heartache of separation from the gratitude of life-saving asylum and come up with a meaningful answer.[52]

But the increasing emphasis on gratitude and the help that was provided by the exceptional few has encouraged the success of a revisionism, led in the Anglo-American cases by William Rubinstein in *The Myth of Rescue*. This work argues that during the 1930s, given the circumstances, all that could have been done was done, and that in the Second World War itself not one single Jew could have been rescued by the Allies.[53] Although most academic responses to Rubinstein have so far been critical, popular reviews, especially (it has to be said) from non-Jews, have been very favourable. Clearly, Rubinstein's work has appealed at an emotional level to many: for those anxious about the moral integrity of the British and American war memory, *The Myth of Rescue* removes any nasty tarnish that, in their minds, has unfairly developed in recent years. Furthermore, it negates the need for further self-reflection.[54] Indeed, a detailed survey of attitudes carried out in 2000 revealed that most believed that Britain had been very generous in helping the Jews of Europe during the Nazi era, with a minority of respondents equally simplistically arguing that nothing had been done to help.[55] This brings me to my final point: Rubinstein lets the reader off from any consideration of the dilemmas facing bystanders, and his success suggests that he has struck a popular chord. It might be added that Rubinstein's Jewishness has perhaps removed any restraint from saying the 'wrong thing'. As Norman Stone, praising what he saw as a 'very good book', stated: 'For the rest of us, common sense and decency make it extremely difficult to offend elderly survivors by suggesting that the picture needs to be amended.'[56]

But choices *were* there for the bystanders. Of course, these need to be placed in their specific contexts, recognising their own particular specific limitations, throughout the Nazi era. Yet there is a danger that, rather than confronting the ambivalence, contradictions and ambiguities of contemporaries, we either increasingly take refuge in the creation of plaster saints or retreat, as with the obsessive interest in the western intelligence world and its knowledge of the Holocaust, into the comfortable fiction that only the privileged few knew of its existence during the war or that nothing at all could be done to stop mass murder. The search for nuance in responses to the Holocaust, certainly in the British case, seems to slip further away as time progresses.[57]

## NOTES

1. 'Pissing in the Wind', Badly Drawn Boy, *The Hour of the Bewilderbeast*, XL Recordings, 2000.

2. Christian Pross, *Paying for the Past: The Struggle over Reparations for Surviving Victims of the Nazi Terror* (Baltimore and London: Johns Hopkins University Press, 1998); Avi Beker (ed.), *The Plunder of Jewish Property during the Holocaust: Confronting European History* (Basingrave: Palgrave, 2001).

3. Public Record Office (PRO), T 236/4312, R.R. Whitty, Custodian of Enemy Property Office, to Gregory, Trading with the Enemy Department, 9 Oct. 1947, quoted in Gill Bennett et al., *History Notes: British policy towards enemy property during and after the Second World War* (London: Foreign and Commonwealth Office, 1998), p.37. For a more critical appraisal, see The Holocaust Educational Trust, '*Ex-Enemy Jews*' – *The Fate of the Assets in Britain of Holocaust Victims and Survivors* (London: Holocaust Educational Trust, 1997).

4. Bennett et al., *History Notes*; The Holocaust Education Trust, '*Ex-Enemy Jews*'.

5. PRO, HO 213/618 E409, H. Prestige memorandum, 21 Sept. 1945.

6. See Donald Bloxham, 'The Holocaust on Trial: The War Crimes Trials in the Formation of History and Memory' (unpublished PhD thesis, University of Southampton, 1998).

7. Tony Kushner, *The Holocaust and the Liberal Imagination: A Social and Cultural History* (Oxford: Blackwell, 1994); Henry Rousso, *The Vichy Syndrome: History and Memory in France since 1944* (Cambridge, MA and London: Harvard University Press, 1991).

8. Ernst Klee, Willi Dressen and Volker Riess, '*Those were the Days*': *The Holocaust through the Eyes of the Perpetrators and Bystanders* (London: Hamish Hamilton, 1991); Christopher Browning, *Ordinary Men: Reserve Police Battalion 101 and the Final Solution in Poland* (New York: HarperCollins, 1992); Daniel Goldhagen, *Hitler's Willing Executioners: Ordinary Germans and the Holocaust* (Boston: Little, Brown, 1996).

9. Bloxham, 'The Holocaust on Trial'.

10. Kushner, *The Holocaust and the Liberal Imagination*, intro., ch.7; Tony Kushner, 'Holocaust Survivors in Britain: An Overview and Research Agenda', *The Journal of Holocaust Education*, Vol.4, No.2 (Winter 1995), pp.147–66.

11. See, for example, Survivors of the Shoah Visual History Foundation, *The Last Days* (London: Weidenfeld and Nicolson, 1999).

12. Amongst the limited literature examining the nature of Holocaust testimony from ordinary survivors, mainly relating to the Fortunoff Video Archive for Holocaust Testimonies at Yale University, see Geoffrey Hartman, 'Learning from Survivors: the Yale Testimony Project', *Holocaust and Genocide Studies*, Vol.9, No.2 (Fall 1995), pp.192–207; Lawrence Langer, *Holocaust Testimonies: The Ruins of Memory* (New Haven: Yale University Press, 1991); Shoshana Felman and Dori Laub, *Testimony: Crises of Witnessing in Literature, Psychoanalysis and History* (New York and London: Routledge, 1992). A less systematic but much more dynamic and sensitive account is provided by Henry Greenspan, *On Listening to Holocaust Survivors: Recounting and Life History* (Westport, CT: Praeger, 1998).

13. Raul Hilberg, *Perpetrators Victims Bystanders: The Jewish Catastrophe 1933–1945* (New York: HarperCollins, 1992), although it should be added that Hilberg does explore the complexity of and slippage between all these categories.

14. An early example was Hannah Arendt, *Eichmann in Jerusalem: A Report on the Banality of Evil* (New York: Viking Press, 1963). From the late 1980s, there has been an immense flood of books using the Holocaust to explore the nature of humanity and morality in the modern world, written both by those with expertise and by those with little knowledge of the subject matter. See, for example, Rainer Baum, 'Holocaust: Moral Indifference as the Form of Modern Evil', in A. Rosenberg and G. Meyers (eds.), *Echoes from the Holocaust: Philosophical Reflections on a Dark Time* (Philadelphia: Temple University Press, 1988), pp.53–90; Zygmunt Bauman, *Modernity and the Holocaust* (Oxford: Polity Press, 1989); Berel Lang, *Act and Idea in the Nazi Genocide* (Chicago and London: University of Chicago Press, 1990); Saul Friedlander, *Memory, History and the Extermination of the Jews of Europe* (Bloomington and Indianapolis: Indiana University Press, 1993); Omer Bartov, *Murder in our Midst: The Holocaust, Industrial Killing and Representation* (New York and Oxford: Oxford University Press, 1996); Michael Burleigh, *Ethics and Extermination: Reflections of Nazi Genocide* (Cambridge: Cambridge University Press, 1997); Norman Geras, *The Contract of Mutual Indifference: Political Philosophy after the Holocaust* (London: Verso, 1998); Jonathan Glover, *Humanity: A Moral History of the Twentieth Century* (London: Jonathan Cape, 1999); David Blumenthal, *The Banality of Good and Evil: Moral Lessons from the Shoah and the Jewish Tradition* (Washington: Georgetown University Press, 1999).

15. Felman and Laub, *Testimony*, p.122.

16. Bauman, *Modernity and the Holocaust*, p.207.

17. Paul Levine, 'Raoul Wallenberg in Budapest: Modern Jewry's Ultimate Hero?', in M. Mor (ed.), *Crisis and Reaction: The Hero in Jewish History* (Omaha, NE: Creighton University Press, 1995), pp.251–67.

18. See Kushner, *The Holocaust and the Liberal Imagination*, part II; for an analysis of these activists, their writings and their impact on state and society, see Tony Kushner and Katharine Knox, *Refugees in an Age of Genocide: Global, National and Local Perspectives During the Twentieth Century* (London: Frank Cass, 1999), ch.6.

19. Tony Kushner, 'The Memory of Belsen', in Joanne Reilly *et al.* (eds.), *Belsen in History and Memory* (London: Frank Cass, 1997), pp.181–205.

20. Edward Linenthal, *Preserving Memory: The Struggle to Create America's Holocaust Museum* (New York and London: Viking, 1995), p.193; Michael Berenbaum, *The World Must Know: The History of the Holocaust as Told in the United States Holocaust Memorial Museum* (Boston:

Little, Brown, 1993). Philip Gourevitch, 'Nightmare on 15th Street', *Guardian*, 4 Dec. 1999 comments on the quote by General Dwight Eisenhower when viewing the mass graves at Ohrduf concentration camp: 'We are told that the American soldier does not know what he was fighting for. Now at least he will know what he is fighting against'. As Gourevitch adds, 'Ike's remarks could serve as the museum's motto'; for a critique of the ethos of the planned Imperial War Museum's Holocaust Exhibition, see Donald Bloxham and Tony Kushner, 'Exhibiting Racism: Cultural Imperialism, Genocide and Representation', *Rethinking History*, Vol.2, No.3 (1998), pp.353–6.

21. For example, Arthur Morse, *While Six Million Died* (New York: Random House, 1968); Andrew Sharf, *The British Press and Jews under Nazi Rule* (London: Institute of Race Relations/Oxford University Press, 1964).

22. David Wyman, *Paper Walls: America and the Refugee Crisis 1938–1941* (Amherst: University of Massachusetts Press, 1968) represented the first account based on detailed, scholarly research.

23. For recent British press coverage, see Denis Staunton, 'Whitehall Sat on 1942 Goebbels Genocide Speech', *Observer*, 21 Nov. 1993; Michael Dynes, 'Nazis Wanted British Troops as Guards at Death Camps', *The Times*, 27 Nov. 1993, partly relating to the release of material in PRO, HW 1/929; Tim Rayment, 'Britain Barred Rescue Plan for Doomed Jews, *Sunday Times*, 8 May 1994; *The Times*, 23 and 30 Jan. 1995, relating to French Jewish orphans and the British government – relating to PRO papers released many years before; Bernard Josephs, 'War Papers Show Britain Knew of Mass Slaughter', *Jewish Chronicle*, 15 Nov. 1996; Richard Norton-Taylor, 'Code Breakers Reported Slaughter of Jews in 1941', *Guardian*, 20 May 1997, and similar reports in the national press on the same day; Richard Norton-Taylor, 'Britain Stymied Help for Jews in Nazi Camps', *Guardian*, 21 July 1999; Barbara Rogers, 'Auschwitz and the British', *History Today*, Vol.49, No.10 (Oct. 1999), pp.2–3; Peter Beaumont, 'British spy's early alert on Holocaust', *Observer*, 8 July 2001.

24. A.J. Sherman, *Island Refuge: Britain and Refugees from the Third Reich 1933–1939* (Berkeley and Los Angeles: University of California Press, 1973), p.267.

25. Ibid, pp.264–5. See also Sherman's comments on later historiography in the new edition of this book (London: Frank Cass, 1994), pp.1–8.

26. Linenthal, *Preserving Memory*, pp.216–28; private information concerning the Imperial War Museum. The public controversies that were such a feature of the Washington Museum, which whilst creating difficulties also made its planning more democratic and openly accountable, have been almost totally absent in the case of the Imperial War Museum.

27. Michael Marrus, *The Holocaust in History* (London: Weidenfeld and Nicolson, 1988), p.157.

28. Louise London, 'British Immigration Control Procedures and Jewish Refugees, 1933–1939', in Werner Mosse *et al.* (eds.), *Second Chance: Two Centuries of German-speaking Jews in the United Kingdom* (Tubingen: J.C.B. Mohr, 1991), pp.485–517; Louise London, *Whitehall and the Jews: British Immigration Policy and the Holocaust* (Cambridge: Cambridge University Press, 2000); Richard Breitman and Alan Kraut, *American Refugee Policy and European Jewry, 1933–1945* (Bloomington and Indianapolis: Indiana University Press, 1987); Paul Levine, *From Indifference to Activism: Swedish Diplomacy and the Holocaust; 1938–1944* (Uppsala: Act Universitatis, Uppsaliensis, 1996).

29. Marrus, *The Holocaust in History*, p.166.

30. Bernard Wasserstein, *Britain and the Jews of Europe 1939–1945* (Oxford: Oxford University Press/Institute of Jewish Affairs, 1979), pp.344, 350–52.

31. See Colin Holmes, *Anti-Semitism in British Society 1876–1939* (London: Edward Arnold, 1979).

32. Tony Kushner, 'The Fascist as "Other"? Racism and Neo-Nazism in Contemporary Britain', *Patterns of Prejudice*, Vol.28, No.1 (Jan. 1994), pp.27–45; Paul Gilroy, *There Ain't*

*No Black in the Union Jack: The Cultural Politics of Race and Nation* (London: Hutchinson, 1987).

33. Kushner and Knox, *Refugees in an Age of Genocide*, conclusion.
34. More generally, see Bill Williams, 'The Anti-Semitism of Tolerance: Middle-Class Manchester and the Jews, 1870–1900', in A.J. Kidd and K.W. Roberts (eds.), *City, Class and Culture* (Manchester: Manchester University Press, 1985), pp.74–102.
35. Kushner, *The Holocaust and the Liberal Imagination*, passim.
36. Ibid., part I; Levine, *From Indifference to Activism*, chs.4, 5.
37. N.J. Crowson, *Facing Fascism: The Conservative Party and the European Dictators 1935–1940* (London: Routledge, 1997), pp.32–3.
38. Kushner, *The Holocaust and the Liberal Imagination*, chs.2, 3.
39. Ibid, pp.233–5; Alan Bullock, *Ernest Bevin: Foreign Secretary 1945–1951* (London: Heinemann, 1983), p.164, see also pp.165, 182, 277–8; Allen Podet, 'The Unwilling Midwife: Ernest Bevin and the Birth of Israel', *European Judaism*, Vol.11, No.2 (1977), pp.35–42 and esp. p.38 dismisses the charge of antisemitism as 'a spurious issue'. More nuanced is Joseph Gorny, *The British Labour Movement and Zionism, 1917–1948* (London: Frank Cass, 1983), p.219, who in analysing Bevin and Attlee concludes that 'If we take antisemitism to imply denial of the rights of Jews to live as equal citizens in non-Jewish society, they were not antisemitic. But if we are speaking of prejudices against Jewish culture, conduct, economic acumen and social "pushiness", they were not innocent.' Nevertheless, Gorny still wants to analyse their 'cool malice' through the prism of the term. Ian Mikardo, a Jewish Labour MP who confronted Bevin in 1947 over Palestine, believed that the Foreign Secretary was a straightforward antisemite and that it related to earlier episodes in his life: Ian Mikardo, *Back-Bencher* (London: Weidenfeld and Nicolson, 1988), pp.97–9.
40. Melvin Shefftz, review of *The Holocaust and the Liberal Imagination*, *AJS Review*, Vol.XXI, No.2 (1996), pp.421–3; Anthony Glees, review of *The Holocaust and the Liberal Imagination*, *Journal of Holocaust Education*, Vol.6, No.1 (Summer 1997), pp.112–14. For an alternative perspective on the thesis of the book, see Steven Beller, '"Your mark is our disgrace": Liberalism and the Holocaust', *Contemporary European History*, Vol.4, No.2 (1995), pp.209–21.
41. Bevin's comments are in PRO, LAB 8/99; David Cesarani, *Justice Delayed: How Britain Became a Refuge for Nazi War Criminals* (London: Heinemann, 1992).
42. Bernard Donoughie and G.W. Jones, *Herbert Morrison: Portrait of a Politician* (London: Weidenfeld and Nicolson, 1973). Morrison, however, objected strongly to his daughter marrying a Jew. He thus had little contact with his grandson, Labour politician, Peter Mandelson.
43. Bryan Cheyette, *Constructions of 'the Jew' in English Literature and Society: Racial Representations, 1875–1945* (Cambridge: Cambridge University Press, 1993); more generally, Geoff Dench, *Minorities in the Open Society: Prisoners of Ambivalence* (London: Routledge and Kegan Paul, 1986). For an insistence on an 'either for or against us' approach to British attitudes towards Jews, limiting antisemitism to extremists, see William Rubinstein, *A History of the Jews in the English-Speaking World: Great Britain* (Basingstoke: Macmillan, 1996).
44. Kushner, *The Holocaust and the Liberal Imagination*, chs.5–7; Kushner and Knox, *Refugees in an Age of Genocide*, ch.6.
45. Levine, *From Indifference to Activism*, part II.
46. Ibid, passim and esp. pp.102, 278. See also Paul Levine's contribution to the present volume, pp.212–36.
47. Beller, '"Your mark is our disgrace"', pp.218–21; Michael Burleigh, 'Synonymous with Murder', *Times Literary Supplement*, 3 March 1995.

48. Michael Smith, *Foley: The Spy Who Saved 10,000 Jews* (London: Hodder and Stoughton, 1999), the paperback addition of which announced that it was the 'book that uncovered Britain's Schindler'. The phrase was used earlier on 'Today', BBC Radio 4, 26 Feb. 1999. On the book's immense success, see *Jewish Chronicle*, 23 July and 19 Nov. 1999. Foley was later granted status by Yad Vashem as a 'Righteous Among Nations'. See *Jewish Chronicle*, 22 Oct. 1999. On Nicholas Winton, see 'Britain's Schindler', BBC Radio 4, 7 June 1999, written and presented by myself. Both the producer and myself objected to the title, but were over-ruled by the BBC. The account of Winton and of British refugee policy was more complex than the title suggested; Anne Karpf, 'The Future Prospects for Remembering the Past', *Jewish Chronicle*, 2 July 1999.

49. Levine, *From Indifference to Activisism*, passim.

50. Smith, *Foley*, pp.vi, 169; 'The Saintly Spy of Berlin', *Jewish Chronicle*, 23 July 1999.

51. *Jewish Chronicle*, 18 June 1999. The dedication is featured in the Oscar-winning documentary on the Kindertransport, 'Into the Arms of Strangers', 2000.

52. Kushner and Knox, *Refugees in an Age of Genocide*, pp.154–7.

53. W.D. Rubinstein, *The Myth of Rescue: Why the Democracies Could Not Have Saved More Jews from the Nazis* (London: Routledge, 1997).

54. In the new introduction to the paperback edition, Rubinstein comments himself how it 'sharply divided critics, and I became used to reading reviews consisting of either fulsome praise or venomous hostility' (London: Routledge, 1999), p.1. David Cesarani has commented on the division representing also those who have and have not carried out archive work on the subject, 'Lateline', Australian Broadcasting Corporation, 20 July 1997.

55. Mass-Observation Archive, University of Sussex: Summer Directive 2000, 'Coming to Britain'.

56. Norman Stone, 'Could the Allies Have Saved Them?', *Guardian*, 3 July 1997.

57. For the increasing fascination in relation to the historiography of the Allies and the Holocaust, see Richard Breitman, *Official Secrets: What the Nazis Planned, What the British and Americans Knew* (New York: Hill and Wang, 1998), a book that has received widespread attention and popular success. See also the second edition of Wasserstein, *Britain and the Jews of Europe* (London: Leicester University Press, 1999), which includes newly available intelligence material and most recently, Richard Overy, *Interrogations: The Nazi Elite in Allied Hands* (New York: Viking Penguin, 2001, forthcoming).

# Constructing Allied Humanitarian Policy

## MEREDITH HINDLEY

Nazi Germany's conquest and occupation of Europe fundamentally altered the lives of civilians and generated a series of humanitarian crises across the continent. The fighting forced millions to flee their homelands, often with nothing more than they could carry. For many of those left behind, the defeat of their country also meant the destruction of their homes, families, and civic society as Hitler's minions implemented brutal occupation policies designed to support the German war machine and fulfil the Führer's vision of racial utopia. Holocaust scholars have poignantly documented how occupation policies provided the Nazis with conditions favourable to their campaign to define, concentrate, and exterminate the Jews of Europe. Indeed, Hitler's decision to implement the Final Solution created the most horrible humanitarian crisis of the war. Although variations in the level of brutality occurred, Nazi occupation policies also created another large-scale humanitarian crisis: the possibility of the body of Europe being destroyed not by armies, but by famine and malnutrition. The Nazi policy of ravaging conquered territories wreaked havoc with local food supplies, a situation compounded by the introduction of rationing and the rise of black markets. Across Europe, civilians living under Nazi rule either experienced or faced the prospect of famine. While far from being the murderous horror of the Holocaust, the European hunger crisis posed a serious threat to the long-term health of Europe.[1]

Throughout the war, Britain and the United States – the Allies – were challenged by humanitarians, representatives of ethnic groups, and governments-in-exile to intercede in both crises. They demanded that steps be taken to provide for the rescue and relief of Jews and to implement feeding programmes in Nazi-occupied

Europe to prevent famine and malnutrition. Meeting these demands required the Allies to assume responsibility for the general welfare of the people of occupied Europe, and more concretely, it compelled them to intervene directly in Nazi-occupied territory. The problem for the Allies was how to balance humanitarian considerations with strategic and political priorities.

Despite the massive outpouring of scholarship on the Second World War, no one has tackled the question of what shaped and influenced Allied humanitarian policy. Admittedly, it is a tricky question. At no time during the war did the Allies consciously formulate a specific policy covering humanitarian activities. Instead, over the course of the war, the Allies made a series of decisions that profoundly affected the well-being of European civilians and the ability of aid organisations to provide assistance. One way to reconstruct Allied humanitarian policy is to compare how the Allies responded to different crises. The Holocaust and the European hunger crisis provide a useful comparison, because they share certain characteristics: civilians in Nazi-occupied Europe were the primary victims, strategic decisions made by the Allies limited the scope of outside intervention, and significant public opposition developed against Allied policies.

By comparing the conditions that generated Allied policies, their effects, and the ability of public opinion to change policy-makers' minds, this essay makes a modest attempt to reconstruct Allied humanitarian policy. The use of a comparison is not intended to discount the magnitude of the Holocaust, but rather as a way of engaging larger questions about Allied attitudes toward intervening in wartime humanitarian crises. It also sheds light on the response of the Allies to the Holocaust.

Over the past 20 years, Holocaust scholars have fiercely debated why the Allies did not do more to help the Jews escape the Final Solution. They take issue with closed immigration quotas for Jews, the decision not to bomb concentration camps and railway lines into the camps, and the failure to devote adequate resources to rescue and relief measures. The explanations offered for these policy choices are unsettling, mainly because of the apparent lack of compassion demonstrated by the British and American governments. The debate, however, has settled down into two major camps: the first argues that antisemitism motivated British and American policies, while the second argues that the decision to put winning the war before all other considerations ultimately determined the Allies' meagre response.[2]

Reconstructing Allied humanitarian policy, therefore, offers a fresh perspective on the debate by engaging the larger question of whether humanitarian intervention was compatible with Allied strategy. Doing so reveals the degree to which Allied attitudes toward humanitarianism were rooted in and shaped by the demands of waging total war. Intervening in both the Holocaust and the European hunger crisis required the Allies to take action in the occupied territories to aid civilians by either sponsoring or permitting others to operate rescue and relief programmes. However, the strategies developed to pursue victory, specifically economic warfare, subordinated humanitarian considerations to political and military objectives. There was, in essence, a fundamental contradiction between the type of war waged by the Allies and the imperative of humanitarian intervention. It was more important to prevent Germany from importing goods to fuel its war economy than it was to provide opportunities for aid to be given to civilians suffering under Nazi rule. Indeed, comparison of the two crises demonstrates that the factors at work in both cases prompted the Allies to make humanitarian intervention a secondary consideration. The principal factors consisted of the absence of a developed body of international law covering the treatment of civilians; how the decision to wage economic warfare against Germany significantly limited the options available for humanitarian intervention; and how public opinion and publicity about the tragedy engulfing Europe failed to shift Allied priorities.

# I

The post-Second World War era has been marked by an international interest in human rights and human rights law. Indeed, the 1945 Charter of the United Nations opens with a statement reaffirming a 'faith in fundamental human rights, in the dignity and worth of the human person, in the equal rights of men and women and of nations large and small'. The Universal Declaration of Human Rights, adopted by the UN General Assembly in December 1948, went on to define civil and political rights, along with economic, social, and cultural rights. While the issue of human rights received some attention in the early part of the century, post-war knowledge of Nazi Germany's conscious decision to ignore the rights of Jews and other populations under its control and carry out mass murder made human rights an emotionally and politically compelling issue. Hence, during the 1945–46 International Military Tribunal at Nuremberg, German high officials were charged not only with 'crimes against peace' and 'war crimes', but also with 'crimes against humanity', a charge encompassing crimes committed against any civilian population. The problem for those advocating humanitarian intervention during the Second World War, however, was that the post-war conjunction of international law and human rights had yet to occur. A substantial body of international law covering the treatment of combatants had developed, but the laws did not cover the treatment of civilians. Instead, international law benefited belligerents by loosely defining their responsibilities toward civilians.

Under the Hague Convention of 1907, a conquering power had a legal duty to refrain from pillage and to limit demands on the resources of the countries it occupied. The Great Powers generally adhered to the convention during the First World War; certainly none of the countries followed a policy of living off the land as practised by the Wehrmacht during the Second World War. The terms of the Hague Convention, however, were sufficiently vague to give humanitarians reason for concern about the plight of civilians during a protracted war. Despite the fact the Great Powers did not engage in large-scale plundering during the First World War, the conflict disrupted European agricultural production, which was compounded by Britain's blockade of Europe. Believing that Belgium would starve it if did not receive outside assistance, an unknown mining engineer by the name of Herbert Hoover organised the Commission for Belgian Relief. By the 1917, the commission was feeding nine million people in Belgium and northern France.[3] Believing that famine should not be a weapon of modern war and that civilians had a basic right to food, Hoover, then US president, made an unsuccessful attempt as part of the preparatory discussions for the 1930 London Naval Conference to have relief ships declared immune from blockade measures. Hoover argued that relief ships, which were engaged in humanitarian activities, should receive the same treatment as hospital ships, meaning unfettered passage through naval blockades. Britain, however, viewed the relief ship proposal as a threat to its belligerent rights and ability to impose an effective blockade. Hoover dropped the proposal in order to preserve improved Anglo-American relations.[4] Consequently, as the Second World War opened, a blockading power still possessed the legal right to prevent the passage of and/or regulate the cargo of a ship carrying relief supplies bound for enemy territory. Those seeking to provide aid to war-torn areas, therefore, had to abide by the demands of the governments administrating the blockade.

While the 1929 Geneva Convention further refined belligerent conduct during war, it did little to address the rights of civilians. Instead, the convention's provisions reflected the experiences and concerns of the Great Powers during the First World War. During that conflict, the treatment of prisoners-of-war (POWs), the use of chemical weapons, and battlefield access by medical personnel proved to be decisive and emotional issues. The primary focus of the convention, however, was on the treatment of POWs. According to the convention, belligerents must humanely treat POWs, supply information about them (including lists of names), and permit representatives of neutral states to visit and inspect camps. Belligerents were also not allowed to use POWs as forced labour.[5]

The implications of the paucity of law covering the treatment of interned civilians became very clear during the Second World War. At the outbreak of the war, Britain, France, and Germany informally agreed to extend to civilian internees of enemy nationality –

'assimilated prisoners' – the same rights accorded to POWs. If their citizens fell into enemy hands, Britain, France, and Germany wanted to ensure that they were treated reasonably well. Consequently, throughout the war, both POWs and assimilated prisoners benefited from outside assistance, particularly the delivery of food parcels designed to supplement meagre rations. The Allies felt that the terms of the 1929 Geneva Convention provided sufficient guarantees that the food sent to these prisoners would not help the German war effort and, therefore, did not pose a threat to the integrity of the blockade.

The convention and the agreement covering assimilated prisoners, however, overlooked the majority of the European population. Unfortunately, there was little to motivate Germany to extend similar protection to other interned nationalities. Germany did not recognise the legitimacy of the governments-in-exile. The exiled governments did not have German citizens under their control, making the possibility of German citizens becoming targets of retaliation for German policies negligible. At the same time, Germany refused to extend any sort of legal protection to Jews, making the plight of an already persecuted group even worse and their chance of receiving outside assistance almost impossible.[6]

Those seeking to aid victims of the Holocaust and the European hunger crisis, therefore, faced a formidable challenge in that those needing aid were civilians. As the Second World War opened, international laws that could provide a framework for facilitating the delivery of aid to civilians under Nazi control were sparse. The vaguely worded Hague Convention allowed for loose interpretations of an occupying power's responsibility. Indeed, for every charge the Allies levelled against Nazi Germany for failing to care adequately for civilians, Nazi Germany argued that it was fulfilling its duties under the Hague Convention and that the blockade of Europe, not Nazi occupation policies, created food shortages. The failure of international law to cover the treatment of civilian internees meant that those interned had little hope of outside intervention improving their fate. For the Jews, the lack of recourse against their captors helped facilitate the Final Solution.

## II

If international law failed to offer aid advocates a useful tool for orchestrating intervention, Allied strategic priorities presented yet another obstacle. In order to aid civilians, groups and organisations needed to be able to ship food and clothing into Nazi-occupied Europe and transfer money to Europe. The Allies, however, adopted a series of policies – economic warfare – which made the task of providing aid all the more daunting. During the inter-war period, British planners developed extensive plans for disrupting Germany's economic ability to wage war. The battle against Nazi Germany would not only be fought with battlecruisers, aircraft, and infantry divisions, but also with financial, trade, and economic sanctions. To wound Germany's economy was to wound its ability to continue fighting.

The key weapon in the Allies' economic warfare campaign was the blockade. Through a combination of financial and trade restrictions – imposed if need be by naval force – the blockade sought to prevent Germany from importing any food, goods, or raw materials considered to be of strategic value from non-European sources. It also sought to limit German importation of *matériel* from neutral European countries. While the blockade was originally only applied to Germany, after the fall of France in the spring of 1940 it was expanded to include all countries under German control.[7]

By using the blockade, the Allies limited to some degree Germany's ability to fuel the Nazi war machine, but this also had the side effect of profoundly affecting the daily lives of European civilians. The blockade cut off overseas imports and limited the flow of goods within Europe itself, thereby compounding local food-shortages brought about by Nazi occupation policies. For Jews and Slavs, two groups that consistently received lower rations, it made maintaining daily calorie levels and some semblance of a balanced diet particularly difficult.

Furthermore, vigilant enforcement of the blockade by the Allies closed down significant avenues for aiding occupied Europe. In 1941 and 1942, the Foreign Office and Ministry of Economic Warfare

(MEW) proposed three different European-wide feeding programmes, generally involving the daily distribution of milk. The proposals were motivated by political considerations, but also because Foreign Office and MEW officials were increasingly worried about the relative health of the European population. The British War Cabinet rejected the proposals, believing that feeding programmes would aid the Nazi war effort by relieving Germany of its responsibility to care for conquered populations. The British would take the same line in 1943, when the newly formed American Office of Relief and Rehabilitation raised the issue of a European feeding programme.[8] Concern for aiding Germany also contributed to Britain's disinclination to allow smaller relief programmes conducted by private aid organisations to operate behind enemy lines. The organisations needed Allied approval in order to ship goods through the blockade or to transfer funds to neutral countries to purchase available surpluses. In addition to overcoming Allied scepticism, any organisation proposing a relief programme had to demonstrate evidence of strict neutral (i.e. non-Axis) control over the importation and distribution of the food or clothing. The Allies were not going to allow food and clothing through the blockade without explicit understanding of who would use it and how. The inability of the organisations to provide evidence of neutral safeguards, generally because Nazi Germany refused to give them, meant that after August 1940, only limited relief programmes operated in Nazi-occupied Europe.

The blockade also limited the number of food parcels that could be sent into occupied Europe. Food parcels were one of the few means available to provide aid to Jews trapped in ghettos and camps. Nevertheless, the Allies were reluctant to allow large-scale food parcel programmes to operate, because of numerous reports that the Germans seized the parcels. The lapse of time between the creation of a mailing list of intended recipients and the sending of the parcels frequently led to invalid addresses, generally caused by deportations and death. Instead of giving the parcel to a relative or another Jew, the Germans seized the parcels and distributed them among soldiers and collaborators. As a means to pacify the increasingly testy governments-in-exile, however, the Allies expanded the food parcel concession in 1942. In practice, the concession proved to be mainly a gesture. Due to preventative buying programmes carried out by both the Allies and Axis, the exiled governments found it difficult to buy food to fill the parcels. The concession is also notable on one other score: Jews were granted the same concession.[9] In a war fought between nation-states, the Allies acknowledged that on some level a transnational group, not just countries, could be in need of aid. The food parcel concession, however, would not be expanded to address specifically the needs of concentration camp and ghetto internees until after the initial successes of the Allied invasion of north-west Europe.

The Allies' economic warfare campaign also limited the ability of private organisations to transfer funds to Europe to support the rescue of Jews. The stringent control of foreign funds derived from the desire to constrict Europe's money supply, to limit Nazi Germany's ability to obtain foreign currency, and to maintain Allied reserves. As the war dragged on, it became harder for the British to approve any sort of funds transfer to Switzerland – even to aid the Allied war effort – because the British Treasury's reserves were dangerously low. In order to transfer funds, organisations had to obtain Allied approval, which was given in the form of a license. Unfortunately, the license approval process offered plenty of opportunity for Allied officials interested in discouraging rescue efforts to construct bureaucratic roadblocks. In particular, the State Department's Foreign Funds Control division dragged its feet on approving licenses for funds used to aid Jews.[10]

The Allied commitment to the blockade in favour of measures that might benefit European civilians reflected a conscious decision by Britain and the United States to place winning the war above everything else. It also represented a strong commitment to the use of economic warfare as a strategic tool. Throughout the war, the Allies resisted any appeal that appeared on the surface to jeopardise the military effort. For Churchill, it was a question of compromise. As he told Minister Hugh Dalton, 'Once we leave the high ground of principle and come down into the valley of compromise we shall face great difficulties.'[11]

## III

In discussions about the Allied response to the Holocaust, scholars have underplayed the relief question in favour of focusing on the question of immigration and rescue. In fact, Allied relief policy has received almost no attention from historians. The majority of the work done on wartime relief efforts focuses on the distribution of relief to liberated areas or on the efforts of non-governmental agencies, such as the International Committee of the Red Cross.[12] The few works that consider the nature of Allied relief policy identify Allied strategic priorities, particularly the blockade of Europe, as the main obstacle to providing both small and large-scale relief to civilians.[13] Scholars writing about the Allied response to the Holocaust and about Allied relief policy, however, share a common complaint. They argue that the Allies failed to comprehend or acknowledge the plight of European civilians. They also question the wisdom of the Allies placing so much emphasis on winning the war that they failed to see the humanitarian crises it wrought. The problem, however, was not that the Allies failed to understand what was happening to European civilians under Nazi control, but that economic warfare was so deeply intertwined with the Allies' political and military strategy that humanitarian assistance posed a threat to the conduct of the Allied war effort. The Allies would only allow organisations to aid civilians in Nazi-occupied territories if it furthered Allied strategic and political objectives.

When the war opened in September 1939, Britain immediately implemented its planned blockade of Germany. Under the terms of the blockade, food was declared 'conditional' contraband, a commodity with both humanitarian and military uses. Since total war made distinctions between enemy armed forces and civilian populations difficult, food destined for occupied territories could legitimately be included in the blockade.[14]

The first challenge to British blockade policy came with pleas for aid to be sent to Nazi-occupied Poland – the *Generalgouvernement*. Both the Commission for Polish Relief, headed by former US president Herbert Hoover, and the American Red Cross wanted to operate relief programmes that would provide food, clothing, and medicine to needy Polish civilians. Britain was not keen on either programme, but agreed to allow relief goods through the blockade providing that Nazi Germany allowed the organisations to control the distribution of relief. Without strict controls, Britain feared that Germany would siphon off the supplies and use them to bolster its war effort. From December 1939 to May 1940, the American Red Cross shipped $500,000 in relief to the *Generalgouvernement*, terminating its programme when Germany's invasion of western Europe prevented the shipment of supplies.[15] Hoover, however, failed to launch a successful programme due to constant bickering with the British and Germans over distribution requirements and his failure to convince Britain and France to provide $1 million each to finance his relief efforts.[16]

The defeat of France, in the spring of 1940, left Britain standing alone against Nazi Germany. Extending the blockade to include all territories under German occupation was one of the few weapons available to Britain. As a result, in June 1940, the Cabinet voted to extend the contraband control system to include countries under Nazi occupation. Britain hoped to strangle Nazi Germany's expanding war effort economically, while buying time to improve its war footing. In a speech before the House of Commons in August 1940, Churchill justified the British government's decision not to allow food to pass through the blockade for the relief of civilians on the grounds that food would 'certainly be pillaged off them by their Nazi conquerors'. Any future food shortages, noted Churchill, would be caused by 'German exactions or German failure to distribute the supplies which they command'.[17] Churchill's House of Commons speech articulated what became the basic Allied position throughout the war: Germany was responsible for feeding civilians in territories under her control and shipping large quantities of food through the blockade would absolve her of that responsibility and aid the Nazi war effort.

Despite British obstinacy, two major blockade concessions were granted for political and strategic reasons early in the war. France received the first concession. By September 1940, France was hungry as German plundering, a spoiled harvest, and the absence of imports led to a contraction of the food supply. The presence of one million refugees within France's borders also compounded the problem. The frequent refrain heard in Washington, DC was that France needed relief. Armed with an American Red Cross plan, Roosevelt proposed to Churchill that France be permitted to receive shipments of milk for children. Roosevelt believed the shipments would bolster internal support for the Vichy government and make it easier for Vichy to resist collaborating with Nazi Germany. While contrary to blockade policy, the milk shipments appealed to the British Foreign Office, which sought to improve relations with France and convince its former ally not to turn over her Mediterranean fleet to the Germans. Roosevelt's request also came at a key juncture in the debate over Lend-Lease. Recognising the political and strategic benefits, Britain agreed to allow through the blockade two shipments of milk in late 1940 and four shipments of wheat during the first four months of 1941. It was a concession Britain soon regretted. Admiral Darlan's decision to turn over 800,000 tons of wheat to the Germans, the very commodity the Allies shipped through the blockade to aid a 'starving France', infuriated the British and made them suspicious of subsequent claims made by exiled governments that their citizens were starving.[18]

Smarting from Vichy's deceit, Britain vowed not to allow the still-neutral United States to seduce her into making further relief concessions, but the plight of Greece soon made that policy untenable. Beginning in the summer of 1941, famine-like conditions developed in Greece due to back-to-back crop failures, the country's dependence on now-halted food imports, and German pillaging. By December 1941, 1,000 people a day were dying in both Athens and Piraeus from malnutrition. Recognising that Germany and Italy would not feed Greece because it possessed little economic value, the Foreign Office pressed for aid to be sent to Greece to preserve Britain's prestige in the region. After an attempt to supply Greece with food from Turkey failed, the Cabinet reluctantly agreed to a blockade concession and, in January 1942, a shipment of Canadian wheat arrived in Greece. Regular monthly shipments of wheat, pulse, and other food items began the following month and continued until the end of German occupation. Conscious of the need to prevent German plundering, Britain and the United States insisted on the creation of a neutral body, the Swedish–Swiss Commission, to oversee the distribution of the imported food. Despite the distribution controls, the Allies felt the Greek relief programme only served to reinforce Nazi occupation.[19]

The concession to Greece brought substantial criticism from other occupied Allied powers, such as Belgium and Norway, which pressed for relief programmes similar to the one in Greece. Both countries assembled panels of experts, which issued reports claiming their citizens were malnourished. The Allies resisted Belgium and Norway's pleas for large-scale programmes, but allowed them to use foreign exchange to purchase food from neutral countries within the blockade. The concession was granted on the grounds that the Allied countries would be buying food that was already available to the enemy within the blockade area. Belgium bought fruit from Portugal, while Norway purchased produce and fish from Sweden. Along with intra-blockade purchases, neutral countries experimented with sending food parcels to civilians, generally in urban areas. After relentless petitioning by Belgium and Norway, Britain and the United States agreed to an expansion of Allied food parcel programmes in the fall of 1942. The expansion of the food parcel programme also provided a new opportunity for Jewish organisations to send relief.[20]

Despite agreeing over the food parcel programme, 1943 proved to be a rocky year for Anglo-American relief policy. Acting independently of the State Department, Roosevelt increasingly showed sympathy for appeals made by the exiled governments to send relief to aid their citizens. At the beginning of 1943, Roosevelt supported a plan to send 750,000 food parcels to Norwegian families.[21] Churchill talked Roosevelt out of pursuing the scheme, but Roosevelt struck back with the creation of the Office of Foreign Relief and Rehabilitation. Created to address post-war relief preparations, OFRRA could not avoid exploring the current relief issue, thereby provoking a series of painful discussions on the feasibility of a wide-scale European feeding programme. The Foreign Office, which had proposed three different European feeding programmes to the War Cabinet only to have them rejected on strategic grounds, found itself defending British blockade policy while deflecting claims of callousness. OFRRA abandoned plans for a European feeding programme after the May 1943 Washington Conference, at which Roosevelt reaffirmed the United States' commitment to maintaining the blockade, but tensions remained high.[22]

The February 1944 passage of the Gillette–Taft resolution in the US Senate calling for the relief of Europe infused new life into the issue. Roosevelt appealed to Churchill in March 1944 to allow a limited feeding programme for expectant and nursing mothers and children in occupied areas.[23] This time, the British Ministry of Economic Warfare, which had privately lobbied the War Cabinet for relief concessions since late 1942, produced a convincing list of reasons *not* to allow the programme: (1) the impending invasion of north-west Europe would disrupt railways and complicate distribution efforts; (2) dried milk was in short supply; and (3) it would take four months to implement the programme and western Europe might be liberated by then.[24] Convinced by the strategic arguments, Roosevelt declined to push the issue further.

In June 1944, the Allies approved a plan to send food parcels to refugee and concentration camps in Europe. The concession was made due to activism by the American War Refugee Board and the presence of a coherent plan – the first of its kind – for providing relief to the concentration camps. Another relaxation of the blockade occurred in August 1944 allowing for small consignments of food to be sent from Sweden to Norway and from Switzerland to Polish urban areas, ghettos, and concentration camps.[25] The concessions, however, did not cover the north-western provinces of the Netherlands. The advance of the Allied armies as part of the Arnhem campaign cut off north-western Holland's access to food imports, while leaving the provinces under Nazi control. The rapidly deteriorating condition of the population sparked a debate over how to address the problem and represented the first time during the war that military officials played a major role in deciding relief policy. General Dwight Eisenhower agreed to allow relief to be sent in, despite the potential benefit to the Nazis. Over the winter, however, protracted negotiations with the Germans, the freezing of waterways, and botched International Red Cross shipments prevented the influx of substantial quantities of relief. The Nazis used Allied POWs as bargaining chips against the Dutch population and, early in the spring, the relief issue became entangled with discussions about surrender terms. As a result, substantial quantities of relief did not reach north-western Holland until the closing days of the war.[26]

Allied relief policy reflected a commitment to uphold the blockade of Europe and the difficulty of reconciling that commitment with humanitarian intervention. While concessions were made early in the war for France and Greece, the uncertain military position of the Allies during 1942 and 1943 made further large-scale concessions incompatible with the war effort. Further large-scale relief programmes were delayed in 1944 in favour of the Allied invasion of north-west Europe. Only after a successful invasion did the Allies allow the influx of modest amounts of relief into Eastern Europe, the heart of Nazi Germany's faltering empire. The decision to pursue a 'no relief except for Greece' policy may have contributed to Allied victory, but for civilians, it reinforced the terrible living conditions and general malnutrition ushered in by Nazi occupation policies.

# IV

In democracies, public opinion plays a prominent role in political decision-making. Politicians, intent on making their constituents happy, worry about how a particular policy will go over in Aberdeen or Houston. Indeed, its sway can be so forceful, that the greatest difficulty facing any politician, observed Jeremy Bentham, comes 'in conciliating the public opinion, in correcting it when erroneous, and in giving it that bent which shall be most favourable to produce obedience to his mandates'.[27] But in wartime, the dynamics of the relationship between politicians, government, and public opinion radically change. In democracies waging war, decision-making becomes more isolated from and less responsive to public opinion. Winning the war, rather than public opinion, becomes the guiding principle. Critics of Allied policies toward the Holocaust and European hunger crisis confronted this hard reality. During the war, significant public opposition developed in both Britain and the United States as individuals, exiled governments, ethnic groups, and humanitarian organisations sought to change Allied priorities. For relief and rescue proponents, Allied fixation on economic warfare and the blockade functioned as an unwavering *bête noire*. No amount of publicity or negative public opinion could provoke the Allies to alter their policies. In part the Allies were stubborn and fearful of concessions. At the same time, none of the campaigns generated enough pressure to force the Allies to yield.

While information about the fate of Jews spurred calls to action, no unified campaign for Allied intervention emerged from within either the British or American Jewish communities. Prior to November 1942, various Jewish groups lobbied the Allies to expand or eliminate the immigration quotas that prevented Jews from leaving Europe. Some Jewish groups also called on Britain to open Palestine to Jewish immigration, an act Britain and the United States feared would provoke an Arab uprising and destabilise the Middle East. While united in concern for European Jews, disagreements within both the British and American Jewish communities over the Zionist movement made it impossible for them to present a united front when lobbying the Allies. And because of the Zionist movement's activism, government officials frequently found it difficult to untangle appeals made for Allied intervention to stop the Holocaust and appeals for the creation of a Jewish state in Palestine. Unfortunately, the intimate link between the two issues provided Allied officials with a formidable set of political and military reasons to discount Jewish appeals. Competition between Jewish groups also frequently led one group to sabotage another group's efforts to publicise the Holocaust.

Although disunity within the Jewish community hampered

efforts to provoke the Allies to action, information and publicity about the Final Solution created public awareness about the killings and at various times forced Britain and the United States to address the issue. Newspaper coverage of the German invasion of the Soviet Union included stories about the killing of Jews, but the stories did not ascribe the killings to a coherent programme of murder. Instead, the reports portrayed the killings as part of a general Nazi programme to eliminate all potential cells of resistance.[28] During the fall of 1942, reports from a variety of sources began to filter to the West, providing a more comprehensive picture of the Final Solution. The information prompted Jewish organisations in Britain to step up their lobbying efforts, but proposals for relief were refused because they would violate the blockade.[29] The first major American newspaper account of the Final Solution appeared on 23 November 1942 in the *New York Herald Tribune* under the headline 'Wise Says Hitler Has Ordered 4,000,000 Jews Slain in 1942'. The story originated from Under Secretary of State Sumner Welles informing Stephen Wise of the World Jewish Congress about the contents of the Riegner telegram. More concentrated press coverage of the Holocaust appeared following Foreign Secretary Anthony Eden's reading of the Allied declaration condemning Nazi Germany's 'intention to exterminate the Jewish people in Europe' in the House of Commons on 17 December 1942. The declaration offered little in the way of concrete plans for action, except to say that 'those responsible for these crimes shall not escape retribution, and to press on with the practical measures to this end'.[30]

In Britain, the declaration was met with wide publicity in both press and radio, but it seems to have had less of an impact on public opinion in the United States. British Jewish groups, supported by the press, church groups, and interested members of Parliament, pushed for His Majesty's Government to follow up the declaration with decisive measures. Ironically, the Foreign Office regarded the declaration a failure at mitigating German treatment of Jews, while opening up the British government to criticism about its policies.[31] Public demand for action to aid the Jews remained strong in Britain during 1943.[32] Feeling the pressure, Britain moved to open talks on general refugee problems, resulting in the Bermuda Conference in April 1943. The conference produced little, if anything, substantial in the way of plans to help European refugees, but gave critics of Allied policy plenty to complain about.[33] In May 1943, the Committee for a Jewish Army of Stateless and Palestinian Jews placed a full-page advertisment in the *New York Times* with the headline 'To 5,000,000 Jews in The Nazi Death Trap – Bermuda Was a Cruel Mockery'. The critical sting of the advertisement abated when the committee was denounced on the Senate floor for printing the names of 33 senators without their approval.[34] Despite the slip-up, American rescue and relief advocates continued to use confrontational advertisements and rhetoric to drum up popular support for intervention, but with lukewarm results. They had to pay for publicity to keep a debate alive, since the American press was largely uninterested in the issue.[35]

Although disunity between Jewish groups played a large role in failing to generate support for intervention, the idea of creating an US agency specifically charged with aiding Jews began to draw adversaries together.[36] The creation of such an agency finally came in January 1944, when President Roosevelt chartered the War Refugee Board. The Board's creation, however, was not a result of pressure from the Jewish community, but rather sprang from the bureaucratic battles waged between the State and Treasury Departments.[37] The Treasury had grown increasingly frustrated with State Department's refusal to approve the use of blocked funds to pay for the evacuation or support of European Jews. The creation of the Board, which seemed to disavow Allied policy on both relief and rescue issues, initially outraged the British. Part of their anger came from having learned about the Board, not from the United States government, but by reading about it in *The Times* (London).[38] After tempers cooled, the Board operated with some success during 1944–45 by channelling Allied and private resources into modest rescue and relief programmes. More importantly, in terms of public opinion, the Allies could point to the Board as evidence of concrete action taken against the Final Solution.

As the war came to a close, public opinion and lobbying efforts had made little impact on Allied policy. Disunity among Jewish groups prevented the development of a lobbying campaign that would have made the Allies uncomfortable enough to act. The close relationship between calls for intervention against the Final Solution and the creation of a Jewish state helped to conflate the two issues in the minds of Allied politicians. Reluctant to engage the issue of Palestine during the war, they shied away from serious consideration of other types of intervention.

Relief advocates failed to alter Allied policies, but for different reasons. Public outcry for the Allies to send relief to Nazi-occupied territories developed in early 1940, more than two years before public knowledge of the Final Solution. While Britons endured the Blitz, Americans voiced their opposition to the blockade in large numbers during 1940–41. A diverse coalition of groups – Christian and humanitarian organisations, groups organised by Herbert Hoover, allied governments-in-exile, ethnic groups concerned about the fate of relatives, the American Red Cross, and isolationists opposing American involvement in the war – argued that the blockade of Europe would do nothing more than ensure the slow death of millions of European civilians. Britain could largely ignore American pleas, except when they came from Franklin Roosevelt, as with the case of France. American entry into the war in December 1941, however, muted criticism of the blockade as attention turned to the business of mounting a war effort. As American interest in the relief issue waned, a significant anti-blockade movement began to develop in Britain in the spring of 1942. News of the terrible conditions in Greece raised questions in the minds of humanitarians about the wisdom of blockade policy. During this period, the Famine Relief Committee (FRC) emerged under the leadership of George Bell, the Bishop of Chichester.[39] The FRC used traditional tactics, such as letter-writing and petition-signing campaigns, newspaper editorials, and speeches, to lobby for blockade concessions. By the end of 1943, the FRC consisted of 182 separate chapters across England and Scotland. The organisation's size and its reliance on reasoned discussion rather than inflammatory rhetoric made it hard for the British government to dismiss it.

In the beginning of 1943, after the success of the North African campaign, American blockade critics resumed their agitation for relief of Nazi-occupied territories. In January, the Federal Council of Churches of Christ endorsed the call for relief. The next month, Herbert Hoover championed the relief cause by holding a mass meeting at New York City's Carnegie Hall and pleading his case in *Collier's* magazine. The publication of Howard Kershner's *One Humanity: A Plea for our Friends and Allies* also fuelled the debate by proposing to send monthly shipments of 51,000 tons of fats, meat, cereals, and milk to needy women and children in Norway, Holland, Belgium and France.[40] Kershner's experience administering relief in Vichy France gave his proposals credibility. Despite the frenzy of anti-blockade rhetoric, British and American relief policy remained unchanged at the end of 1943. The presidential campaign of 1944 raised the relief issue in the United States to fever-pitch. While various resolutions calling for the relief of Europe had been introduced to Congress since the beginning of the war, the progress of the Gillette–Taft resolution through the Senate Foreign Relations Committee and the Senate's eventual endorsement generated unprecedented attention for the relief issue. Prior to 1944, the American press assumed a neutral stance on the relief issue, but as the Allied military situation improved, editorials began calling for the United States to create post-war goodwill in Europe by supplying areas still occupied by the Nazis with relief. Pro-relief groups used paid full-page advertisements in leading newspapers to reinforce the messages contained in anti-blockade editorials.[41]

Despite the lobbying of various groups in Britain and the United States, Allied relief policy remained substantially unchanged as the war closed. Public opinion and interest groups were unable to rewrite Allied blockade policy. Widespread agitation in the United States prior to American entry in the war did little to influence relief policy, and, even after Pearl Harbor, relief advocates struggled to make a convincing case. Significantly, the creation and activism of the Famine Relief Committee came after the decision to embark on the Greek relief programme. Relief advocates saw the Greek programme as a model for others, but the Allies viewed it as an exception rather than a precedent. They had already granted what concessions there were to be made.

## V

This article has explored two humanitarian cataclysms during the Second World War engulfing large numbers of European civilians – the Holocaust and the European hunger crisis. Comparing the crises reveals certain similarities in the conditions influencing outside intervention. International law did not address the needs of civilians, leaving them at the mercy of the political and strategic priorities of belligerent governments. A more developed body of international law could have served as a mobilising tool for aid advocates by offering a framework for humanitarian intervention and shaping public opinion. The paucity of international law proved to be no match for the decision by the Allies to pursue total war, a decision that made all other considerations secondary and severely limited the possible avenues of aid. Finally, the lobbying efforts by intervention advocates and publicity about the suffering of civilians failed to provoke anything more than minor changes in Allied policy.

Not surprisingly, we are left with the conclusion that Allied humanitarian policy was driven by political and strategic considerations. No amount of public pressure could provoke Allied leaders to change their priorities, leaving little room for addressing the needs of civilians. When concessions were made, they were granted to achieve specific political and strategic objectives. Relief was sent to France in the hopes of staving off Vichy France's collaboration with Nazi Germany. The Greek relief programme derived from an appreciation of Greek suffering, but also out of fear that Britain's prestige in the region would decline if it failed to take action. After the Greek concession, nothing occurred that the Allies believed demanded a significant revision of their policies or provided political incentives to do so. Intervening on behalf of Holocaust victims carried with it few political and strategic benefits, due to the disenfranchised status of European Jews. Aiding the Jews meant aiding a group rather than a specific country. In a war that was fought based on alliances between nations, a transnational group had little to offer and no room to bargain. Using such a litmus test left little room for moral considerations.

Why did concern for civilians occupy such a small place in Allied sensibilities? The answer lies, in part, in the revolutionary nature of the scope of the Second World War. Nazi Germany's occupation policies and pursuit of the Final Solution represented a conscious decision to blur the line between combatant and non-combatant. The Allies naively assumed that they could place the burden of caring for civilians on Nazi Germany because it was obligated to care for them under international law. As the war progressed, the Allies failed to come to terms with the idea that civilians, like soldiers, were targets in their own right. The other part of the answer lies in Allied fears about losing the war. Having decided on a blockade policy, which had proven for centuries to be an important tool in waging European wars, the Allies could not conceive of granting concessions that might weaken the blockade's integrity and forestall victory. During 1942 and 1943, when the ebb of the war seemed uncertain, the Allies cannot be faulted for clinging to a strategy that had allowed them to stay in the war. But as the Soviet armies pushed Nazi Germany back into central Europe and British and American armies advanced into north-west Europe, lifting the constraints that hampered rescue and relief programmes should have been the subject of thoughtful consideration. Fear of concessions ensured malnutrition and death for millions of civilians. What does Allied humanitarian policy suggest about the Allied response to the Holocaust? At the very minimum it reinforces the need to see decisions made by Britain and the United States in response to knowledge about the Final Solution as firmly grounded in what they believed to be the most effective way to wage war. After the fall of 1942, high-level Allied policy-makers knew with great certainty that Jewish civilians trapped in Nazi-occupied territories faced the prospect of death. But while the officials knew the Jews had little time, they remained reluctant to alter policies engineered to produce the defeat of Nazi Germany. Such clarity of purpose suggests the need to carefully reconsider the charge that antisemitism, above all over factors, determined the Allied response to the Holocaust. While antisemitism was a feature of British and American bureaucratic cultures, claims of it determining the Allied response are overdrawn. Before the Allies had knowledge of the Final Solution, they established a pattern of action in which political gains outweighed moral considerations.

## NOTES

I would like to thank Talbot Imlay, Andrew Apostolou, and David Cesarani for their helpful suggestions in developing this essay.

1. A healthy body of scholarship has developed on the effect of Nazi Germany's occupation of Europe. Landmark works include Alexander Dallin, *German Rule in Russia, 1941–45: A Study in Occupation Polices* (London: Macmillan, 1957); Theo Schulte, *The German Army and Nazi Policies in Occupied Russia* (Oxford: Berg, 1989); Robert Paxton, *Vichy France: Old Guard and New Order, 1940–1944* (New York: Columbia University, 1982); and Mark Mazower, *Inside Hitler's Greece: The Experience of Occupation* (New Haven, CT: Yale University Press, 1993). The plight of Poland, Norway, and France captured the attention of Allied decision-makers and the public. For Poland, see Richard Lucas, *The Forgotten Holocaust: The Poles Under German Occupation, 1939–1944* (Lexington, KY: University of Kentucky Press, 1986); Jan Tomasz Gross, *Polish Society under German Occupation: The Generalgouvernement, 1939–1944* (Princeton, NJ: Princeton University Press, 1979); and Hans-Christian Harten, *De-Kulturation und Germanisierung: Die Nationalsozialistische Rassen- und Erziehungspolitik in Polen, 1939–1945* (Frankfurt: Campus, 1996.) There are few works on the occupation of Norway in translation, but Richard Petrow's *The Bitter Years: The Invasion and Occupation of Denmark and Norway, 1940–1945* (New York: Morrow, 1974), while uneven, offers a useful starting point. English-language accounts of the Nazi-occupation of France, notably Robert O. Paxton's, *Vichy France: Old Guard and New Order, 1940–1944* (New York: Columbia University Press, 1982) and John F. Sweets, *Choices in Vichy France: The French Under Nazi Occupation* (New York: Oxford University Press, 1986), have set the agenda for discussing life in Vichy. Swiss scholar Philippe Burrin, in *Living with Defeat: France under German Occupation, 1940–1944*, trans. Janet Lloyd (London: Arnold, 1996), has recently challenged the idea that the French were either 'functional collaborators' (Paxton) or 'functional resisters' (Sweets), arguing that these categories fail to capture the complexity of occupation.
2. David S. Wyman, *The Abandonment of the Jews: America and the Holocaust, 1941–45* (New York: Pantheon, 1984); Monty N. Penkower, *The Jews Were Expendable: Free World Diplomacy and the Holocaust* (Chicago: University of Illinois, 1983); Richard Breitman and Alan M. Kraut, *American Refugee Policy and European Jewry, 1933–1945* (Bloomington: Indiana University, 1987); Bernard Wasserstein, *Britain and the Jews of Europe, 1939–1945* (Oxford: Clarendon Press, 1979); William Rubinstein, *The Myth of Rescue: Why the Democracies Could Not Have Saved More Jews from the Nazis* (New York: Routledge, 1997).
3. George Nash, *The Life of Herbert Hoover: The Humanitarian, 1914–1917* (New York: W.W. Norton & Co., 1988) p.362–4
4. B.J.C. McKercher, *Transition of Power: Britain's Loss of Global Pre-eminence to the United States, 1930–1945* (Cambridge: Cambridge University Press, 1999), pp.40–41, 44.

5. The texts of the Hague and Geneva Conventions can be found in Adam Roberts and Richard Guelff (eds.), *Documents on the Laws of War* (Oxford: Oxford University Press, 2000).

6. Ronald W. Zweig, 'Feeding the Camps: Allied Blockade Policy and the Relief of Concentration Camps in Germany, 1944–45,' *The Historical Journal*, Vol.41, No.3 (1998), p.827. According to Zweig, three categories of individuals were prohibited from receiving parcels: Jews, those incarcerated as a 'Nacht und Nebel' prisoner (one who has been officially vanished), and those charged with serious crimes against the Nazi state or under protective custody of the Gestapo (*Schutzhäftlinge*).

7. W.N. Medlicott, *The Economic Blockade*, Vols.I and II (London: HMSO, 1952–59), pp.1–54.

8. Selborne to Eden, 13 April 1943; Memo by Worsfeld, 22 March 1943; Memo by Foot, 11 April 1943, PRO, FO837/1214. War Cabinet, WP(43)186, 30 April 1943; War Cabinet, WM(43)63, 3 May 1943; Telegram, Churchill to Halifax, 30 May 1943, PRO, FO837/1214; 'Journal of Mission to London', by Jackson and Lehman, 8–23 April 1943. NA, RG 169, Entry 124, Box 41, Reports London.

9. War Cabinet, WP(41)176, PRO, FO371/28825. Medlicott, *The Economic Blockade*, Vol.II, p.578.

10. Breitman and Kraut, pp.185–91.

11. Ben Pimlott (ed.), *The Second World War Diary of Hugh Dalton, 1940–45* (London: Jonathan Cape, 1986), p.175.

12. For the official histories see: C.R.S. Harris, *Allied Military Administration of Italy, 1943–45, History of the Second World War* (London: HMSO, 1956); F.S.V. Donnison, *Civil Affairs and Military Government in North-West Europe, 1944–46, History of the Second World War* (London: HMSO, 1956); R.M. Titmuss, *Problems of Social Policy, History of the Second World War* (London: HMSO, 1950). To avoid duplicating the work of their British counterparts, the US Army chose to publish a document collection, Harry Coles and Albert K. Weinberg (ed.), *United States Army in World War II: Civil Affairs – Soldiers Become Governors* (Washington, DC: GPO, 1964). The International Red Cross has issued a variety of official histories on its role in the Second World War, the most recent of which is *Inter arma caritas: The Work of the Red Cross during the Second World War* (Geneva: The Committee, 1973). An outside perspective is offered by John F. Hutchison, *Champions of Charity: War and the Rise of the Red Cross* (Boulder, CO: Westview Press, 1996) and David Forsythe, *Humanitarian Politics: The International Committee of the Red Cross* (Baltimore, MD: Johns Hopkins University Press, 1977). David Hinshaw, *An Experiment in Friendship* (New York: G.P. Putnam's Sons, 1947) provides an overview of the work of the American Friends Service Committee. The most comprehensive account of the work of the United Nations Relief and Rehabilitation Administration remains its three-volume report, UNRRA, *Economic Recovery in the Countries Assisted by UNRRA* (Washington: GPO, 1946). For a general summary, see House Select Committee on Foreign Aid, United States Congress, *Final Report on Foreign Aid* (Washington: GPO, 1948).

13. W.N. Medlicott, *The Economic Blockade*, Vols.I and II (London: HMSO, 1952–59). Joan Beaumont, 'Starving for Democracy: Britain's Blockade of and Relief for Occupied Europe, 1939–1945', *War and Society*, Vol.8, No.2 (Oct. 1990), pp.57–82; Bob Moore, 'The Western Allies and Food Relief to the Occupied Netherlands, 1944–1945', *War and Society*, Vol.10, No.2 (Oct. 1992), pp.91–118. The relief issue has also been taken up tangentially by biographers of Herbert Hoover, who debate whether Hoover was committed to the relief issue or viewed it as a way to rehabilitate his image in the wake of his handling of the Great Depression. See Gary Dean Best's *Herbert Hoover: The Postpresidential Years, 1933–1964*, 2 vols. (New York: Oxford, 1988) and James H. George, Jr., 'Another Chance: Herbert Hoover and World War II Relief', *Diplomatic History*, Vol.16, No.3 (Summer 1992), pp.389–407.

14. The blockade, along with bombing, propaganda, and subversion, were the four 'weapons' in which the British government placed its hopes following its defeat at Dunkirk. During the war, the British used the blockade as a form of contraband control. In the early years of the war, ships were intercepted on the high seas and diverted to ports where their cargoes were checked for contraband. Later in the war, this technique was replaced with a complex system of 'navicerts' or commercial passports, which ships received at their place of origin as a guarantee that they were not carrying contraband. See David Reynolds, 'Churchill and the British "Decision" to fight on in 1940: Right Policy, Wrong Reasons', in Richard Langhorne (ed.), *Diplomacy and Intelligence during the Second World War* (Cambridge: Cambridge University Press, 1985), pp.157–8; and W.N. Medlicott, *The Economic Blockade*, Vols.1–2 (London: HMSO, 1952–1959).

15. Telegram No.216, Kirk to State, 28 Nov. 1939, F375; Amcross News Service Press Release, 28 Nov. 1939, F400, NA, RG59, 840.48 Refugees, M1284, Roll 1. Telegram No.941, Taylor to Davis, 13 April 1940, F261, NA, RG 59, 840.48 Refugees, M1284, Roll 3. Minute [W5630/37/48] by Humphrys, Cadogan, and Halifax, 8–9 April 1940; Letter [W5630/37/48], Seymour to Mounsey, 11 April 1940; Telegram No.578, FO to Washington, 15 April 1940, PRO, FO371/25237. Telegram No.620 Arfar, MEW to Lothian, 27 April 1940, PRO, FO371/25238.

16. Hoover's request that Britain contribute money to fund his relief programme for the *Generalgouvernement* was extensively debated in the spring of 1940. See PRO, FO371/25237.

17. Hansard, House of Commons, 20 August 1940.

18. The American appeal to Britain for a French relief programme and the implementation of that programme can be found in NA, RG 59, 840.48 Refugees, M1284, Rolls 5 and 6. The debate over blockade concession within the British government can be found in PRO, FO371/25201–2 and FO837/1226–7.

19. Britain's attempts to bring relief to Greece can be traced in PRO, FO371/28825–35, FO371/32455–65, and FO837/1230–37. American involvement in the Greek relief programme can be glimpsed through the correspondence between the State Department and the US Embassy in Stockholm in NA, RG59, 868.48.

20. War Cabinet, WP(41)176, PRO, FO371/28825. Medlicott, *The Economic Blockade*, Vol.II, p.578.

21. Telegram R-243, Roosevelt to Churchill, 22 Dec. 1942. Warren Kimball, *Churchill and Roosevelt: The Complete Correspondence*, Vol.II (Princeton: Princeton University Press, 1984).

22. Selborne to Eden, 13 April 1943; Memo by Worsfeld, 22 March 1943; Memo by Foot, 11 April 1943, PRO, FO837/1214; War Cabinet, WP(43)186, 30 April 1943; War Cabinet, WM(43)63, 3 May 1943; Telegram, Churchill to Halifax, 30 May 1943, PRO, FO837/1214; 'Journal of Mission to London', by Jackson and Lehman, 8–23 April 1943, NA, RG 169, Entry 124, Box 41, Reports London.

23. Telegram, Roosevelt to Churchill, 15 March 1944. Warren Kimball (ed.), *Churchill and Roosevelt: The Complete Correspondence*, Vol.III (Princeton: Princeton University Press, 1984).

24. War Cabinet, WP(44)177, 30 March 1944; WM(44)43, 3 April 1944.

25. War Cabinet, WM(44)147. Telegram No.2197 Arfar, MEW to Berne, 24 June 1944, PRO, FO837/1217.

26. The negotiations and false starts for supplying north-west Holland with relief can be found in PRO, PREM3/221/11-12 and FO371/50135-45.

27. Catherine Pease-Watkin and Michael James (ed.), *The Collected Works of Jeremy Bentham: Political Tactics* (Oxford: Clarendon, 1999).

28. See for example *The New York Times* from July to December 1941.

29. Breitman, *Official Secrets*, pp.140–41.

30. Hansard, House of Commons, 17 Dec. 1942.
31. Wasserstein, *Britain and the Jews of Europe, 1939–45*, pp.159, 163.
32. FO note to Cabinet Committee on Refugees, 18 Feb. 1943, PRO CAB 95/15.
33. UK delegates to Eden, 28 June 1943. PRO PREM 4/51/3.
34. US Congress, House, 78th Congress, 1st Session, Congressional Record, 4044–7.
35. Wyman, *Abandonment of the Jews*, p.152.
36. Wyman, *Abandonment of the Jews*, p.146.
37. Breitman, *Official Secrets*, pp.192–201.
38. Telegram No.644, Foreign Office to Washington, 24 Jan. 1944; Telegram No.413, Washington to Foreign Office, 26 Jan. 1944; PRO, FO371/42727.
39. Bell had a reputation for campaigning on behalf of politically sensitive issues, such as the immorality of area bombing; 'Note on Blockade Policy Respecting Relief', 24 Feb. 1943; PRO, FO837/1214. The Famine Relief Committee also included William Patton of the World Council of Churches and Edith Pye of the Society of Friends. The FRC was very careful to disassociate itself from the pacifist movement, which offered one of the earliest critiques of the blockade.
40. Howard Kershaw, *One Humanity: A Plea for our Friends and Allies* (New York: G.P. Putnam and Sons, 1943).
41. 'Report on American Opinions,' 1–15 January 1944; memo by Professor Allardyce on 'Feed Europe Now', forwarded by the British Embassy in Washington, 16 Jan. 1944; PRO, FO837/1216.

# Switzerland, National Socialist Policy and the Legacy of History

## JACQUES PICARD

This article deals with the relationship between National Socialism's foreign and economic policy, on the one hand, and Swiss models of behaviour in dealing with Nazi Germany, on the other. Finally, it examines explanations of this period in Swiss memory and historiography after the war. For the period of Nazi rule, this relationship boiled down to the options available to any small state when confronting the policies and war economies of a large power. However intensively it was nurtured and carefully managed, this co-existence remained an unequal relationship. So the link between the significance of Switzerland (long considered peripheral) and the pivotal, apparently irresistible and powerful centre of strength (Berlin) must always be described as problematic. This problematic character has became manifest on various levels in the historiography and collective memory of Switzerland.

The first part of this article will briefly recapitulate some aspects of National Socialist policy and its underlying economic ideology. The starting point here is the National Socialist project of a 'Germanised' Europe and the concept linked with that of a 'Greater Germany' based on racial foundations. In this context, antisemitism is an important factor in the complex web of ideology and had an effect on various policies and aspects of life. The second part of the article will consider three features of the Swiss state of affairs, namely aspects of the history of Swiss policy with regard to military matters, economic issues and the attitude towards refugees. What emerges is that the state of knowledge concerning these three features under investigation differs greatly. The bracketing of the three areas through the question of how the National Socialist ideology of *Lebensraum* was perceived, and the Swiss response to it, is not intended to disguise this fact.

## I

During the phase when Hitler was establishing his power, he succeeded in claiming credit for the temporary stabilisation of the economy and winning the confidence of wide circles in industry and finance both inside and outside Germany. This was crucial to his early success. Compromise with the old elites in state and society was essential for the stabilisation of his own position as leader. Hitler's decision to opt for an alliance with the Army and against his party's own organisation, the SA, is significant in this context. The interests of the various institutions of the 'Führer-state' were involved in partial competition with one another in the process of establishing power and making it secure, and in the course of further development this produced varied moments of radicalisation.[1]

In his conception of politics Hitler linked radical and universal antisemitism and racism with the declared goal of stage-by-stage expansion within Europe. National Socialist racism was linked with the notion of Germany's assuming a position as a world power within Europe and ultimately on the world's oceans as well. This entailed an intention to profit from the expected splitting up of the British colonial empire. Elements of this planned foreign policy can be discerned in the efforts of senior members of the National Socialist movement to oblige the United States to maintain a neutral position by talking of a German 'Monroe Doctrine' and leaving no room for doubting National Socialist intentions.[2] In Europe itself the primary aim was to acquire *Lebensraum* for the Germans in the East, in order to provide the Third Reich with the preconditions for achieving the status of a world power.[3]

It is significant that the beginning of the war against the Soviet Union in 1941 coincided with the beginning of a systematic slaughter of Russian Jews and other 'degenerate' minorities and thus represented an important step towards the physical annihilation of other races. National Socialist extermination policy was also designed to realise the concept of *Lebensraum*. Indeed, as Saul Friedländer maintains, the ideological goal which Hitler and his fellow party members shared had been adumbrated early on as a philosophically-based 'anti-Semitism as redemption', distinct from other traditional forms of enmity towards the Jews. Friedländer points to the fact that Hitler was driven by ideological obsessions which were anything but the calculable manoeuvres of a demagogue, inasmuch as he took a 'quite specific type of popular anti-Semitism to its most extreme and most radical boundaries'.[4] The conditions of warfare and colonisation in the East allowed for a great deal of latitude in carrying out the mass murders of Jewish men and women and other groups among the population. Racism and territorial expansion were turned into reality by the politics of power.[5]

The notions of dominance as a world power and a colonial power corresponded with the usurpation of power within the state. In their ultimate logic they were directed against everything that was, as Heinrich Himmler put it, *gesellschaftsfremd* (hostile to society), and destroyed the constitutional bases of a power-sharing democracy.[6] The dissolution of alternative power centres within government and society had drastic consequences. The polycratic structure of the National Socialist state meant that Hitler could play off various subordinate, opportunistic groups and party fractions against one another. Corruption and misapropriation were the practices of elites, parvenus and profiteers and had inhibiting effects when a part of the German population, especially the Jews, was robbed and expropriated.[7] The principle of competition, which was calculated according to power politics, and which was to have fateful consequences for the society and economy of the National Socialist state, produced numerous wielders of power, both big and small, who contributed to the independent radicalisation of particular measures. Precisely in the new *Lebensraum* of the East, but also in occupied areas, this 'select among the elite' found far-reaching possibilities open to them. These opportunities were turned into reality without the slightest moral inhibition and produced acts of exploitation, plunder and murder. The initiation of the 'Final

Solution' in east Polish Galicia shows, for example, how the radicalisation of policies towards the Jews could lead to a region becoming 'literally a slaughter-house'.[8]

The rationalisations and justifications for their actions used by the Nazis before and after the war give the impression that the National Socialist regime pursued a kind of tactic of legality, veiling its destructive intentions behind constant proclamations of its peaceful intentions while using the façade of due legal process and conformity with the constitution. However, this perception is countered by the fact that the National Socialist regime declared more or less openly its policy of intensive rearmament, the preparation of aggression, and internal terrorism and specially legalised discrimination directed against individuals and ethnic groups. As early as 1939 two contemporary witnesses, Ernst Fraenkel and Franz Neumannn, who were active in the legal profession in Germany before their flight, described National Socialist rule as a combination of imposed specific norms and specific measures, simultaneously with the existence of different structures of the same power.[9] In view of the multi-faceted power structure, its racist basis and the anti-democratic methods of government, the question arises: on what economic principles and trade policies was National Socialism supposed to rest?[10]

If the democratic state had hitherto been identified with the principle of free trade, oriented towards the world market, National Socialist rule was eventually equated with a new 'alternative' economic order which was based on state direction and control of private enterprises. Therefore National Socialist economic ideology favoured the concept of a closed trading state, which bore the features of a *Planwirtschaft*, a planned economy. This ideal became attractive in several European countries where financial problems had disrupted society. For many of the 'front generation' who had fought in the First World War, authoritarian policy and planned economy represented more 'modern' forms of organisation than liberalism or reform socialism. But in other countries, like England and Belgium, authoritarian state intervention and nationalistic economics were seen not as a solution but as the root of these problems.[11] In Germany, the conviction that an authoritarian approach and planned economy would work rested on a pact between major elites of the economy and the army as well as Wilhelmenian conservatism and National Socialism, which had emerged through the experience of the economic crisis. Economic reconstruction after the First World War was weakened by the tensions between London and Paris over the desirability of fostering recovery in Germany, an issue related to the burdens of war reparations. The declared aim of the alliances inside Germany, as far as the National Socialists were concerned, was to provide a new military and economic basis for Hitler's goals of territorial and economic expansion.[12]

## II

The dream of an economic order based on 'autarchy' was promulgated by 'reformers' well before 1933, before it was used as an element of ideological explanation by the National Socialists from 1936 onwards, when the Four-Year Plan began. The earlier ideas of 'autarchy' were given their essential stamp by three elements whose conservative utopianism rapidly reveals the contradictions in it. First, the 'autarchy' movement was motivated by the desire, in terms of economic policy, to remove Germany from its links with the international currency market and thus avoid all monetary disruptions. The experience of the crises and inflation of the 1920s as well as the burdens of debt and reparations from the First World War which lay behind these, and the increasing difficulties in transferring money internationally necessarily strengthened a policy which consisted of presenting compulsory exchange controls (justified as an emergency measure) as an expression of allegiance to an 'autarchic' order of things. Second, the autarchy movement is distinguished by a conception of exaggerated nationalism whose political arguments were based on agrarian considerations and issues concerning raw materials; at the same time, there was a partial harking back to doctrines from popular economy, originating from the era before liberalism. These could be combined with neo-corporatist concepts which were linked to the principle of the 'estates of the realm' and a hierarchical society. Finally, the notion of autarchy was aiming at the creation of a large economic area, in the sense of a supranational trading area, but one with fixed boundaries, which should be conceived of as 'pan-European'. Thus a counterweight would be created to the economic and hegemonic areas outside Europe. Increasingly, this process was understood not only in terms of the declining British empire, but also with an eye on the Soviet Union, which was considered economically successful in the 1930s.

The debate about 'autarchy', which is marked by such mutually contradictory elements, was expressed in extensive writing on economics which mirrored the intellectual response to the crises since the end of the First World War. Such discussions took place in Switzerland, too. They were not always welcomed, but could not be ignored. A critique of the doubts expressed about Free Trade, which appeared in the *Schweizerische Rundschau* of 1933, shows evident unease about the newly propagated views:

> Autarchy, in terms of the policy of trade, which is the sense in which the expression is most frequently used and in which it is used here, means, to speak with the words of its defenders, to withdraw; means national self-sufficiency, the closing of the borders; means supplying one's own demands oneself; means limitation to the national economic sphere; and means independence from the rest of the world.
>
> The word *national* itself, which recurs in numerous combinations in the rephrasing of these concepts, points to the fact that autarchy as an economic postulate emerges for many, probably for the vast majority, of its proponents not as the ripe fruit of reflection on and understanding of the science of economics but from quite different trains of thought, that is to say national, or, more correctly, *nationalistic* ones. The hypertrophied nationalism of our times is the best source from which the dubious growth of the autarchy movement draws its nourishing juices.

> Understandably – since whoever feels a relationship with pre-Christian antiquity in terms of his attitude to everything that is not part of his race; whoever sees in the members of other nations and states inferior semi-barbarians, if not simply enemies; whoever finds every attempt to satisfy the world foolish and every attempt at international understanding offensive, for such a person even the products of everywhere that is foreign must be a horror, and even the desire to avoid every contact as far as possible seems to follow self-evidently and with the most compelling logic. And yet in another respect autarchy directly contradicts this nationalistic megalomania, since trading with the world increases a people's significance and esteem. What would Switzerland be in economic terms without its lively foreign trade and high-quality exports, which have carried its name to the ends of the earth?[13]

This article demonstrates the ambiguity and wide applicability of the concept of 'autarchy'. The National Socialist conception of economics had to latch on to an old debate because it had no original economic policies at its disposal.[14] It found in older slogans such as 'autarchy', *Lebensraum* and 'Greater Germany' things it could hang on to in order to promote an allegedly alternative, that is stable, economic and social, order on the basis of an economic policy that actually depended on state expenditure. The National Socialists took over the existing 'reformist' slogans and combined them with plans for expansion in racist and colonising terms which were part of their foreign policy and their power politics.[15] Pan-European ideals and peacekeeping European projects that were earlier formulated with the purpose of securing peace, particularly the notion of *Mitteleuropa*,[16] were rejected and replaced by their own conceptions of a 'New Europe' or 'New Order'. From this point on, the NSDAP conceived of a 'Germanic Europe' on the basis of an 'Aryan master race'.[17] In other words, Hitler preferred a racist and territorial hegemonic policy to expanding Germany's political position in terms of world trade in concert with the other European powers. Thus the global market-economy system of free trade with its division of responsibilities had to be replaced by a national economy tied to one particular area and under state control. Against the background of altered power relationships the shift in the meaning of the old notion of Europe[18] was made clear. The optimism about peace, which went hand in hand with free trade in the nineteenth and early twentieth centuries, was replaced by the perspective of a 'continental block' under the influence of National Socialist racial ideology.[19]

There was a dramatic shift of emphasis between 1929 and 1933. If the economic goals of the crisis cabinets under Heinrich Brüning and Franz von Papen still envisaged bringing public finances into balance or stimulating entrepreneurial initiative, under Kurt von Schleicher, and then under Hitler, state control of the economy took over completely.[20] Following the introduction of compulsory exchange controls in 1931, the German government issued ever stricter emergency decrees dealing with the laws governing currency exchange and wavered in terms of banking policy between market economy and state control.[21] In terms of internal and foreign policy, this approach harmonised with the institutional goals of National Socialism: firstly through the intensive rearmament of the military and then through close economic cooperation with neighbouring states. Foreign trade was supposed to take place as far as possible without currency exchange, on the basis of bilateral treaties. Naturally it was clear to the National Socialists that 'autarchy' in the narrow sense of complete self-sufficiency was out of the question. But the logical consequence of the ideology underpinning their economic policies was to imagine individual economies as a kind of barter system and to see in them an instrument for their plans for hegemonic domination. Above all, from the National Socialist point of view, it was necessary to pursue a trading policy which would facilitate the opening up of markets and sources of supply. The central European economic area, initially directed towards the south and east, would, according to this conception, signify the anticipation of territorial expansion, that is the policy of *Lebensraum*. The heart of the economic and political pipe-dreams of the National Socialist regime was the Four-Year

Plan, by means of which the National Socialist arms economy was supposed to be coordinated by the internal direction of labour, wages and consumption, in addition to industrial mobilisation and the securing of raw materials through foreign economic policy.

The Four-Year Plan as an expression of totalitarian economic policy, whose goal was to secure the necessary political stability within the country by a kind of 'organised capitalism', was matched in the sphere of foreign policy by a system of alliances with the states that were dependent on Germany. Faced with war, a dedicated policy of exploitation was eventually pursued. Military supremacy and big-business opportunities, shared values and symbiotic attraction – all this was destined (as can be read in the 'Yearbook of the German Society for European Economic Planning and Large-Scale Economy' of 1941) to turn the 'New Europe' into an 'eternal, central living area for the peoples of the white race, as a natural unity in accordance with the laws of life and territory'.[22]

Such a vision necessarily had consequences in terms of economic policy. The place of the liberal 'most-favoured nation status', that is the equal treatment of native and foreign investors, was replaced by political, racial and geographical preferences. In its foreign trade policy the Reich pursued a politically-motivated bilateralism, which as far as possible excluded free trading in currency. In this so-called 'clearing system' sums due for payment in external trade were mutually credited and balanced out against one another, creating inside each state two 'independently' working streams of money. From the point of view of trading policy, free trade was corsetted in accordance with the principle of reciprocity: goods of the same value or the same quantity were supposed to be exchanged. In terms of power politics – and this seemed to be decisive as far as Hitler was concerned – it was believed that such a foreign trade policy would automatically lead to an amalgamation of neighbouring states and areas.

In this sense, the 'clearing' system was believed to be a multi-dimensional instrument of control, which could be applied in a bilateral way to dealings with individual states or even conquered areas. Essentially, however, as far as Berlin was concerned, it represented a repertoire of unilateral techniques for trade on the basis of exchange and payment. It appeared to the decision-makers that German power politics and economic interests had been optimally combined in the system of clearing relationships. In an essay circulated by Walther Funk, Reichsminister for the economy and president of the Reichsbank, which appeared in July 1940 in the *Südost-Echo* and was available in Switzerland, the clearing system is discussed in greater detail and becomes significant as an instrument of financial and trade policy within the National Socialists' plans for power.[23]

The various schools of the 'Greater Germany' theory provided geopolitical justifications, fantasies for social Darwinism and universally applicable socio-political arguments in order to provide a rational basis for the drive to economic and colonial expansion. Not least, an anticipatory thinker like Carl Schmitt also provided the new 'structures' for a corresponding German legal system.[24] The opening up of markets and *Lebensraum* as envisaged and planned by the National Socialist regime was entirely achievable with the range of tools inherent in trading policies, though these were anything but peaceful or cooperative and in the end would necessarily provoke confrontation with the USA. Where the trade policy card would not succeed, military expansion remained part of the calculations.[25] At the centre of the economic plans stood the *Volksgemeinschaft*, 'the community of the people', which was linked with the policy of *Lebensraum*. The notion of life as 'the struggle between the races' meant that war could be perceived not only as a goal of policy but also as a maxim of economics, and thereby of economic relations with foreign powers.

The state of the German economy, in the meantime, did not look as it was supposed to according to the National Socialist economic policy as promulgated in the Four-Year Plan. A study prepared in Switzerland in 1939 on the basis of accessible documentation of German origin, which undertook a comparative evaluation of economic circumstances in the case of war, concluded that for economic reasons it would be impossible for Germany to wage a successful war. On the other hand, this publication, which emerged from emigrant circles and was published by *Europa-Verlag* in Zurich and New York (the anti-fascist Swiss publisher Hans Oprecht) estimated the reserves of Germany's possible enemies as 'beyond calculation'! The study, written by Heinz Rosinski under the pseudonym 'Miles', comes to a realistic conclusion in its judgement of the economic capacity of the Third Reich and its true ability to sustain a war economy.[26] This estimate by a contemporary witness has been partly vindicated by research; some historians have come to the conclusion that the National Socialist leadership was clear about the consequences of the artificial boost given to armament production and the uneconomic nature of the system of state organisation and *Wehrwirtschaft*.[27] Admittedly, the inclusion of southern and eastern Europe in the economy of Greater Germany might generate increases in production and open up important sources of raw materials. But this was balanced by general problems related to the difficult financial situation, the overheating of production and losses through inefficiency within the planned economy. Another factor was that German armament itself was directed towards short and fast campaigns of conquest and fast movement, and not towards armament in depth for long-term conflicts, with the classic warfare of fixed and fortified positions.[28]

Germany needed gold and convertible currencies because the imports that were relevant to rearmament could not be paid for solely by the 'clearing' method. But by 1939 the National Socialist state had used up almost all of its gold and currency reserves. As a state in debt with 'doubtful credit status and minimal gold reserves', as Rosinski formulates it, Germany was dependent on imports from abroad. France and Great Britain, on the other hand, had unhindered imports at their disposal from their possessions overseas. Germany's dependence on imported food and raw materials, the real Achilles heel of the Third Reich, was relieved for a short time thanks to the conquests achieved by *Blitzkrieg*. The inclusion of conquered states or those that had come under German hegemony through trading policy, and systematic, unscrupulous exploitation and confiscation, made the problems of supply less acute at first glance. Yet, the economic losses caused by military service and the reduction of the numbers employed in industry could not be made good. In the end, the invasion of the Soviet Union exposed the exhaustion of strength and reserves and necessitated a mobilisation campaign of vast dimensions in Germany itself.

## III

National Socialist *Judenpolitik*, policy directed at the Jews, as well as policy towards Roma and Sinti and other minorities in Europe, had as one of its aims the involvement of the occupied and Axis states in a vast crime as a result of which they would be sundered from the free world. The policy of expulsion and annihilation created, as an ideological aim, a 'hegemony' which went far beyond the classical meaning of controlling politics and economy. Here the real character of the *Lebensraum* policy becomes manifest, as a 'race war'. In the year that war broke out Georg Hahn came up with the formulation, in his 'Basic Questions of European Order'. Besides the revision of the 'dictated treaty' of Versailles and the struggle against Bolshevism it was the 'exclusion of Jewry' that created a 'binding community of fate' for all European peoples. Only involvement in the 'solution of the Jewish question', as he claimed, 'would create the basic pre-requisite for the 'integration of European states into a larger economic region'.[29]

We are therefore concerned with a project of European conquest that goes hand in hand with a 'siege economy'.[30] In retrospect, it becomes increasingly clear *how* the National Socialist regime compensated for the inadequacy of its war economy and *how* it realised the 'solution of the Jewish question'. Initially, it followed the logic of economic hegemonisation, namely in the north and in the south-east. Then, with short and initially effective 'lightning wars', it opened up the areas which were charged with racial significance in National Socialist ideology. At the same time, during this looting foray through the occupied territories it acquired gold, currency, valuable investments and raw materials for itself. The property that was looted and confiscated was converted into negotiable forms and the owners who had been robbed of it were murdered. Even before the outbreak of the war, the policy of exploitation as an initial step in the measures for dispossession and expulsion had become discernible. It is worth recalling the close correlation between the failure of the third issue of state loan bonds on the German finance market in autumn 1938 and the demand imposed on the German Jews in the wake of the *Kristallnacht* to provide an 'expiatory milliard' of Reichsmarks.[31] The 'aryanisation' of Jewish property was continuous from 1933 onwards, but intensified in 1937–39.[32] The linkage between racial policy, economic policy and conquest was visible in the other ways that the Third Reich exploited its territorial acquisitions. Production was partially coordinated while foreign workers and enslaved men and women – 'Eastern workers', forced labourers, POWs and concentration camp inmates – were used for its war economy inside and outside Germany.[33]

The regime also utilised those areas which did not provide any direct opportunity for exploitation, either as satellites or as occupied territories, but offered an indispensable service as neutral ground. Essentially, business that required a large number of contacts to be made all in one place was transacted there, as far as possible under war conditions. In this context, the Reich had various ways of acquiring convertible currencies, which were used individually or in combination with one another. Access to currencies which were convertible throughout the world and important for the war economy could take place via the sale of gold to foreign note-issuing institutions and merchant banks.[34] In addition, there was the export of goods and services, the sale of plundered property such as bearer bonds, jewellery and works of art. It also includes the extortion of 'ransom' for people persecuted by the National Socialist regime, though this mostly failed.[35] From the National Socialist point of view, neutral countries such as Sweden and Switzerland appeared to be attached in a useful way to 'Greater Germany'. For the National Socialist regime, every territory available to them was important so long as it fulfilled the purpose of meeting their needs in terms of currency and raw materials and other important resources required for German industry and finance.[36]

## IV

Historical writing in Switzerland since 1945 gives the initial impression of an officially commissioned and, moreover, politically controlled historiography. The evil of this 'history in chains' is that it fostered a belief that Swiss neutrality was undamaged.[37] From this point of view, the role of Switzerland during the National Socialist period remained limited to emphasising the preservation of neutrality. The markers for this period were the start and finish of the war, but not the years before and especially after this time. Those aspects of the National Socialist period which concerned the policy of expulsion and annihilation and the questions of economic history as a whole were, for a long time, not a theme for Swiss historiography. However, the creation of links between National Socialist and Swiss patterns of action has been permitted since the 1950s and 1960s, leading to intermittent discussions about the ways in which Switzerland and the Third Reich distanced themselves from one another and the ways in which they were involved with one another.[38]

In the debate about the past, questions of political and military history initially occupied the foreground. Vague indications from Hitler's so-called table-talk such as the statement that neutral Switzerland was a 'pimple on the face of Europe' that ought to be removed, gave shape to the picture of a Switzerland under immediate threat.[39] Yet, the controversy over the military 'redoubt' in the Alpine region of central Switzerland made it clear that policy towards the Third Reich had not been simply a matter of armed neutrality. Consideration of foreign policy and economic relations gave rise to questions that went even further, since it became evident that here political, financial and ideological interests were mutually entangled. Finally, research into policy concerning foreigners and refugees revealed a political culture which both before and after 1933 was ideologically loaded, and which even after 1945 remained taboo.[40] Most surprisingly, Swiss victims of National Socialism were largely ignored in the early historiography.[41]

With the more recent insights into refugee, military and

economic policies, questions are now being raised about differing features of Swiss political and legal practice during and after the National Socialist period. It is important to emphasise that just one central question, namely the relationship of Switzerland to the Third Reich and the National Socialist ideology, always lay behind the various themes of historiography. But the marginalisation in Switzerland of concern with the National Socialist system, its *Lebensraum* policy and the direction of its economic ideology, and especially the lack of any real discussion of the history of the Holocaust, retarded Swiss historiography. It is abundantly clear that using 'neutrality' uncritically is not conducive to explanation and narrows the analysis down to internal Swiss problems. It can be said that the old fixation with the question of neutrality represents an extension of the apologetics of the last years of the war and the immediate post-war years.[42]

## V

It is now evident that Switzerland's neutrality, armed or otherwise, was never unconditional and that its relations with the Third Reich followed a pattern set in its relations with other powerful neighbours, France in particular. Initial discussions about cooperation between the French and the Swiss general staffs in 1939, papers about which had fallen into the hands of the German troops, were based on 'Case North', the assumption that Hitler would unleash war on Switzerland. Switzerland wanted to make sure, in the event of an attack, that it would have an ally. Above and beyond these technical and military considerations, however, the discussions represented a breach of the laws of neutrality, in this case in favour of the Allies.[43] Accordingly, the Swiss army was mobilised for a short time from autumn 1939, but after the fall of France in June 1940 the situation was reassessed. The negotiations with France show the army acting in a political context which later, in the case of Germany, assumed a predominantly economic character. This can only mean that the basic principle of armed neutrality was applied very flexibly in accordance with the degree of threat and the state of the war. Implicitly the option to act in favour of the German side always remained open, and open to interpretation, and represented an invitation to make a gesture in the direction of Germany, if not necessarily a military one.[44] The decision to effect a partial demobilisation of the army, accompanied by a far-reaching review of the geopolitical and strategic situation, was a pivotal moment in Swiss history.

When in summer 1940 the army was demobilised by two-thirds to a figure of 150,000 men and withdrawn into the Alps, the so-called 'redoubt', the Swiss turned to economic cooperation with the great powers. There is a subtle but vital linkage between the 'redoubt', and the myth of 'armed neutrality', and the reality of economic cooperation with National Socialism. The commander of the army, General Henri Guisan, put a few Germanophile officers out to grass and projected himself as a symbol of order and resistance. He was able to attract the support of those parts of the population who were uncertain which way to turn.[45] But demobilisation benefited the labour market and the supply of raw materials, and freed up the resources necessary for economic cooperation. The implications of the decision to withdraw to the central alpine fortress did not go unchallenged among the army leadership at the time. The commander of the 2nd Army Corps, Fritz Prisi, was afraid the army could be starved out and saw no sense in 'defending alpenstocks and glaciers, if the central area with its rich economic production and the majority of the Swiss people are given up to the enemy without a fight'.[46] It was rather a matter of fighting, he said, for 'constitution, honour and freedom', because even at that moment there was a point in dying for an *idea*. Many people who experienced the war years may have been very conscious of the threatened handing over to Germany of old people, women and children who lived in the *Mittelland*, the non-alpine central area. So the decision in favour of a withdrawal to the 'redoubt' hardly warrants Guisan's veneration, despite his success in promoting the 'intellectual defence of the country' and styling himself as a symbol of national resistance.

The conflict between Prisi and Ulrich Wille, who was soon

removed from the scene, anticipated, as it were, the dispute among historians on the question of whether the retreat into the Alps was really a matter of defending the country, in the sense of 'neutrality and waging war', or whether it merely offered an illusion of heroism that was useful as a myth of legitimation during and even after the war. The 'redoubt', as recent research shows, must be understood largely as a tactical deterrent and a gesture of resistance which had value only within political equations so long as there was no real war. The demobilisation of large parts of the army made possible the release of workers who set the apparatus of production in motion in the central area which was slated to be given up in case of invasion.[47] Economic motives played only a minor role as far as General Guisan was concerned, but they counted all the more in the circles of industry and the National Bank, who demanded demobilisation.[48]

The subtle connection between military and economic elements, which long remained unexplored, explains why in the past military aspects were more visible than economic ones. Research into Switzerland's financial history since 1980 shows that during the war the allocation of funds to the army, precisely for the building of the 'redoubt' would not have been possible without profitable trade connections to Germany.[49] The thesis of authors critical of the army has recently been confirmed from the military side. New work shows that the tension between the 'military and economic defence of the country' was subsumed under the heading of the 'war economy'. In effect, this denoted the export economy 'demanding special dispensations' for army men to work for the industry and stringent state control of the distribution of raw materials.[50] This connection finally deprived the army's self-justification of the weight it carried in historiography throughout the Cold War. In the debate about the history of the war years, critics perceived the 'redoubt' as a myth through which the army, even after 1945, was legitimised as a masculine, Swiss and Christian elite group. It was a fight about fixed images of history and thus about the question of the appropriateness of a policy of collective security to the life of the individual and how such a policy should be understood in the present.

Behind these later debates about military history, however, there stands the question of 'interactions between military, economic and ideological factors' in the Swiss elites at that time.[51] In concrete terms, this concerns the significance of the exporting economy, technological production and the delivery of war-materials – before, during and after the Second World War. Peter Hug has stated in a recent study that in wartime Swiss companies exported 80 per cent or SFR 820 million of their war material production to Germany, Italy and Romania. The most important of these companies had their origin in the period after the restrictive Versailles treaties of 1918–19 when the Germans saw a way out to maintain their war material production by relocating capital and technology into neutral countries.[52]

## VI

Streams of capital and knowledge are not bound by national borders, but, under the conditions of relatively free trade, follow transnational 'areas' which are determined by systems of various kinds. The chances and risks which affect political and entrepreneurial action are constantly re-evaluated in the course of events.[53] Even where the preferences for entrepreneurial action are dictated by economic advantage, political risks also play a role in decision-making by economic elites. In decisions of foreign economic policy – for example the Swiss rejection of exchange control or their advancement of state credit to the Axis powers and the Allies – basic values become the subject of conflicts between states and of conflicts of a social nature within states. Seen in retrospect, neutrality could turn into a theoretical trap: outside Switzerland its 'neutrality' took on a negative value because it affected foreign economic decisions. The attitude adopted in the last two years of the war, 1944–45, of not freezing relations with Germany, but rather of investing in the expected 'normality' of the post-war order, was read by the Allies, in view of the criminal nature of National Socialist policies and economics, as a moral concession by Switzerland to a hostile ideology (though such a reading lasted only a few years).

Swiss attitudes in the face of the racist and expansionist economic policy of the National Socialist state are comprehensible only if we consider political decisions as the expression of a complex mixture of political calculation, ideological determinants, carefully controlled information and economic interests. We can distinguish three levels to the system of rules behind such decisions. First, there is the micro-structural area of entrepreneurs and firms, which cultivated links and supplied markets within the geographical power areas of the Third Reich and the Allies; second, a middle level with state organisations and quasi-state organisations which controlled activities with the Reich and the Allies; and third, on the macro-economic level, there are the basic economic and political conditions of the global situation and the ideological perspectives of the men in power. National Socialist antisemitism, that is to say the measures of discrimination, justified by racist ideology, and the advantages of exploitation that result from it, produced different effects on these differing levels. It was only in the post-war period that these financial and economic relationships became visible as problematic political situations. Whether in current discourse the past should be interpreted against the background of Auschwitz and human rights, or exclusively as a politically 'necessary' calculation in a particular situation, as a question of economic risk, and appealing to the law as it stood at that time, has been the cause of heated discussions since the 1990s.

In Swiss economic history, the facts and aspects of finance, currency, industry and trade appear relatively synchronised factors.[54] In brief, during the war the Swiss franc was a freely convertible currency of reserve and exchange. The net inflow of currency which resulted from the surpluses of the balance of payments determined to a large extent the monetary basis. The growth of the monetary reserves by 9.5 per cent annually during the war years contrasts with the indices of prosperity, which described a largely stagnating national income and exports that had been falling since the 1930s. In contrast to this recessive general development, there was a relative increase in the quantities of exports to the two Axis states. In the years 1940 to 1942 Swiss exports to Germany and Italy amounted to over 45 per cent of the country's total exports. Germany had long since assumed a leading position in Swiss foreign trade: in the ten years before the outbreak of war, its share of the goods imported by Switzerland was one-quarter of the total value, and its share of exports over the same period wavered between an eighth and a fifth. The balance of trade with Germany was largely equalised by the provision of services, which included the transfer of capital and the granting of licences.

In terms of financial policy, through the acceptance of gold, which was centralised after 1943, the government pursued a policy of creaming off money. This policy was continued after the war. From the National Socialist point of view, the Swiss rejection of exchange control made Switzerland into an important market for currency and goods. On the basis of the strong Swiss franc and a high internal savings rate, the National Socialist state not only had the possibility of being able to secure the desired deliveries of high technology items and electricity in exchange for gold and raw materials, but also of having credit for its imports. These credits linked to goods were presented from the Swiss side as a 'weapon' in the politics of neutrality, an argument that was also presented with reference to the Allies. Looked at more closely, they were a continuation of Switzerland's role as a country that exported capital and were a war-time form of export or transfer guarantee for the Swiss economy, whose interests as creditor were principally covered by taking up gold of German as well as Russian origin.[55] Seen in this light, even the wartime rationing of food consumption inside Switzerland represents a form of state-enforced savings.

The system of export and transfer guarantees also had its genesis in the financial crisis of Germany at the end of the 1920s, which made the Swiss economic elites pessimistic. The behaviour of the banks in Germany generated scepticism inside and outside the country. But the National Socialists played up the antisemitic myth of the 'Jewish' character of banking.[56] As a reaction to the bank crashes, which led to a dramatic reduction of Germany's gold and currency reserves, in 1933 the German government declared a moratorium on the transfer of financial payments to foreign creditors. Negotiations between Germany and Switzerland began shortly afterwards and led in 1934 to the conclusion of a clearing agreement. The legal basis of the clearing agreements was the law passed by the Federal Government, 'Über wirtschaftliche Massnahmen gegenüber dem Ausland' of 14 October 1933, which empowered the Federal Government to take measures to protect national production, to promote exports and to equalise the balance of payments; inside Switzerland, the industrial sector was given clear preference over the financial side. A special aspect of this agreement concerned the Swiss export of electricity produced by hydroelectric power stations, which was indispensable for the southern Germany industrial area. This was not only an economic issue, but also a strategic and political one.[57] Another example of the impact of the clearing policy is the fact that German Jews were not allowed to transfer their assets out of the Reich. They were forced to smuggle currencies or, in some cases, invest their money in works of art.[58]

An important consequence of the clearing system in foreign trade was that payments were henceforth not made directly between importers and exporters but between two state institutions. Only recently has research shed light on the complex legal and financial 'techniques' of this bilateral payments system.[59] A precondition for the functioning of the system was an approximate balance between what the two sides had to offer. The exchange of goods and services was therefore limited as to quantity and value and subject to a quota. The establishment of appropriate quotas then became the subject of regular bilateral negotiations. Within the spectrum of the Swiss clearing system, rivalries developed between various areas of trade and various firms which always wanted to be given preferential treatment in the payment arrangements. This ultimately required political decisions which were largely taken in favour of 'work and capital', that is to say exportable industrial production. Internal Swiss arguments over the available funds for clearing were aggravated by Germany's demand for Swiss francs within the framework of the so-called currency overlap.[60]

The bilateralism which characterised the Swiss-German exchange arrangements from 1934 onwards, with the clearing system modelled on the planned economy, was not significant for technical financial reasons alone. The system had an inclusive political and legal character which became dramatically visible under wartime conditions. Jakob Tanner sums up the structure of the clearing system at the intersection of financial, trade and war-policies as follows:

> Together with the so-called Clearingmilliard, a credit [of more than one thousand million] given by Switzerland to Germany within the framework of the trade and finance clearing system, trade in gold formed the monetary counterpart to the largely concrete economic integration of the Swiss production base into the German war economy in the years 1940 to 1944.[61]

At the end of the war, German clearing debts amounted to 1.19 billion francs, the highpoint of export credit having been reached immediately before the German attack on the Soviet Union. To be fair, critics of this historiographical analysis have recently pointed out that Switzerland also gave credit of around 800 million to the British during wartime.[62]

From the German point of view, Swiss trade policy corresponded to the necessity of the war economy. Switzerland became a place for production and finance, and increasingly turned out to be a useful channel for acquiring currency, transferring gold and converting assets that had been acquired by theft or extortion.[63] In a similar way, Switzerland was a haven for tax evasion from Germany, France and other countries, and for Jews who smuggled currency out of Germany. All this was regarded as an illegal practice by the National Socialist authorities.[64] Admittedly, Switzerland was in an extremely difficult position because it lacked raw materials of its own, but the corresponding attitude of Switzerland during the pre-war and war years required some explanation even at the time for those involved. This is indicated by a broad range of statistics, accounts and reports of both an official and private character, which became available after the war.[65]

One example: Heinrich Homberger, the influential

representative of the Swiss Association of Trade and Industry and a member of the standing committee of the negotiating delegation of the Bundesrat, judged the clearing system to be 'extremely useful in order to deal appropriately with the interests that are at issue'. It is interesting that he gives a hint in this document (whether concealed or unintended) that the clearing system itself was practised within the area under the control of the National Socialist state between Germany and the states it occupied: 'since in the *occupied* territories payments were permitted in only Reichsmarks, Germany wanted without further ado to go over to that method in its clearing relations with Switzerland.'[66] This had to be all the truer for unoccupied states which nevertheless participated closely in German policies, such as Romania or Hungary. In any case, from Homberger's point of view, the fact that Switzerland practised the clearing system with Germany while insisting on the validity of the strong Swiss franc beside the Reichsmark as a 'double currency' in their exchange relations, was a decisive 'attribute of an independent state'. However, he did not deal with the implications, in terms of looting and extermination, of National Socialist occupation policy.

During and after the war the clearing credit system was depicted as a 'weapon' of trade policy, as Homberger's document shows. It was alleged that the Swiss government's action in making credit tied to goods available to the Allied side as well as to the Axis powers had been for the 'economic defence of the country'. But the oft-quoted phrase 'economic defence of the country' is contradictory. Providing the criminal German state with credits and armaments could extend the capacity of the Third Reich to wage war and thus extend the potential threat to Switzerland. This is the origin of the present-day dispute about the 'war extension thesis' which is itself problematic because of variables which are not always clarified and which implies questions about factors that were important for the war, the characteristics of exports and financial services, and questions about ideological and political motives.[67]

If one were writing a 'what if?' history one could hypothetically ask: if the National Socialist state had won its 'final victory' would not the Swiss clearing credit have been written off and would not

Switzerland, as a *Lebensraum* that was already economically integrated into Germany, simply have 'dropped into the National Socialists' lap' politically and territorially? From the National Socialist state's point of view, would the strategy of expansion, based on the ideology of *Lebensraum*, and in which the clearing system was a powerful political instrument for the 'absorption' of neighbouring states, have achieved its ultimate success? These questions cannot be answered, but the far-reaching intentions of the National Socialist regime can be established. According to a quip by Joseph Goebbels, the Minister for Popular Enlightenment and Propaganda, Switzerland laboured for six days for Germany and on the seventh prayed for an English victory. To him it was clear enough that 'we must take up a credit with Switzerland for 800 million francs for goods that have been delivered'; the Führer, he said, was of the opinion that Switzerland would in any case 'collapse any day now'.[68]

# VII

From current research it is clear that at the interface between money and gold policy, trade policy and armament finance, questions about the history of ideology can also be illuminating – even if the effects of Swiss financial and economic policy have been ignored for all too long because of the historiographic filter of 'neutrality'.[69] Switzerland obviously developed the principle of state financing of exports with its clearing credits at a time when the constraints of German exchange control and the Allied blockade policy were beginning to take effect. Indeed, the Swiss attempt to keep out of the warfare between the Axis and the Allies cannot be understood exclusively from the perspective of Swiss self-perception, according to which Switzerland had remained neutral in terms of international law. Here – as never before – the legal position, the reality of war, and the metaphorical use of neutrality failed to coincide.[70] A rigorous distinction must be made between them, just as the legal position and the real policy of neutrality differed from the employment of 'neutrality' as imagery in contemporary explanations, polemics and historiographical apologetics. There is no doubt that, from a historical point of view, the long cherished 'model of being equidistant in terms of economic and financial policy from both camps in the total war can no longer be maintained'.[71]

This much became accepted historiographical knowledge when Daniel Bourgeois established the importance of transnational analysis with his book *Le Troisième Reich et la Suisse 1939–1941*.[72] Further research brought a more accurate estimate of the mutual interests and economic relations with the Axis powers[73] and the Allied states.[74] Details are less clear about the German perspective, especially with reference to questions in the areas of financial and economic history.[75] However, it can be stated that National Socialist policy itself necessarily had a strong interest in external trade links with Switzerland. From the point of view of the National Socialist state's opening up of markets and *Lebensraum*, Switzerland could be considered initially an economic backyard which, as a *Lebensraum* that gave no cause for concern in 'völkisch–racial' terms, would fit into a Germanised Europe anyway. In the course of the war, especially with the invasion of the Soviet Union, the mobilisation of the war economy was intensified, while the system of theft and plunder was actively pursued in the occupied territories. Switzerland increasingly appeared an indispensable economic partner. In contrast to the other hegemonised and conquered states, especially in eastern and southern Europe, which from a National Socialist point of view needed to be exploited and disposed of as 'racially and ethnically inferior', Switzerland, with its anti-Bolshevist attitude, scarcely offered much reason for an attack. It must rather have been considered a country that would have been naturally hegemonised, at best analogous to Sweden or perhaps even to Vichy France.

From the Swiss point of view, the policy of granting credit to the National Socialist state was to be understood 'only' as a transfer guarantee for export quotas. This policy and the corresponding economic negotiations with the Axis and Allied states were proclaimed and justified as 'multilateral'. Despite this illusion, and according to the logic of the credit system policy, however, the clearing system with Germany could function during wartime only as long as it formed part of political bilateralism. With the defeat of the Third Reich, the advance of Allied troops and the failure of the German counter-blockade, the system of mutually promised deliveries and the balancing out of demands for payment broke down. The economic collapse of the Third Reich, the turning away from the clearing system and credits linked to goods and the opening of Switzerland's western border naturally meant that Allied demands for an end to deliveries and transits were automatically fulfilled. In this way, the symbiotic structure of the clearing agreements was dissolved, but not the political significance of the remaining mutual demands and debts. Heinrich Homberger's testimony makes clear his amazement when he realised the price of the 'economic defence of the country' and the neutrality that was characterised in this way.[76] The adoption of the Bretton Woods resolution in 1944, in which neutral states were required to hand over assets of the enemy which had been stolen, made it clear that the symbiosis which had been undertaken in the name of neutrality had been watched by outsiders with suspicion.

The vacuum left by the implosion of 'Greater Germany', which had been 'planned' in terms of economic ideology and realised as a campaign of robbery and murder, made it clear to the Swiss decision-makers that their policy of remaining economically and financially linked to Germany for far too long had been imprinted by more than bad taste. Justifications in terms of neutrality seemed unbelievable in the eyes of the American government. The risky nature of Switzerland's relations with the Third Reich turned out to be – as Harold James formulated it when speaking about the gold market – 'a trap of good faith which it laid for itself', inasmuch as the Swiss justified their policy to themselves, against their better knowledge.[77] Such self-deception could never obscure the fact that this policy carried a cost. The Swiss agreed to pay SFR 250 million in compensation for the purpose of reconstruction in Europe, and the Allies declared that they would forego any claims against the Swiss for gold which they received from Germany, though the issue of how to implement this agreement remained open. Additionally, in a settlement finalised at the end of August 1952, an agreement was reached on the liquidation of frozen German assets in Switzerland in return for a lump-sum payment to the Allies.[78] But the Washington treaty of 1946, as well as the London conference on war debts, marginalised restitution and the compensation of victims in favour of inter-state war reparations. These arrangements were heavily determined by the new international conditions at the beginning of the Cold War. The failure to address the missing assets of Nazi victims in Switzerland[79] or to solve that crucial problem between 1962 and 1972 provoked international discussions in the 1990s, pressures on the country from outside, payments by Swiss banks in favour of Holocaust victims, and investigations by two international commissions.[80]

In Switzerland, an international commission of historians began to investigate the general relations between the country's economy and the National Socialist state; it presented its results in 2001.[81] It is important to state that the investigations covered the period before 1945 as well as the time after the defeat of the National Socialist regime. This approach revealed several dimensions to the handling of the assets in banks and the life insurance policies of those who were persecuted by the National Socialists. On the one hand, the National Socialist practice of confiscation and stealing bonds, stocks, shares and insurance policies, and the many promises to create new *Lebensraum* and large areas for future economic expectations, obliged the Swiss to decide whether they intended to profit and cooperate or not. On the other hand, the administration of unclaimed assets and life insurance policies after the war was part of a Swiss and international policy on the past (*Vergangenheitspolitik*) which includes not only restitution and compensation but also more recent questions of historical and legal legitimacy.[82]

The newly discovered history of I G Farben and the so-called Interhandel affair is a good example of this. Founded in 1910, this German company had come under 'Swiss' control during the 1930s. Only now can we see how, after the war, it became a subject of conflict between a Swiss bank and American interests.[83] This collapsing together of different times and interests places historiographical continuity and discontinuity in a new light. Many other issues illustrate this development. The enforced auction of works of Jewish-owned art collections and 'degenerate' works from German museums, the role of Swiss and German Jewish emigrants as intermediaries in dealing with art works, and the restitution of stolen art works after the war have similarly erupted into the present.[84] The employment of forced labourers by subsidiaries of some Swiss companies inside Germany and the amnesia concerning their role in recent years is another example.[85] Or, the question of how the Swiss behaved in view of the wave of 'aryanisation' in Austria in 1938, which was raised anew because of the compensation made by Austria in recent years.[86] The latest investigations include case studies of how National Socialist criminals escaped at the end of, and just after, the war and managed to reach Latin American countries by using Swiss financial intermediaries or the help of Swiss governmental officials.[87]

In view of the long collective amnesia since 1945 it scarcely needs to be stressed that the attitudes towards Jews and antisemitism, as well as towards Gypsies, in Swiss society must play a substantial part in such an analysis.[88] This is not simply a matter of examining the active or quiescent adoption of antisemitic attitudes or measures, as for example when German business partners pressured Swiss firms to get the authorities to ensure that Swiss citizens of Jewish extraction were removed from certain functions.[89] Resistance to antisemitism, the defence of human rights, and genuine, often risky efforts to help must not be left out of the analysis, either. Swiss courts resisted National Socialist authorities by denying them access to assets which had been 'Aryanised' in Germany in 'legal' terms, but which in reality had been deposited by their Jewish owners in Switzerland.[90] For those German and Austrian Jews who had a fortune outside the National Socialist realm this often meant that they had some prospects – if they were lucky enough to escape to Switzerland and be accepted as refugees seeking asylum.

# VIII

Since refugees in Switzerland were subject to a general employment prohibition and the transfer of funds from abroad was extremely difficult, they could support themselves only if they had assets in Switzerland. The short-term residence permits for refugees entering Switzerland during the 1930s which were issued by cantonal authorities often demanded collateral and pledges of payment. Jews were welcome as business partners, tax-payers or guests in the crisis-ridden tourist industry. For most refugees, however, this was not the case. They were dependent on foreign aid, which was extended through the great efforts of Swiss, American and Jewish relief organisations and many Swiss individuals who were moved by their fate. Between 1933 and 1947 these relief organisations paid out about SFR 70 million. The share of this sum attributable to Jewish organisations inside and outside Switzerland amounted to SFR 46 million. The issue of costs became acute after the *Anschluss* in 1938. The Swiss Federal authorities initially refused to contribute to these costs and their own financial involvement began only after binding in the relief organisations – although their funds were increasingly exhausted. A special tax was imposed on wealthy refugees and emigrants in 1941, and in 1943 the Federal Council decided to confiscate the assets of refugees who had entered Switzerland 'illegally'. In 1945 the deficit spending of the Swiss Federal state reached SFR 83 million.[91] In wartime, around 110,000 civilians, including refugees, emigrants and children recovering from war as well as 103,000 military internees, lived for shorter or longer periods in Switzerland.[92]

On 30 August 1942 Eduard von Steiger, Minister of Justice and Police, declared in Zurich at a meeting of the Young Church that there was no more room in the Swiss 'lifeboat' – a speech which was diametrically opposed to the one made on the same day in the same city by Max Wolff, the President of the Synod of the Evangelical-Reformed Landeskirche.[93] Von Steiger's phrase, which at the time bore a large share of the responsibility for the Swiss government's policy towards refugees, is quoted nowadays as a striking metaphor for the failures of refugee policy. It inspired the titles of Alfred A. Häsler's book (1967) and Markus Imhof's film (1982) *The Boat is Full*, and provides a phrase under which a critical consideration of the history of refugees in Switzerland has become possible.[94]

In the eyes of those who were persecuted, Switzerland, after 1941, was not a peripheral place, but had become central to their hopes of survival. Von Steiger's phrase and the metaphor linked with it undoubtedly give vivid figurative expression to the substitution of 'space' for 'life', and the juxtaposition of economics and refugees, bread and strangers.[95] Within this framework the Swiss response to the refugee crisis has been looked at in terms of competition for food, or, when seen from the perspective of population policy, of sexual envy.[96] It can also be examined as a question of principles determining the membership of the communal household of an ark. The image of the boat that is allegedly full begs the question: who exactly would or would not find a place in it? It is the question about the unwanted 'species', the category of those human beings who, from the 1920s onwards, were increasingly declared 'unwanted' in Switzerland as well as in other European countries which shifted their alien policy in an illiberal direction.

Through the metaphor of the boat it becomes clear to us that the Swiss reaction to National Socialist antisemitism and its claim for *Lebensraum*, justified by economic and racial ideology, was shaped by the concept of spatial and economic constriction. The metaphor of the 'full boat' points to a vital dimension of *Lebensraum*, inasmuch as it excludes certain human beings from their right to life in a small state. The decisive place where the act of inclusion or exclusion occurred, that decided life or death, was the frontier. The preconditions and factors which characterise this event have long been treated as a chapter of Swiss history exclusively concerned with refugee policy, rather than a policy directed against a particular minority – in reality a policy against the Jews. Going back beyond the events of 1938 (the 'J' stamp) and August 1942 (the refusal of asylum and the sending back of refugees), it is possible to discern the structural and cultural conditions influencing these decisions. They show that the 'Jew' as a stereotype had always been 'present' in an ambivalent or negative way in the consciousness of the people who had power or implemented policy. The 'images', the dream of a national state, cleansed of everything that was 'alien in its essence', were there in potential before they became reality as a consequence of practical choices.

The antisemitic element of Swiss refugee policy in the period from 1933 to 1950 has a dialectical stamp, inasmuch as different 'normalities' are in a mutual relationship with one another. An ambivalence, rejection or practice of discrimination towards male and female Jews, which is already partially present within the country, is actualised across the borders by a foreign state which promotes and practises policies of antisemitic persecution and extermination. This frame of reference for Swiss policy towards foreigners and refugees during the National Socialist period of European history was shaped by the temporal caesuras and individual phases of persecution and extermination carried out by the Third Reich. But even before 1933 the rejection of the 'Jew', especially of the 'foreign' Jew, is discernible as a leitmotif in the sources. Research has revealed continuities in the public media, institutions and the authorities of hostility to the Jews, since the founding of the confederation in 1848 and the emancipation of 1866.[97] Antisemitism is, moreover, linked with further problematic areas of research, which have not been sufficiently clarified and point to expanded discourses. Among these are questions of 'eugenics' or medical and population policy, naturalisation policy or international police cooperation since the First World War; included, as Regula Ludi and Thomas Huonker have stated, are the attitudes and eugenic practice of Switzerland and other governments towards Gypsies since 1910.[98] Concerning antisemitism, there are likewise questions about the diplomatic protection of victims during the Second World War and the connection between antisemitism and the way in which assets in Swiss banks untouched since 1945 have been handled.

For the period from 1933 to 1945, the basic conditions in which hostility to Jews and other minorities could become manifest changed radically. A stylised hostility to the Jews for the purpose of carrying out social and cultural policy was countered by the necessity of publicly suppressing the appearance of a so-called 'Jewish question' in order to minimise demands, from within and without, to emulate the Third Reich.[99] This duality finds expression in a double and contradictory procedure. The desire to avoid importing National Socialist ideology, by which Switzerland would appear as an accomplice of the Third Reich, was matched by a constant appeasement of German policy. Policies that were hostile to Jews were implemented allegedly as a way of opposing antisemitism. The alleged opposition to antisemitism consisted precisely in the rejection of the foreign 'race' and in categorical discrimination against the victims of National Socialism. The authorities responsible for the official implementation of this policy were the Federal Alien Police and especially the Swiss Foreign Ministry. But right-wing civil guards with a nationalist turn of mind and antisemitic parties with the collective name *Frontismus* did not feel discouraged. On the contrary, their imprecise slogans against the 'Jew' could mean either the foreign refugee or the Swiss citizen of Jewish extraction – especially when they were of eastern European origin and had settled or been naturalised in Switzerland since two generations.

The ambivalence discussed here, which characterises the discourse that began as early as 1900, about allegedly being 'overrun by foreigners', manifested itself in the practice of attributing socio-economic problems or questions of population policy to particular groups of the populace. The history of the Federal Alien Police shows the effort, designed to secure power, to bring order not only to policy dealing with foreigners, but also into Switzerland's own social policy and population planning.[100] The obsessive fear of a *Verjudung* ('jewification') of their own culture, of a 'failure of the Jews to be assimilated' to the 'essential nature' of the Swiss, was conveyed in the illusory logic of scientific language. It could refer to what was foreign as well as to what was home-grown and it found its expression after the First World War, for example in the following statement: 'Sick people who constitute a public danger, then swindlers, layabouts, loan-sharks, in short: the carriers of economic infection must all be eliminated.'[101] The demand for a 'radical cleansing' amalgamates in its terminology biological, cultural and economic variants of the discourse, not least as a reaction to the fear of indefinite and therefore uncontrollable processes of social change. This also brings it into the context of international eugenic discourses, where there is also talk from the 1910s onwards of the sterilisation of 'asocial elements' – in the United States as well as in European countries.[102] By means of statistics and scientific argumentation a counter-image was created, for the purposes of population policy, of an 'overpopulated' country which was threatened by 'jewification'. In this conception of things, it was considerably harder for Jewish men and women to become citizens. These harsher provisions were complemented by expectations of assimilation from Jews who were citizens already, or the imposition of stringent regulations for transit and the strict refusal of permission to refugees to work.

Against this background, Switzerland's refugee policy was predetermined by characteristics related to social, economic and cultural policy. These preconditions, which in turn operated against the background of the *Lebensraum* ideology, characterise the readiness to receive refugees and, on the other hand, the expulsions of refugees which tragically occurred at the very time when it was a matter of life or death. After 1933 the policy towards foreigners and naturalisation, which was conceived as an instrument of a long-term policy designed to create order, ran into an opposing argument, namely the humanitarian policy of the country which had been declared a tradition of neutrality. The ambivalence between the policy towards foreigners on the one hand and the belief in the humanitarian policy of the neutral state on the other become evident in contrasting figures for the years 1933 to 1945. They document the two opposite dimensions, the controlled admission with *Lagerhaltung* in refugee camps and, on the other hand, the antisemitically tinged rejection and the refusal to rescue people in distress. In round figures, Switzerland saw for shorter or longer terms around 295,000 refugees, among them 100,000 military internees, 60,000 children recovering from war, while 51,000 civilian refugees survived in Switzerland during the National Socialist period, of whom 21,000 were Jews.[103] Against this must be set a documented 25,000 expulsions and refusals to admit refugees at the border, of whom a very large number must have been Jewish.[104] Although the Swiss elites were increasingly better informed about the systematic extermination policy of the National Socialists after 1941, the change in refugee policy – in contrast to Sweden – took place only gradually and only in 1944.

Two policies illuminate the mixture of social, cultural, economic and biological arguments that were used to bolster particular measures. On the one hand, there is the treatment of long-term asylum, on the other the policy on the admission of Jewish children. The right to long-term asylum for Jewish men and women (who as stateless persons often did not wish to return to their countries of origin, where they had been stripped of citizenship and persecuted), was finally granted in 1949, but only to people who were over 52 years of age. These Jewish men and women, who were past the age of reproduction, could scarcely pose any kind of danger in terms of population policy for the Swiss *Lebensraum*. Moreover, this decision extended the financial obligations of the Swiss Jews to the refugees, who were mostly in need of assistance, further into the post-war period, without the Jewish community in Switzerland gaining any opportunity to strengthen its own human or structural resources.

The refusal to admit Jewish children to Switzerland for holidays displays a similar antisemitic model which is in contrast to the normal generous arrangement of these matters. The idea that foreign children should recover in healthy Alpine air from the sufferings of war harked back to notions from the time of the First World War. During the Second World War, Jewish children were expressly excluded from the scheme on the basis of an antisemitic instruction by the Justice and Police Department. At the same time, the rescue plans of Jewish and Christian charitable organisations operating in Vichy France also failed because of international obstructions.[105] Charitable organisations of the most varied origins and religious affiliations were therefore compelled to organise secret or 'illegal' ways to bring in the children.[106] A similar inappropriateness is evident at the end of the war, too, when child survivors from Buchenwald were kept behind barbed wire by the Swiss Red Cross.[107]

# IX

In this article I have sketched various models of reaction and orientation which became characteristic in Switzerland in the face of the National Socialist *Lebensraum* ideology. The bearers of responsibility in Switzerland found themselves confronted after 1944–45 not only by changed conditions, but above all by a different set of basic values in accordance with which to orient their actions. This confrontation makes it clear that the point at issue in the Swiss relationship to National Socialist crimes was a question not only of politics but of values. The United Nations' Universal Declaration of Human Rights set the guarantee of individual and universal rights against the National Socialist ideology of *Lebensraum* and extermination . The shift from the old international law – merely a law between two states – and the feebly defended concept of minorities' protection dating from the Versailles treaty into a new international law put the human rights of individuals at the centre. This was no abstract or merely intellectual formula, but a declaration that had been fought for and won on the basis of realities. Among the factors that contributed to its genesis was the failure of earlier attempts to protect minorities by international law, as envisaged in the Versailles treaties of 1918–19 but which in practice ran up against political boundaries.[108] It is notable that Jewish jurists, among them the Swiss Paul Guggenheim, made substantial contributions to the formulation of minority rights and procedures to protect minorities.

Switzerland had difficulty finding its proper place in the new international system of the immediate post-war period.[109] Geneva, the seat of the old League of Nations, partially lost its importance, and New York became the headquarters of the United Nations. The American domination of Germany, which developed initially under the occupation, began to have a strong influence on the model of

Swiss reorientation. It became clear that the implementation of the new order must shed light on earlier Swiss practices and policies. That this would recur more than 50 years after the sacrosanct Washington Agreement was beyond the grasp of the leadership from a generation which was in the grip of a kind of collective amnesia. Meanwhile, more than 20 per cent of the inhabitants of Switzerland today are non-Swiss, but the country has partially failed to naturalise and integrate them. It is obvious that Switzerland has become a multicultural, multireligious and multiethnic society. History and the present remain interlocked in a surprising manner.

*Translated by Mike Rogers*

### NOTES

1.  Ludolf Herbst, 'Die NS-Wirtschaftspolitik im internationalen Vergleich', in Wolfgang Benz, Hans Buchheim and Hans Mommsen (eds.), *Studien zur Ideologie und Herrschaft des Nationalsozialismus* (Frankfurt am Main, 1994), p.153ff.; Martin Broszat, *Der Staat Hitlers: Grundlegung und Entwicklung seiner inneren Verfassung* (Munich, 1969/1986); Norbert Frei, *Der Führerstaat, Nationalsozialistische Herrschaft 1933 bis 1945* (Munich, 1987); and a number of the contributions to Gerhard Hirschfeld and Lothar Kettenacker (eds.), *Der 'Führerstaat', Mythos und Realität, Studien zur Struktur und Politik des Dritten Reiches* (Stuttgart, 1981).

2.  Lothar Gruchmann, *Nationalsozialistische Grossraumordnung, Die Konstruktion einer deutschen 'Monroe-Doktrin'* (Stuttgart, 1962).

3.  Dan Diner, 'Rassistisches Völkerrecht, Elemente einer nationalsozialistischen Weltordnung', *Vierteljahreshefte für Zeitgeschichte*, No.37 (1989), p.23ff.

4.  Saul Friedländer, *Das Dritte Reich und die Juden, Die Jahre der Verfolgung 1933–1939*, Vol.1 (Munich, 1998), p.13.

5.  Götz Aly and Susanne Heim, *Vordenker der Vernichtung, Auschwitz und die deutschen Pläne für eine neue europäische Ordnung* (Hamburg, 1991). Cf. the contributions in Karl Dietrich Bracher et al. (eds.), *Nationalsozialistische Diktatur 1933–1945. Eine Bilanz* (Düsseldorf, 1983), and Richard Breitman, *Der Architekt der 'Endlösung', Himmler und die Vernichtung der europäischen Juden* (Paderborn, 1996).

6.  Diemut Mayer, *Grundlagen des nationalsozialistischen Rechtssystems: Führerprinzip, Sonderrecht, Einheitspartei* (Stuttgart, 1987), includes the legislative project which Himmler sketched out in January 1945 for the elimination of Germans who were 'foreign to society', that is 'Aryan' citizens regarded as undesirable.

7.  Frank Bajohr, *'Arisierung', in Hamburg, Die Verdrängung der jüdischen Unternehmer 1933–1945* (Hamburg, 1945).

8.  Thomas Sandkühler, *'Endlösung' in Galizien. Der Judenmord in Ostpolen und die Rettungsinitiativen von Berthold Beitz, 1941–1944* (Bonn, 1996), pp.406ff.

9.  The Third Reich as 'Fassadenwerk' was first analysed by Ernst Fraenkel, *The Dual State,*

*A Contribution to the Theory of Dictatorship* (New York, 1941), calling up the German 'Normenstaat' and the National Socialist 'Massnahmenstaat'. A further analysis written during the National Socialist period itself was Franz Neumann, *Behemoth, Struktur und Praxis des Nationalsozialismus 1933–1944* (Frankfurt am Main, 1977); the American original appeared in 1942 and in expanded form in 1944. For the place of Neumann's work in the discussion on fascism, cf. the essay by Gert Schafer in the 1993 German edition of Neumann, pp.682ff.

10. For a survey of the relevant literature of that time, see Hans-Erich Volkmann, *Wirtschaft im Dritten Reich, Eine Bibliografie, Teil 1:1933–1939* (Munich, 1980).

11. See Mark Mazower, *Dark Continent: Europe's Twentieth Century* (London, 1998), pp.136ff.

12. For further information, compare Hans-Erich Volkmann, 'Wirtschaft und Aufrüstung unter dem Nationalsozialismus', in Manfred Funke, *Hitler, Deutschland und die Mächte, Materialien zur Aussenpolitik des Dritten Reiches* (Düsseldorf, 1976), pp.269–91.

13. Theo Keller, 'Sinn und Unsinn der Autarkie', in *Schweizerische Rundschau, Monatszeitschrift für Geistesleben und Kultur*, No. 33 (1933/34), pp.769–83, quotation from pp.769f.

14. Werner Krause, *Wirtschaftstheorie unter dem Hakenkreuz, Die bürgerliche politische Ökonomie in Deutschland während der faschistischen Herrschaft* (Berlin, 1969).

15. Avraham Barkai, *Das Wirtschaftssystem des Nationalsozialismus, Der historische und ideologische Hintergrund 1933–1936* (Cologne, 1977); and Hans-Erich Volkmann, 'Das aussenwirtschaftliche Programm der NSDAP 1930–1933', *Archiv für Sozialgeschichte*, No.17 (1977), pp.251–74, esp. 262f.

16. Reinhard Frommelt, *Paneuropa oder Mitteleuropa, Einigungsbestreben im Kalkül deutscher Wirtschaft und Politik 1925–1933* (Stuttgart, 1977). The concept of 'Mitteleuropa' was already widespread before 1933; as a series of contemporary publications document, in which the integration of Europe as a production economy appears the real goal, compare Wilhelm Gurge and Wilhelm Grotkopp, *Grossraumwirtschaft, Der Weg zur europäischen Einheit* (Berlin, 1931); Herbert Gaedike and Gert von Eynern, *Die produktionswirtschaftliche Integration Europas, Eine Untersuchung über die Aussenhandelsverflechtungen der europäischen Länder* (Berlin, 1933).

17. Gruchmann, *Grossraumordnung*, p.71ff.

18. Charles Tilly, *Coercion, Capital and European States, 990–1990* (Cambridge, 1990).

19. Compare the contributions in Reinhard Opitz (ed.), *Europastrategien des deutschen Kapitals* (Cologne, 1977).

20. On this see Helmut Marcon, *Arbeitsbeschaffungspolitik der Regierungen Papen und Schleicher, Grundsteinlegungen für die Beschäftigungspolitik im Dritten Reich* (Bern/Frankfurt am Main, 1974).

21. For an account in terms of financial history see Christoph Kopper, *Zwischen Marktwirtschaft und Dirigismus, Bankenpolitik im 'Dritten Reich' 1933–1939* (Bonn, 1995).

22. *Jahrbuch der Gesellschaft für europäische Wirtschaftsplanung und Grossraumwirtschaft, "Nationale Wirtschaftsordnung und Grossraumwirtschaft"*, Bd.1 (Dresden, 1941), pp.9ff.

23. Walther Funk, 'Wirtschaftliche Neuordnung Europas!', *Südost-Echo*, No.30, 26 July 1940. A copy of the corresponding offprint can be seen in the Archives of the Schweizerischer Handels- und Industrie-Verein at the Archive für Zeitgeschichte der ETH Zurich.

24. On Schmitt, cf. the thorough study by Raphael Gross, *Carl Schmitt und die Juden, Eine deutsche Rechtslehre* (Frankfurt, 2000).

25. Gerhard Kümmel, *Transnationale Wirtschaftskooperation und der Nationalstaat* (Stuttgart, 1995) analyses the trade relationships between Germany and America and between German and American firms in the 1930s, demonstrating the shift from cooperation to increasing confrontation; Hans-Erich Volkmann, 'Zum Verhältnis von Grosswirtschaft und NS-Regime im Zweiten Weltkrieg', in Bracher et al., *Deutsche Diktatur*, pp.480ff.

26. Miles [Herbert Rosinski], *Deutschlands Kriegsbereitschaft und Kriegsaussichten* (Zurich/New York, 1939).
27. Willi A. Boelke, *Die Kosten von Hitlers Krieg, Kriegsfinanzierung und finanzielles Kriegserbe in Deutschland 1933–1948* (Paderborn, 1985), pp.66ff, and Hans-Erich Volkmann, 'Die NS-Wirtschaft in Vorbereitung des Krieges', in Wilhelm Deist et al. (eds.), *Ursachen und Voraussetzungen des Zweiten Weltkrieges* (Freiburg, 1979), p.211ff. are both early analyses of the German military 'Wehrwirtschaft'.
28. Cf. also the contributions in Friedrich Forstmeier and Hans-Erich Volkmann (eds.), *Wirtschaft und Rüstung am Vorabend des Zweiten Weltkrieges* (Düsseldorf, 1975).
29. Georg Hahn, *Grundfragen europäischer Ordnung* (Berlin/Vienna, 1939), pp.47ff.
30. John Pinder, 'Europa in der Weltwirtschaft 1920–1970', in C.M. Cipolla and K. Borchardt (eds.), *Europäische Wirtschaftsgeschichte*, Vol.5 (Stuttgart, 1986), p.389.
31. Basic to this are the contributions in Walter Pehle (ed.), *Der Judenpogrom 1938, Von der 'Reichskristallnacht' zum Völkermord* (Frankfurt am Main, 1988); and Hermann Graml, *'Reichskristallnacht', Antisemitismus und Judenverfolgung im 'Dritten Reich'* (Munich, 1988).
32. Avraham Barkai, *Vom Boykott zur 'Entjudung', Der wirtschaftliche Existenzkampf der Juden im Dritten Reich, 1933–1943* (Frankfurt a.M., 1988); Helmut Genschel, *Die Verdrängung der Juden aus der Wirtschaft des Dritten Reiches* (Göttingen, 1968); Gerhard Kratzsch, *Der Gauwirtschaftsapparat der NSDAP, Menschenführung, 'Arisierung', Wehrwirtschaft in Westfalen-Süd* (Münster, 1989).
33. Ulrich Herbert (ed.), *Europa und der Reichseinsatz, Ausländische Zivilarbeiter, Kriegsgefangene und KZ-Häftlinge in Deutschland 1938–1945* (Essen, 1991). Ulrich Herbert, *Fremdarbeiter, Politik und Praxis des 'Ausländer-Einsatzes' in der Kriegswirtschaft des Dritten Reiches* (Berlin and Bonn, 1986).
34. Independent Commission of Experts Switzerland – Second World War, *Switzerland and the Gold Transactions in the Second World War* (Berne, 1998), pp.61–134.
35. Bettina Zeugin and Thomas Sandkühler, *Die Schweiz und die deutschen Lösegelderpressungen in den besetzten Niederlanden, Vermögensentziehung, Freikauf, Austausch 1940–1945* (Zurich, 2001), ed. by Independent Commission of Experts Switzerland – Second World War.
36. An early, Marxist-inspired three-volume study is Dietrich Eichholtz, *Geschichte der deutschen Kriegswirtschaft 1939–1945* (Berlin, 1969).
37. Sacha Zala, *Gebändigte Geschichte, Amtliche Historiografie und ihr Malaise mit der Geschichte der Neutralität 1945–1961* (Berne, 1998).
38. Georg Kreis (ed.), *Switzerland and the Second World War* (foreword by David Cesarani) (London and Portland, 2000), pp.1ff.
39. Hitler's alleged utterance quoted after H.R. Trevor-Roper in Gerhard L. Weinberg, *A World at War: A Global History of World War II* (Cambridge, 1994), p.982 n.222.
40. Independent Commission of Experts Switzerland – Second World War, *Switzerland and the Refugees in Nazi Era* (Berne, 1999), pp.15ff.
41. Regula Ludi and Anton-Andreas Speck, 'Swiss Victims of National Socialism, An Example of How Switzerland Came to Terms with the Past', in John K. Roth and Elisabeth Maxwell, *Remembering for the Future: The Holocaust in an Age of Genocide* (London and New York, 2001), pp.907ff.
42. Two rather different perspectives are presented by Thomas Bohrer and Hanspeter Mock, 'The Recent Holocaust Era Debate and Beyond: A Swiss Perspective', and Daniel Wildmann, 'The Second Persecution, Legal Discourse and the Construction of History', both in Roth and Maxwell, *Remembering for the Future*, pp.876ff. and 938ff. See also Daniel Wildmann, 'Wo liegt Auschwitz? Geografie, Geschichte und Neutralität', in Arbeitskreis Armenien (eds.), *Verdrängung und Verdrängung, Der Genozid an den Armeniern – die Schweiz und die Schoah* (Zurich, 1998).
43. Georg Kreis, *Auf den Spuren von 'La Charité', Die schweizerische Armeeführung im Spannungsfeld des deutsch–französischen Gegensatzes* (Basel, 1976).

44. Jakob Tanner, '"Reduit national" und Aussenwirtschaft, Wechselwirkungen zwischen militärischer Dissuasion und ökonomischer Kooperation mit den Achsenmächten', in Philipp Sarasin and Regina Wecker (eds.), *Raubgold, Reduit, Flüchtlinge* (Zurich, 1998), pp.81–103, esp. pp.86ff.

45. On this see Georg Kreis and Henri Guisan, 'Bild eines Generals, Glanz und Elend einer Symbolfigur', *Schweizerische Monatshefte*, No.5 (1990), pp.413ff.

46. Willi Gautschi, *General Henri Guisan. Die schweizerische Armeeführung im Zweiten Weltkrieg* (Zurich, 1989), pp.310f.

47. Jakob Tanner, Or and Granit, 'La défense nationale et les liens économiques entre la Suisse et le Troisième Reich durant la Seconde guerre mondiale', in *Les Annuelles, Histoire et société contemporaines*, No.1 (1990), pp.31–48.

48. Cf. *Documents Diplomatiques Suisses*, Vol.13 (1939–40) (Berne, 1991), pp.889ff.

49. Jakob Tanner, *Bundeshaushalt, Währung und Kriegswirtschaft. Eine finanzsoziologische Analyse der Schweiz zwischen 1938 und 1953* (Zurich, 1986) and Markus Heiniger, *Dreizehn Gründe, warum die Schweiz im Zweiten Weltkrieg nicht erobert wurde* (Zurich, 1989).

50. Hans Wegmüller, *Brot oder Waffen, Der Konflikt zwischen Volkswirtschaft und Armee in der Schweiz 1939–1945* (Zurich, 1998), pp.103ff. and 134ff.

51. On the dispute on this issue cf. Rudolf Jaun, 'The Military National Defense, 1939-45', in Kreis, *Switzerland and Second World War*, pp.202ff.

52. Peter Hug, *Schweizer Rüstungsindustrie und Kriegsmaterialhandel zur Zeit des Nationalsozialismus: Unternehmungsstrategien, Marktentwicklung, öffentliche Kontrolle*, ed. by Independent Commission of Experts Switzerland – Second World War (Zurich, 2001). See also Marc Perrenoud, 'Foreign Trade and Swiss Politics, 1939–45', in Kreis, *Switzerland and Second World War*, pp.26ff.; and Peter Hug, 'Biologische und chemische Waffen in der Schweiz zwischen Aussen-, Wissenschafts- und Militarpolitik', *Studien und Quellen*, Vol.23 (Berne, 1997), pp.115ff.

53. See Jakob Tanner, 'Switzerland's International Financial Relations, 1931–50', in Kreis, *Switzerland and Second World War*, pp.42ff.

54. *Historische Statistik der Schweiz*, ed. Heiner Ritzmann-Blickenstorfer under the direction of Hansjörg Siegenthaler (Zurich, 1997), pp.698ff, 805ff. Cf. also an early analysis of Max Steiner, *Die Verschiebung der schweizerischen Aussenhandelsstruktur während des Zweiten Weltkrieges* (Zurich, 1950).

55. Compare the figures in Independent Commission, *Switzerland and the Gold Transactions*, p.39.

56. Harold James, 'Die Deutsche Bank und die Diktatur 1933–1945', in Lothar Gall et al., *Die Deutsche Bank* (Munich, 1995), p.334.

57. Jean-Daniel Kleisl, *Electricité suisse et le Troisième Reich, 1939–1945* (Zurich, 2001), ed. by Independent Commission of Experts Switzerland – Second World War.

58. See the studies of the Independent Commission of Experts Switzerland – Second World War, as indicated below, note 81.

59. On this see Stefan Frech, *Clearing, Der Zahlungsverkehr der Schweiz mit den Achsenmächten*, ed. by Independent Commission of Experts Switzerland – Second World War (Zurich, 2001).

60. Martin Meier, Stefan Frech et al., *Schweizerische Aussenwirtschaftspolitik 1930–1948: Strukturen, Verhandlungen, Funktionen*, ed. by Independent Commission of Experts Switzerland – Second World War. See also the two articles by Peter Hug/Martin Kloter and Thomas Gees in Peter Hug und Martin Kloter (eds.), *Aufstieg und Niedergang des Bilateralismus, Schweizerische Aussen- und Aussenwirtschaftspolitik 1930–1960, Rahmenbedingungen, Entscheidstrukturen, Fallstudien* (Zurich, 1999), pp.13–139, 141–72.

61. Jakob Tanner, 'Finanzwirtschaftliche Probleme der Schweiz im Zweiten Weltkrieg und deren Folge für die wirtschaftliche Entwicklung nach 1945', in Rolf Caesar et al. (eds.),

*Probleme der Finanzgeschichte des 19. und 20. Jahrhunderts* (Berlin, 1989), p.84.

62. See Oswald Inglin, *Der stille Krieg, Der Wirtschaftskrieg zwischen Grossbritannien und der Schweiz im Zweiten Weltkrieg* (Zurich, 1991).

63. Cf. Marc Perrenoud, Florian Adank et al., *La place financière et les banques suisses à l'époque du nationalsocialisme* (Zurich, 2001), ed. by Independent Commission of Experts Switzerland – Second World War.

64. An example is given in the documentary story of Israeli novelist Roman Frister, *Ascher Levys Sensucht nach Deutschland* (Berlin, 1999), pp.10, 299ff.

65. See also Perrenoud, *Foreign Trade and Swiss Politics*, pp.26ff.

66. Heinrich Homberger, *Schweizerische Handelspolitik im Zweiten Weltkrieg* (Zurich, 1970), p.54 (emphasis added).

67. Heinz-Albers Schönberg, *Hat die Schweiz den Krieg verlängert? Handels-, Gold- und Verkehrspolitik gegenüber Deutschland im Zweiten Weltkrieg* (Zurich, 1999). Schönberg does not offer new insights but shows that many questions are still awaiting an answer. A consideration which seems far more appropriate to me is the opposite question, namely whether Switzerland could have shortened the war.

68. *Die Tagebücher von Joseph Goebbels, Im Auftrag des Instituts für Zeitgeschichte und mit Unterstützung des Staatlichen Archivdienstes Russlands herausgegeben von Elke Fröhlich, Teil II: Diktate 1941–1945*, Vol.7 (Munich, 1993), pp.38, 141 and Vol.2, p.536.

69. Georg Kreis, 'Die Schweiz und der Zweite Weltkrieg. Bilanz und bibliografischer Überblick nach dreissig Jahren', in *La seconda guerra mondiale nella prospettiva storica a trent'anni dall'epilogo* (Como, 1977), p.231.

70. See Jacques Picard, 'Switzerland as a "Bystander" of History, On Neutrality in a Time of Global Crisis and Genocidal War', in Roth and Maxwell, *Remembering for the Future*, pp.71ff.

71. Linus von Castelmur, 'Aspekte der Wirtschafts- und Finanzbeziehungen der Schweiz im Zweiten Weltkrieg', in Hans Werner Tobler (ed.), *Die Schweiz im Zweiten Weltkrieg, Forschungsstand, Kontroversen, offene Fragen* (Zurich: Kleine Schriften ETH Zurich 23), p.23.

72. Daniel Bourgeois, *Le Troisième Reich et la Suisse 1939–1941* (Nuremburg, 1974). See also articles by Bourgeois, *Das Geschäft mit Hitler–Deutschland* (Zurich, 2000).

73. Robert Urs Vogler, *Die Wirtschaftsverhandlungen zwischen der Schweiz und Deutschland 1940 und 1941* (Zurich, 1998); Klaus Urner, 'Die schweizerisch–deutschen Handelsbeziehungen während des Zweiten Weltkrieges', *Neue Zürcher Zeitung*, 27 Nov., 2 and 6 Dec. 1968.

74. Marco Durrer, *Die schweizerisch–amerikanischen Finanzbeziehungen im Zweiten Weltkrieg. Von der Blockierung der schweizerischen Guthaben in den USA über die 'Safehaven'-Politik zum Washingtoner Abkommen (1941–1946)* (Berne/Stuttgart, 1984); Neville R. Wylie, *The Riddle of the Swiss: British Policy towards Switzerland 1940–1943* (Cambridge, 1994).

75. Willi A. Boelcke, 'Zur internationalen Goldpolitik des NS-Staates. Ein Beitrag zur deutschen Währungs- und Aussenwirtschaftspolitik 1933–45', in Funke, *Hitler, Deutschland und Mächte*, pp. 292–309.

76. Homberger, *Handelspolitik*, pp.119f.

77. Harold James, 'Der Goldmarkt als "Landesverteidigung"', *Tages-Anzeiger*, 26 Sept. 1996. The 'trap of good faith' concept is to be understood as the result, for which they have only themselves to blame, of a Swiss discourse of self-justification. Otherwise, the misleading impression could arise that it was a 'trap' set by the National Socialist state into which Switzerland fell to a certain extent 'in good faith' – which would present Switzerland as a putative victim.

78. Linus von Castelmur, *Schweizerisch–alliierte Finanzbeziehungen im Übergang vom Zweiten Weltkrieg zum Kalten Krieg, Die deutschen Guthaben zwischen Zwangsliquidierung und Freigabe,*

*1945–1952* (Zurich, 1997), p.255. This author mainly ignored the questions of unclaimed assets of Nazi victims raised during and after the Swiss–American negotiations. In his study, the agreement seems to be a victor's success of Swiss diplomacy.

79. Jacques Picard, *The Assets of Missing Nazi Victims in Switzerland* (Zurich: Bank Julius Baer, 1993); in a German version, 'Die Vermögen rassisch, religiös und politisch Verfolgter in der Schweiz', Swiss Federal Archive, 'Die Schweiz und die Flüchtlinge 1933–1945', *Studien und Quellen*, Vol.22 (Berne, 1996), pp.233ff.; Peter Hug, 'Unclaimed Assets of Nazi Victims in Switzerland: What People Knew and What Else They Ought to Know', in Kreis, *Switzerland and Second World War*, pp.81ff.; Independent Committee of Eminent Persons (ICEP), *Report on Dormant Accounts of Victims of Nazi Persecution in Swiss Banks* (Berne, 1999).

80. *Année politique/Schweizerische Politik 1996*, ed. Institut für Politikwissenschaft, Universität Berne (Berne, 1997), SS.119f.; *The Disposition of Assets Deposited in Swiss Banks by Missing Nazi Victims, Hearing before the Committee on Banking and Financial Services, House of Representatives, US Congress, December 11, 1996* (Washington, 1997).

81. The Independent Commission of Experts Switzerland – Second World War are the editors of 20 volumes of research, published under the names of the authors, mainly in German and partly in French, by the Zurich Chronos-Verlag. A synthesis report of the Commission will appear in 2002. The research programme began in 1997. See Jacques Picard, 'Das Forschungsprogramm der Unabhängigen Expertenkommission Schweiz–Zweiter Weltkrieg', in Philipp Sarasin and Regina Wecker (eds.), *Raubgold, Reduit, Flüchtlinge*, pp.169ff.

82. See the recent research contributions edited by the Independent Commission of Experts Switzerland – Second World War as follows: Barbara Bonhage, Hanspeter Lussy, Marc Perrenoud, *Nachrichtenlose Vermögen bei Schweizer Banken, Annahme ausländischer Gelder seit 1931 und Restitution von Opferguthaben seit 1945* (Zurich, 2001); Stefan Karlen, Lukas Chocomeli et al., *Expansion, Konfiskation, Nachrichtenlosigkeit, Schweizerische Versicherungsgesellschaften im Machtbereich des 'Dritten Reiches'* (Zurich, 2001); Hanspeter Lussy, Barbara Bonhage and Christian Horn, *Schweizerische Wertpapiergeschäfte mit dem 'Dritten Reich', Handel, Raub und Restitution* (Zurich, 2001).

83. Mario König, *Interhandel: Die schweizerische Holding der IG Farben und ihre Metamorphosen, Eine Affäre um Eigentum und Interessen, 1910–1999* (Zurich, 2001); Barbara Bonhage, *Schweizerische Bodenkreditanstalt: 'Aussergewöhnliche Zeiten bringen aussergewöhnliche Geschäfte'* (Zurich, 2001); both volumes edited by Independent Commission of Experts Switzerland – Second World War.

84. Esther Tisa Francini, Anja Heuss and Georg Kreis, *Fluchtgut-Raubgut, Der Transfer von Kulturgütern in und über die Schweiz 1933–1945 und die Frage der Restitution* (Zurich, 2001), ed. by Independent Commission of Experts Switzerland – Second World War.

85. Lukas Straumann and Daniel Wildmann, *Schweizer Chemieunternehmen im 'Dritten Reich'* (Zurich, 2001); Christian Ruch et al., *Geschäfte und Zwangsarbeit, Schweizer Industrieunternehmen im 'Dritten Reich'* (Zurich, 2001); both volumes edited by Independent Commission of Experts Switzerland – Second World War.

86. Gregor Spuhler, Ursina Jud et al., *'Arisierung' in Österreich und ihre Bezüge zur Schweiz* (Zurich, 2001), ed. by Independent Commission of Experts Switzerland – Second World War.

87. Christiane Uhlig, Petra Barthelmess et al., *Tarnung, Transfer, Transit: Die Schweiz als Drehscheibe verdeckter deutscher Operationen, 1939–1952* (Zurich, 2001), ed. by Independent Commission of Experts Switzerland – Second World War.

88. Jacques Picard, 'Investigating 'Anti-Semitism'? On the Concept and Function of 'Anti-Semitism' and Problems Involved in Research', in Kreis, *Switzerland and Second World War*, pp.132ff.

89. An example of the effectiveness of National Socialist attempts to exert pressure in the interplay between firms and authorities is illustrated by the following case. The German client of an insurance firm complains on a visit to Switzerland that he has confirmed the presence of a Jewish doctor at the border control and threatens to pass on this information to the Foreign Office in Berlin. The Swiss insurance firm contacts the Political Department in Berne, which instructs the Federal Office for Military Welfare that 'there should be no employment of Jewish officials or medical personnel on the German–Swiss border.' Cf. the files in the Swiss Federal Archives, Berne, BAR 2001 D 3, Vol. 48, correspondence of 30 Jan. and 10 Feb. 1942.

90. Frank Vischer, 'Das nationalsozialistische Recht im Spiegel einiger Entscheidungen schweizerischer Gerichte', in *Festschrift für Ulrich Drobnig* (Tübingen, 1998), pp.455ff.; and the expertise of Adolf Lüchinger, in Independent Commission of Experts Switzerland–Second World War (ed.), *Juristische Beiträge zur Forschung, Privatrecht*, Vol.19 (Zurich, 2001).

91. See Independent Commission of Experts, *Switzerland and the Refugees in the Nazi Era* (Berne, 1999), pp.175ff.

92. Carl Ludwig, *Die Flüchtlingspolitik der Schweiz seit 1933 bis zur Gegenwart* (Berne, 1959), p.318.

93. *Evangelisch–reformierte Landeskirche des Kantons Zürich*, 'Sonst ist alles Beten um den Frieden nur Geschwätz', *Kirchensynode 1939–1946, Eröffnungsreden des Präsidenten Max Wolff* (Zurich, 1997), pp.20–24.

94. Alfred A. Hasler, *Das Boot ist voll. Die Schweiz und die Flüchtlinge 1933–1945* (Zurich, 1967); Markus Imhof, *Das Boot ist voll. Ein Filmbuch. Mit Standphotografien von George Reinhart und einem Vorwort von Friedrich Dürrenmatt* (Zurich, 1983).

95. The boat metaphor can also be found in *National-Zeitung*, 20/21 Feb. 1943. The 'boat', an allusion to Goebbels's speech about 'total war', refers to the German people whose members are about to embark on an uncertain 'voyage of destiny'. By 'total war' is meant, as was explained above, the all-inclusive mobilisation of the reserves for the war economy within Germany.

96. May B. Broda, 'Verbotene Beziehungen. Polnische Militärinternierte und die Schweizer Zivilbevolkerung während des Zweiten Weltkrieges am Beispiel auch des Internierten-Hochschullagers Herisau/St.Gallen', in *Appenzelhische Jahrbücher 1991*, pp.1–55; see the same author's 'Oral History – nichts als Fragen?', *Traverse* (1994/1), pp.131ff.

97. Friedrich Külling, *Bei uns wie Überall? Antisemitismus in der Schweiz 1866–1900* (Zurich n.d). (1977); Aaron Kamis-Müller, *Antisemitismus in der Schweiz 1900–1930* (Zurich,1990); Aram Mattioli (ed.), *Antisemitismus in der Schweiz 1848–1960* (Zurich, 1998).

98. Thomas Huonker and Regula Ludi, *Roma, Sinti, Jenische, Schweizerische Zigeunerpolitik zur Zeit des Nationalsozialismus*, ed. Unabhängige Expertenkommission Schweiz – Zweiter Weltkrieg (Berne, 2001).

99. See also Jacques Picard, *Die Schweiz und die Juden 1933–1945. Schweizerischer Antisemitismus, jüdische Abwehr und internationale Migrations- und Flüchtlingspolitik* (Zurich, 1994); in the French version: Picard, *La Suisse et les Juifs*, preface by Saul Friedländer (Lausanne, 2000).

100. On population policy, see the two essays by Stefan Mächler, 'Kampf gegen das Chaos, Die antisemitische Bevölkerungspolitik der eidgenössischen Fremdenpolizei und Polizeiabteilung 1917–1954' and Patrick Kury, 'Ostjudenfeindschaft und die Erstarkung des Antisemitismus', respectively in Mattioli, *Antisemitismus*, pp.357–443. The history of the Federal Police is discussed by Uriel Gast, *Von der Kontrolle zur Abwehr, Die eidgenössische Fremdenpolizei im Spannungsfeld von Politik und Wirtschaft 1915–1933* (Zurich, 1997).

101. Ernst Delaquis, 'Der neueste Stand der Fremdenfrage, Öffentlicher Vortrag' in St. Gallen, 22 Oct. 1921 (Berne, 1921), p.19. Delaquis was until 1929 Chief of the Federal

Police Department before resuming his academic career in Hamburg as a criminal law professor. Cf. Gast, *Kontrolle zur Abwehr*, p.284ff.

102. See especially Stefan Kühl, *Die Internationale der Rassisten, Aufstieg und Niedergang der internationalen Bewegung für Eugenik und Rassenhygiene im 20. Jahrhundert* (Frankfurt and New York, 1997). On this issue inside Switzerland cf. Nadja Ramsauer/Thomas Meyer, 'Blinder Fleck im Sozialstaat, Eugenik in der Deutschschweiz 1930–1950', *Traverse* 1995/2, p.117ff., and Urs Germann, *Psychiatrie und Strafjustiz. Umfeld, Entwicklung und Praxis der forensischen Psychiatrie im Kanton Bern* (Ms. Universität Berne, Berne, 1998). See also Huonker and Ludi, *Roma, Sinti und Jenische, 2000*, pp.25ff. The evaluation of such issues in the relationship between eugenics in Switzerland and National Socialist Germany requires further research.

103. This figure depends, as do all statistics, on the manner in which the categories are compiled. In these figures Jewish and Christian 'non-Aryans', as well as children, are included in the total estimate.

104. Compare Guido Koller, 'Entscheidungen über Leben und Tod. Die behördliche Praxis der schweizerischen Flüchtlingspolitik während des Zweiten Weltkrieges', *Studien und Quellen*, No.22 (Berne, 1996), pp.91ff. Note that the figure for refusals is not necessarily identical with the figure of refugees. A refugee could have been refused more than once if he or she tried to cross the Swiss border again. Otherwise, a presumed figure of refugees did not reach the border because they may have feared being handed over to the Germans.

105. Picard, *Schweiz und Juden*, pp.428ff.; Donald A. Lowrie, *The Hunted Children* (New York, 1963), esp. p.226; *US Department of State, Foreign Relations. Diplomatic Correspondence* (Washington DC, 1963–69), Vol. 1942–41, pp.466ff.

106. Jacques Picard, 'Hilfe, Selbsthilfe und Solidarität entlang der Grenze', in Wolfgang Benz and Juliane Wetzel (eds.), *Solidarität und Hilfe während der NS-Zeit*, Vol.1 (Berlin, 1996), pp.252ff.

107. Andre Lasserre, 'Les réfugiés de Bergen-Belsen et Theresienstadt, ou les dédoirs d'une politique d'asile en 1944–1945', *Schweizerische Zeitschrift für Geschichte*, No.40 (1990), pp.307ff. Cf. *Documents Diplomatiques Suisses* (Berne, 1997), Vol.16, pp.18ff.

108. Chaim Guterman, *Das Minderheitenschutzverfahren des Völkerbundes* (Berlin, 1979).

109. Cf. the contributions in Georg Kreis (ed.), *Die Schweiz im internationalen System der Nachkriegszeit 1943–1950* (Basel,1996). See also my final remarks in Jacques Picard, *On the Ambivalence of Being Neutral, Switzerland and Swiss Jewry Facing the Rise and Fall of Nazi State* (Washington: United States Holocaust Memorial Museum, 1998), pp.14ff.

# The Lost Honour of Bystanders?
# The Case of Jewish Emissaries
# in Switzerland

## RAYA COHEN

> In the circle of violence in which all moral values and the
> basic principles of humanity are lost, only one thing remains
> to guide our paths through this inferno, and that is all of
> those individuals, in the positive meaning of the word, who
> are prepared to give up their lives, their existence, for others.
>
> (Gisi Fleischmann, Slovakia, 27 August 1942)[1]

## I

The term 'bystander' has earned a place of distinction in Holocaust
historiography: having become one of the pillars of Holocaust
research, it now stands alongside the very perpetrators of the crimes
and their victims. Accusatory questions such as why Auschwitz was
not bombed, or why the flight of Jewish refugees to the USA or
Palestine was made so difficult during the war, have recently been
joined by questions regarding the role of Switzerland during the
war. The mask of neutrality having been ripped from Switzerland's
face, the financially and economically active role that country played
in assisting the Nazi regime has been exposed. The Swiss historian
Jacques Picard has performed a deconstruction of the term 'Swiss
neutrality', showing that Switzerland is rapidly moving from the
position of a witness to that of one of the accused.[2] This in itself
indicates the fundamental question as to whether in a war whose
main paradigm has become Auschwitz, it is possible to justify a
position of neutrality or any passive stance at all.

*The Fall*, by Albert Camus, is perhaps a good starting point for an analysis of the role of 'bystanders' in the Second World War. In that novel, written in the early 1950s, Camus tells of a man standing on the edge of a bridge who witnesses a young woman commit suicide by jumping from it. This event dramatically alters the life of the narrator, a respected and successful lawyer, for no apparent reason. The fact of his accidental presence at the place and that he did nothing to assist, trouble his conscience, despite his clear knowledge that he could not have saved the woman anyway. He quits his home, his city, his profession, but all in vain: he cannot escape the terrible event. In contrast with the hero of Camus's novel *The Plague*, in which the bystander is the classical hero, an altruist who endangers his own life by saving others, this bystander can do nothing but keep returning to the tormenting memory of that moment.[3]

And indeed, despite the years that have passed, the memory of Auschwitz continues to dominate reflections of the past in Europe, and Europe cannot free itself of that memory. Dormant bank accounts, looted art treasures, expropriated real estate and legal actions against collaborators – all these prevent the past from passing. As Germany completes its process of reunification and removes the last vestiges of defeat, it sometimes appears as though it is the bystanders – Switzerland, the Vatican, the Municipality of Paris or the Jewish leadership – that are occupying the seat of the accused in place of the actual perpetrators. Perhaps this phenomenon is due in part to the assumption that the 'accounts have already been closed' with the Nazis and their followers, wheareas with the bystanders, this process is only just beginning. It would seem that the term 'bystander' has been transformed into a historically pejorative term.

The term 'bystander' was not always so central to Holocaust consciousness. In the first two decades after the war, the legal focus was on punishing the perpetrators of war crimes and this left no room for the witnesses – the bystanders. On the other hand, the sheer immensity of the horror and the huge number of victims made it impossible to consider the survivors, let alone those who had performed rescue feats.[4] The very concrete opposition of the 'righteous gentile' to the collaborator was a clear expression of a 'black and white' view of the past. But as the dichotomous view of the past began to wither away, the picture became more complicated.[5] It seems that the time was ripe for a change in the conclusions that were being drawn with regard to the Holocaust – away from the parochial view that 'the entire world is against us' to an emphatic recognition of the fact that 'rescue, and attempted rescue, were in the main conditioned by the activities and good intentions of non-Jewish political and public bodies and institutions both inside and outside Europe.'[6] Thus, we attest to the appearance of rescuers of Jews on the agenda of mainstream research. The second Yad Vashem international conference in 1974 can be seen as a symptom of a more general change vis-à-vis the past.

There was now room to expand Holocaust research into a 'broader area, exceeding the bounds of the Jewish context, to what was going on in other nations, international institutions, and the relationship between Jews and their non-Jewish environments'. Further, as the editorial to the published proceedings says, 'the results in the area of rescuing lives were paltry given the size of the disaster that befell the Jewish people', yet historians must look at 'who did what'.

This view made no distinction between Jews and non-Jews and included 'what the Jewish organisations did [outside of the areas of Nazi rule] within the limits of their abilities, in their roles of voicing protest and exercising influence upon non-Jewish bodies'. Like other 'bystanders', it was those (few) who did something to help the Jews who thus became, in their turn, heroes of the past. The 1974 Yad Vashem conference also discussed the roles played by Saly Mayer, the representative of the American Jewish Joint Distribution Committee (the 'Joint') in Switzerland; the World Jewish Congress; the Jewish Leadership ('Working Group') of Slovakia; the Yishuv mission to Kushta (Istambul); and the part played by the International Red Cross, Roosevelt's refugee policy, and the policies of the governments of Great Britain, Italy, the USSR and others.[7]

However, the new place in the historiography occupied by the bystanders concurred with a negative image of bystanders that had

1 Eleanor Rathbone, champion of refugees (The Illustrated London News Picture Library).

2 Gösta Engzell headed the Legal Division of the Swedish Foreign Office throughout the war. He was primarily responsible for the dramatic and positive switch in the Swedish government's response to the genocide of Europe's Jews (Hans Gösta Engzell).

3 Count Folke Bernadotte arriving at Bromma airport, Stockholm, after successfully negotiating an agreement with Heinrich Himmler for the release of thousands of inmates from concentration camps in northern Germany (Pressens Bild).

4  A ferry with several 'White Buses' and recently rescued women arrives in southern Sweden
in May 1945. These women probably come from Ravensbrück concentration camp
(Nordiska Museet and K.W. Gullers).

been created by non-academics such as Rolf Hochhut, the author of the play *Der Stellvertreter* (The Deputy) on Pope Pius XII, and the journalist Arthur Morse, the author of the book *While Six Million Died*. In Israel, S. Bet Zvi, a schoolteacher, in a breakthrough study, accused the Zionist leadership of passivity in the Holocaust period despite their knowledge of the extermination.[8] During the 1980s and 1990s the extermination of the Jews as the principal issue of the war gained a central place among historians of the Nazi area. The Holocaust's industrial dimensions, technological organisation and racial Utopia were increasingly seen as a *Zivilisationsbruch* (break with civilisation).[9] Given the new understanding of 'Auschwitz' as an unprecedented phenomenon it was no longer possible to ask questions such as 'Who rescued?', 'Who did not?' and 'Why?' with the same simplicity as before. Now such questions as 'What did they know?' and 'What was understood?' took precedence over all other questions. Historical research now demonstrated that the 'terrible secret' had in fact been leaked and was known to the Allies, the Vatican, the Red Cross and other neutral bodies. The issue was no longer 'What did they know?' but 'When did they find out?'[10] and whether the information was ignored, or withheld, or just misinterpreted.[11] The positivistic approach of 'Who did what?' was now being replaced by one that was more complicated both in content and scope. As formulated by the historian Leni Yahil, there were three distinct stages to be considered in the historical analysis of the bystanders (which include the Yishuv in the context of immigration and illegal immigration, as well as the neutral countries of Europe as 'islands of refuge'): the receipt of information, the interpretation of this information, and the making of decisions based on it.[12] The emphasis thus placed on the difficulty of interpreting or internalising the information that had come to light blurred the unequivocal boundaries that separated perpetrators, victims and rescuers. It implicated people who, until then, had been considered righteous victors, as well as anyone who had previously been left out of the historical puzzle of the annihilation of the Jews. The part played by bystanders became increasingly relevant as it became more and more apparent that knowledge of the annihilation had indeed reached many circles. Because the Allies were now being painted as bystanders, on an equal footing with neutral states, their war effort became a secondary factor.[13] As Michael Marrus put it, the historiography of bystanders developed a focus on what was *not* done.[14]

One of the sources of this difficulty stems from the fact that while the 'bystander' became contextualised in respect of news and the ability to respond to it, the concept of 'rescue' remained as positivist as previously: the actual rescue of *life* is largely considered the only way of measuring the acts of the bystanders. Seen in this light, I would like to propose, the sense of the term 'bystander' is limited from the outset. On the one hand, the Allied declaration of 17 December 1942 regarding the Nazis' annihilation is viewed as a turning point after which the claim that 'We didn't know' about the extermination became untenable. Therefore, bystander historiography focuses mainly on the years that followed: 1943 and, principally, 1944 and 1945. On the other hand, we know that, as of the end of 1942, much less could have been done than previously. Until the summer of 1941 it was still possible to leave Nazi Europe, and the annihilation machine had not yet been put into operation; later, even the possibility of using Jewish life as commercial currency to try to sway Germany from its sure path to total devastation was no longer available.[15] Hence, there is little sense in measuring the efforts of bystanders to actually rescue people after 1942, when the dimensions of the extermination were publicly recognised.

Yet there may well be another sense to the emphasis of the historiography on both rescuing people and the awareness of the annihilation – a sense of a post-Auschwitz world that wrestles with its past, and in which public recognition of the extermination of the Jews of Europe serves as 'the Fall', a moment after which everything is judged in different terms. As in *The Fall*, the plot is based on the awareness that it takes place once it is too late: 'il est trop tard, maintenant, et il sera toujours trop tard', as Camus puts it in his closing sentence, adding 'heureusement!'[16] As in *The Fall*, it is the traumatic memory of the events which becomes the fulcrum of the story, not the drowned woman. The emphasis placed on the cognitive aspect of internalising an unprecedented truth, and the exclusive emphasis placed on the rescue of life by the historiography of the bystanders, tends to reflect the point of view of the heirs of both victors and survivors, not necessarily the point of view of those who 'drowned'. Primo Levi reminds us that no one can explain the experience of a drowned person, just as no one can describe or document their own death. Yet we have a great deal of material prior to the extermination which enables us to attempt to get closer to the world of those who were 'drowned'.[17]

In dealing with the issue of bystanders before the end of 1942, before knowledge of the extermination of Jews became public knowledge, one must bear in mind that it was not possible to distinguish between knowledge and rumour regarding extermination. On the contrary, knowledge and rumour were active ingredients of the process of coming to terms with what was actually occurring: genocide.[18] The focus of research on what 'real' information had reached the free world and at what time distorts the historical picture. False information or rumour, imagination and political considerations as much as real information were instrumental in acknowledging the reality of genocide. Thus, for example, the file of evidence provided by Gerhart Riegner and Richard Lichtheim to the Americans in November 1942, which is commonly seen as corroborating the existence of a 'general plan' to exterminate the Jews, relied mainly on mistaken and contradictory information. For instance, it contained reports of transports of Jews from western Europe that, on arrival in Germany, contained only corpses and 'evidence' of annihilation orders made, apparently, at the beginning of 1941. Yet it was a mixture of this type of 'evidence' and other political considerations that finally coalesced into the material that formed the basis of the public declaration of the 'truth' about the German policy towards the Jews of Europe in December 1942.[19]

In reconstructing the pre-Auschwitz word, one must also consider the weight of expectations that Jewish organisations stimulated among the Jews under Nazi oppression, expectations that were part of the ideological solidarity they had advocated in the pre-war period. In this respect, the Jewish leadership in the free world occupied a special place. Moreover, bystanders' awareness of the expectations of victims – the question of what they could do and how they rationalised their answers – played a role, and gives rise to various, often contradictory, interpretations of what bystanders said as against what they did. While it is clear that it was not always possible to meet the expectations of the victims – whether because this entailed risking other vital interests, or because such expectations were actually impossible to fulfill – we can clearly state that the concrete demands of the victims on the 'bystanders' were not fantastic: they emanated from a realistic view of the war and the assumption that liberation was impossible before an Allied victory. This perception is reflected in the ironic story told in the Warsaw ghetto in spring 1942 about Churchill summoning the Rabbi of Gur and asking his advice as to how to destroy Germany. According to the story, the Rabbi of Gur replied that there were two ways: a natural one and a miraculous one. The natural way was for one million angels bearing burning swords to rise up against Germany and smite her; the miraculous way would be for one million Englishmen to land in Germany and put her to the sword.[20] However, the Jews expected help despite the ongoing war, so as to help them to survive it.

Therefore, in contrast to the emphasis on public recognition of the extermination of the Jews and of rescue attempts from 1943 onwards, I suggest drawing attention to bystanders in the period from June 1941 to September 1942, in the phase preceding the full awareness of what was happening and the hopelessness of the position. In the summer of 1941 most of European Jewry was still alive, whilst during the following year the extermination reached its peak. It was therefore also the period in which victims' hopes for assistance were at their height. By the end of that year, only about 300,000 Jews out of a total of three million were left living in Poland.

## II

The historiography of the Holocaust is not the first example of the attempt to historicise the conduct of perpetrators and bystanders.

Another model exists. Prior to the Second World War, there had been a different link between war, genocide and bystanders. In the pre-war historiography, it was the Germans, allies of the Turks, who were considered to have been bystanders to the genocide of the Armenians in Turkey during the First World War. Following the signing of the treaties of Versailles and Sevres, the memory of the Armenian genocide was erased from the international agenda in order to enable the acceptance of Turkey as a western ally. 'The Asian Deed' was forgotten. Those who remembered the Armenian genocide saw it as the apex of the horrors of the Great War. It evoked propaganda against war and in favour of pacifism. 'The genocide of a people-of-culture that was hidden by the Kaiser of Germany from his subjects'[21] was understood as a dreadful event that had been concealed in order to permit the war to continue. It was presumed that had it been known, many more people would have called for an end to the war. When Franz Werfel attempted to rekindle awareness of the Armenian genocide in the 1930s, he put the victims at the centre of his novel, and those who gave the orders and the bureaucratic machinery behind the execution of those orders in opposition to them. The role of the 'bystanders' was conceived in a very limited manner, although morally it was unequivocally negative. It was held that Germany did not interfere in what was officially declared the 'internal affairs of a friendly allied power'. And although France and England protested against the murderous Turkish policy, they were also represented as disingenuous, their crocodile tears disappearing along with their changing interests in Turkey, 'who held good cards'. Yet the fact that genocide was being committed was known to the policy-makers, who all had their own information channels. They did not 'benefit' from any of the cognitive doubts raised today about the understanding of or belief in information at the level of political decision-makers. The men of 1915–16 were politicians acting in defence of interests, not of moral principles.[22] The concept was thus of genocide not as fundamentally unprecedented or unbelievable, but rather as a human disaster, the dimensions of which were so shocking that they could be ignored only by crude political cynicism. This is the same cynicism to which

Hitler referred in his rhetorical question to army commanders in Obersalzburg: 'who still remembers the Armenian slaughter?'.[23]

In retrospect, the Armenian genocide is an example of the role played by public opinion in supporting such a memory or limiting it to an ethnic concern. Yet in the period between the wars, Werfel's ideas were representative of broadly accepted theories on evil, politics and the mass murder of helpless minorities. Among the Jews of Europe in particular, the memory of the Armenian genocide came flooding back from the depths of oblivion the more they became aware of the 'Final Solution'.[24] The Jewish leadership in the Warsaw ghetto was convinced that the world was not reacting to the systematic slaughter because it was unaware of it. Concealment of the murder was seen as a central device in the Nazis' annihilation strategy, and therefore a huge effort was invested in attempting to disclose the 'Terrible Secret' to the free world. In this regard, it is common to cite Emmanuel Ringelblum, the renowned organiser of the underground archives in the Warsaw ghetto, who was convinced that he and his friends were fulfilling an historical mission by revealing the systematic murder that was taking place on Polish soil. 'We have dealt the enemy a blow', he wrote in his diary in June 1942, after hearing radio broadcasts from London, 'we have foiled [the enemy's] plans and revealed his cards.'[25] Yet less emphasis tends to be placed on the enormous hope they pinned on making their fate known in the free world and their assumption that its revelation would be a deterrent factor: '[Even] if foreign countries satisfy themselves with speeches and empty threats, salvation will perhaps come as a result of fear of German public opinion.'[26] With hindsight, their expectations turned out to be naive but, again, not unrealistic.

It is difficult to recover the sense of the expectations that the victims had of the free world and its bystanders. We can glimpse what the Jews of Poland hoped for in 1941–42 from the efforts they made to inform representatives of the Jewish leadership in the free world of those expectations. In Geneva, a small number of people were listening to what was coming from 'there'. Those people noted what was being claimed and passed the information on to the headquarters of the Jewish organisations in New York and Tel

Aviv.[27] The fact that historians now concentrate on the process of corroborating information regarding the extermination blurs the context in which these efforts were taking place. This is also what happened in the case of the well-known Riegner telegram regarding the existence of an plan to murder some 4 million Jews 'in one blow' by industrial means. The telegram was sent by Riegner on 8 August 1942, and was based on information revealed by a German industrialist named Eduard Schulte. Like Jan Karski, the Polish underground emissary, Schulte and Riegner hoped that breaking the veil of secrecy surrounding the planned systematic extermination would lead to concrete measures being taken to oppose it. It was principally expected that public threats would be made, aiming to deter, or at least impose restraint on, persons who collaborated directly or indirectly with the murder – from high-ranking politicians to the general population, Germans and non-Germans alike, allies of the Nazis and, above all, those who were still resisting Nazi pressure.[28] However, Schulte aimed at more than merely making the information public, which was later achieved in part by the public declaration of December 1942. Above all, he hoped that by engaging the assistance of Rabbi Stephen Wise and the Archbishop of Canterbury it might just be possible to delay the execution of the plan or 'to stop something'. This is why, at risk to himself, he passed on the information he had to the Jews and not to the British secret service, with which he had previously been in contact.[29]

In the 1930s and 1940s persecuted Jews expected the Jewish leadership outside Europe, especially in the United States and Palestine, not only to engage in protest actions and to apply diplomatic pressure, but also, and perhaps principally, to provide material assistance to their hard-pressed brethren. Since it was possible to write to and from Switzerland, representatives in Geneva became the central points of contact between the two halves of the divided Jewish world. What can be seen from the thousands of letters and postcards that arrived in Geneva is that until awareness of the annihilation penetrated Polish-Jewish consciousness, and while this was happening, Polish Jewry expected material and moral assistance. The more a person was politically and ideologically engaged, the more he expected from his colleagues in the various social groups, be they *Landsmanschaften* (associations of emigrants from the same township), political parties or, above all, youth movements.

For instance, the failure of the HeHalutz movement in the free world to send money to the HeHalutz Zionist youth movement in the Warsaw ghetto was seen despairingly as abandonment. As Ziviah Lubetkin, who was in charge of contacts with the outside world on behalf of the HeHalutz Centre in the Warsaw ghetto, explained, the money was required not only for alleviating the hunger that had stricken members of the HeHalutz movement but also to assist young people in escaping from Poland to Slovakia. Once she realised that the much-needed money was not going to arrive, she stopped writing to Nathan Schwalb, the HeHalutz representative in Geneva, charging him with disloyalty. However, by the end of 1941, it became clear to Lubetkin that Schwalb was the only address for her complaints – he was her sole contact with the outside world, and with the Yishuv in Palestine in particular, so she was forced to continue writing to him. Schwalb, for his part, understood Lubetkin's disappointment and sought to convince her that he was doing everything he could. He explained that no budget had been allocated to him, so he had sent whatever he could collect personally:[30] 'I know only one thing [and I hope that] you will be convinced of it sometime, that whatever I can send to the family [the HeHalutz movement] comes from the pennies that I manage with difficulty to scrape together myself.'[31]

But Lubetkin could not believe him. She could not imagine that Schwalb could be continually submitting budget proposals to the offices of the Jewish Agency and the Histadrut (the workers' organisation that organised the HeHalutz movement) without receiving any attention. But the truth was that those institutions curtailed the allowance of expenses to Europe, and the budget of the immigrant (Aliyah) department of the Jewish Agency for the HeHalutz movement was cancelled altogether in 1941. Apart from two sums (about $1,000 and $2,000 respectively), Schwalb received no support from institutions in Palestine for the HeHalutz movement in occupied Europe until the end of 1942. Yet he was the main – if not the only – contact with the tens of thousands of members of that movement in central Europe, in western Europe, and in particular in Poland itself.[32]

The victims' expectations provoked a harsh judgment on their fellow Jews in the outside world. Members of youth movements who had succeeded in reaching Palestine and had severed contacts with their comrades were seen as treacherous, as a poison that spoiled the life-source of past solidarity.[33] The more dramatic failure to send some tens of thousands of dollars to save approximately 20,000 Slovak Jews, after 60,000 had already been expelled to Poland, resulted in an even harsher condemnation of their co-religionists, who were accused of indifference towards the death of their own family.[34] In Slovakia, money was needed to bribe those responsible for the expulsions, and to carry out the plan of the local leadership of the remaining Jews, known as the 'working group'. Gisi Fleischmann, who was responsible for fundraising on behalf of the 'working group', called on the Joint to consider the fact that her community had already lost 75 per cent of its members and that in the past it had generously contributed to other communities in distress, and had been making donations to Polish refugees since the outbreak of the war. She understood that the Joint had many more communities to assist, and that the suffering of the Slovak community was 'like a drop in the infinite ocean of tears'. However, as the danger of expulsion came closer, she wrote to Saly Mayer, the Joint's representative in Switzerland: 'I will go so far as to say that I do not view the partners [Slovak officials whom they had not succeeded in bribing in autumn 1942] as 100 per cent responsible for this', a clear hint at Mayer's responsibility for failing to prevent the deportation of some 4,000 more Jews.[35]

The harsh expression of these charges was not only an attempt to motivate the people reading these letters, who were 'in another world'; the accusation gained strength from the author's commitment to the ideology of the various movements. They stemmed from a more general belief in fraternity and solidarity.

It was also clear to the leaders of these organisations in the free countries that it was important to maintain contact with Jews in Europe in whose name they were acting, despite the constraints of war, if they were to be true to what they claimed to represent: that the Jewish Agency was the representative of the Jewish people as a nation; the World Jewish Congress was the 'fixed and legitimate address for representing 16 million Jews'; and the Joint was the Jewish 'Cornucopia'. As Geneva was the base for efficient and centralised action in respect of central and eastern Europe, liaison bureaux were set up there and existing offices expanded. The role of these bureaux was to report on what was happening in Europe, to maintain the organisational infrastructure, to mediate between the organisations and the Jews trapped in occupied Europe, and to provide aid to the refugees. Richard Lichtheim was appointed head of a new office set up to represent the leadership of the Jewish Agency. He was the most senior of the representatives and his role was to establish contact with the Zionist leadership in occupied countries, on the one hand, and to transfer money from Zionist funds into Palestine, on the other. The HeHalutz movement's contact office in Geneva was set up with the aim of establishing contact with HeHalutz youth centres in eastern and central Europe, to provide them with information on what was occurring in Palestine, to supply them with propaganda materials relating to the Zionist movement, and to achieve other ideological aims. Gerhart Riegner was appointed to manage the office of the World Jewish Congress in Geneva, and in particular to report on developments in war-time Europe. Alfred Silberschein concentrated on providing assistance on behalf of RELICO, a new institution he had constituted under the auspices of the World Jewish Congress office in Geneva.

This is the context in which Jewish emissaries in Switzerland, some of whom were three times removed from the actual organisational leadership, took upon themselves the position of 'bystanders'. Even when they found themselves alone, from summer 1940 onwards, on an 'island' surrounded on all sides by the armies of Germany and its allies, they continued to believe that they should be fulfilling their mission, to serve as a 'very narrow bridge' between the two halves of the Jewish world split by the war. Thus, for instance, when Silberschein's friends urged him to emigrate to Palestine or to the United States, as many of his colleagues who had managed to escape from Poland had done, joining the leadership in Jerusalem or in New York, he replied: 'our place is not in Palestine, but outside of it, so as not only to act for the sake of Palestine, but also for the survival of the remnant of destroyed Jewry.'[36]

However, the emissaries' destiny was different from what they had imagined. Their geographical proximity to the fields of hunger, oppression and death and the daily stream of mail that arrived, did not permit them to be passive despite their powerlessness and despair. Instead, they went about their tasks with fortitude, and tried to continue to maintain contacts and provide aid, not always aware that they were witnesses to a systematic extermination. In historical perspective, their engagement and efforts at that time stand out in relief against the marginal place occupied by the fate of European Jewry on the agenda of organisations in Palestine or in the United States during the same period. Away from the political and social problems that troubled the various Jewish communities outside Europe, and further from the political discussions and festive conferences that were held after the war regarding the future of the Jewish people, they were exposed to the constant flow of information that pierced the ghetto walls, censorship and their own routines.

It is against this background that I would like to introduce an alternative story of bystanders to the Holocaust.

## III

Until the summer of 1940 the Jewish organisations outside occupied Europe were mainly involved in assisting refugees who still hoped to be rescued from Europe. The plight of the refugees illustrated the distress of European Jewry, and their presence behind locked doors attracted public attention. Activists from the Joint, the Jewish Agency, the illegal immigration organisation HeHalutz, and the World Jewish Congress who were in Europe were instrumental in gathering information and obtaining assistance for the needy.

After the summer of 1940, when the Middle East became a theatre of war, and it became apparent that Europe's Jews were trapped under the Nazi jackboot, calls were made to various activists to leave Europe and go either to the United States or Palestine. Even the HeHalutz leadership in Palestine, which saw itself as the spearhead of Zionist operations and had educated its members in an ethos of self-sacrifice for the sake of the movement, recalled its emissaries. Once the link with them had been severed, the Jews of Europe were taken off the agenda of the Jewish organisations in the free world. This was the beginning of a period of 'silence', as Hava Eshkoli's book is entitled – the deafening silence of Jewish leadership in Palestine and the United States regarding European Jewry up to the end of 1942.[37] Until that time, the common view was that Jews in the free world could do nothing but wait for the end of the war. The Jews of Europe, it was thought, would be an immense mass of refugees seeking a place to reconstruct their lives. A sovereign country was considered to be the most desirable solution by many, not only from the point of view of the Jewish community in Palestine, but also from the point of view of the Jewish community in the United States, which had already given up the battle to open their country's gates to their brethren.

The importance the leaders of the organisations attached to their representatives in Geneva diminished in direct proportion to the view that nothing could be done for the Jews in Europe until the end of the war. Richard Lichtheim, the special emissary to Europe of the executive of the Jewish Agency, received replies to his reports only from the secretary of the executive, Dr. Lauterbach. The situation of Nathan Schwalb, the representative of the HeHalutz movement, was even worse: he received no budget, his letters to the movement's leaders were seldom answered, and even the dispatch of propaganda material ceased. The most organised office was that of the World Jewish Congress in Geneva, which, prior to the outbreak of the war, had been one of that organisation's two central offices. However, after the fall of France, the headquarters of the organisation was moved to New York and its European office in Geneva lost its importance, its budget also being gradually cut. By the summer of

1942, it was allotted the sum of $500 – an amount sufficient only to fund the salaries of Alfred Silberschein, Gerhart Riegner and two part-time assistants. The costs of posting the information that Riegner collected regarding the economic and legal situation of Jews in various countries were covered only several months later. The emissaries who remained in Geneva were expected to do nothing but wait in their posts until the end of the war. As Lichtheim put it, they felt like Noah, waiting for the flood waters to recede.[38] Yet, despite this universal feeling of helplessness, bystanders in Geneva adopted a view different from that of bystanders in New York and Jerusalem. An interesting example in this context is that of RELICO, the Committee for the Relief of the War-Stricken Jewish Population.

The activities of the offices of the World Jewish Congress in Geneva between 1941 and 1942 revolved around assistance: the provision of legal aid, mainly material, and the dispatch of food packages to Jews in occupied countries. These activities had already begun at the end of 1939, and for various reasons were set up from the outset in a separate framework. They were carried out under the auspices of RELICO, which Silberschein operated from the Geneva offices of the World Jewish Congress. However, in April 1941 the leadership of the World Jewish Congress in New York decided to impose a complete halt on all aid shipments to Jews in occupied countries, in apparent compliance with the strict terms of the economic boycott of Germany and its allies, under which every food package was seen as direct or indirect assistance to the enemy.[39]

Not that the World Jewish Congress leaders thought that the food sent to the ghettos would fall into German hands, as the British claimed. RELICO supplied clear proof that every food package reached its destination. The apparently 'patriotic' surrender to the boycott stemmed mainly from the political considerations of the American-Jewish leadership regarding its view of its relations with Britain at the end of the war. Rabbi Stephen Wise, though far from indifferent to the fate of his people, used his considerable political influence to ensure that his way of thinking was accepted, despite the moral difficulty he experienced:

This business of food packages and money transfers, I repeat, must stop at once. It is stopped. I do not want any more memoranda or any more discussion. As president of the American Jewish Congress, I lay down the order of immediate discontinuance.

Even if some members of the Governing Council choose to withdraw from it, because of the order, the order will stand. I shall not for one hour longer remain the President of the American Congress if it is to continue to run the risk of alienating the already too dubious goodwill of the British Government to our people.

What I have written about this bears with equal force upon the Geneva office. I shall cable today, after talking to Dr. Goldmann, that all these operations with and through Poland must cease at once and at once in English means AT ONCE not in the future.[40]

It was thus due neither to patriotism nor to some naive belief that valuable food parcels damaged the war effort to the benefit of the Nazis, as was thought at the time, that the office in Geneva was required to stop sending food parcels. Henceforth, the office was to concentrate only on reporting what was going on in Europe and to send material that might assist Congress in making claims for compensation after the war and re-establishing Jewish rights.[41]

Riegner protested against the decision. 'Over a pot of meat', he argued, it is easy to decide to stop the shipments of food parcels that save thousands of people from starvation, to continue to speak for European Jewry and come to terms with the fact that 'the list of Jewish victims was getting a bit long; nothing more.' However, from then on he did accept the stringent position taken by his superiors, and concentrated on collecting information. Alfred Silberschein rebelled. A qualified attorney and one of the leaders of the Zionist movement in Galicia, a representative of the Zionist Socialist Party in the Polish parliament, and founder of the Jewish Cooperative Movement in Poland (the National Cooperative Society for Credit and Savings), he remained in Geneva precisely because he wanted to assist 'destroyed Jewry'. Therefore, he decided to continue sending as many parcels as he could, even without the backing of the World Jewish Congress. When he began to despair, due to the poor response by former friends in the United States and Palestine in support of his actions, he stopped writingto them all altogether. Perhaps it was better that way because when the leaders of the World Jewish Congress found out about his continued activities in contradiction of their instructions, they demanded a severance of all formal contacts with him. As a result, Silberschein was ousted from the office in Geneva and, in the summer of 1942, he began to work alone. Now, both the World Jewish Congress and Silberschein were using the name RELICO.

Only in July 1942 did the WJC leadership attempt to enter into negotiations with the economic embargo authorities, the American Finance Ministry (which had, in the meantime, imposed its own limitations on the transfer of money to Europe) and the Red Cross, in order to obtain a licence for dispatching food to the ghettos and camps. And only then did it become apparent how many obstacles to such activities the various Allied bureaucracies had erected.[42]

Although Silberschein also dealt with forged passports, provided legal and other assistance to refugees, and corresponded with as many people in occupied Poland as he could, this next section will focus on his activities in the area of food packages.

When it became clear that smaller packages arrived more quickly, RELICO began sending packages of ½ kg containing coffee, chocolate and sardines, or tea, cocoa and tuna. RELICO was only one of the agencies that operated through Lisbon. Other private agencies also took advantage of the breach created there by sending food surplus to occupied countries. But RELICO earned the name of a trustworthy agency and therefore succeeded in selling its services to various institutions and private individuals, in particular within Switzerland itself. With the money it collected for its services, and with the assistance of loans, it funded the dispatch of packages to people who applied to it directly from Poland, especially to people without means.

Between January and June 1942 more than 50,000 kg in food was sent by RELICO in more than 100,000 packages. From the spring of 1942 some of these food packages were sent as collective parcels to the Yiddishe Soziale Alleinhilf (JSA). Branches of the JSA had been recognised by the occupying authorities as an aid organisation in the large ghettos as of November 1941, and their addresses had been given to Silberschein as an appropriate method of assisting the weakest people and aiding Jews who had been expelled from Germany and Slovakia to Poland, whose addresses could not be found. Silberschein therefore explained to members of his party in the Warsaw ghetto that the JSA parcels were intended for 'distribution to the needy' and not necessarily for 'my family' (that is, members of his party). In total, some $200,000 worth of food and cash parcels were sent by RELICO in the third year of the war; only about $3,000 of this was provided by the WJC (the sum having been transferred in July 1941).[43]

Through Yitzhak Weisman, a contact in Lisbon, RELICO succeeded in reaching an agreement with the German Red Cross in Berlin, which was to guarantee the distribution of collective food parcels to JSA branches in the ghettos (an agreement that became operative in 1942). In fact, from then on, as a result of relief operations arranged for RELICO by Weisman, further food dispatches were limited only by the amount of money available to RELICO. However, in summer 1942, they ran into difficulties, and only gradually did it appear that the reason for these difficulties was that there was no longer anyone to whom food could be sent.

For a long time, the food packages were seen in the ghettos as protection from death by starvation. With hindsight, historiography recognises that this was only an illusion and tends to dismiss aid operations as acts that pale into insignificance in light of the annihilation. What, therefore, is the significance of the dispatches of food in an historical retrospective?

In any judgment of the significance of rescue attempts as large-scale operations intended to save the masses during this period, the rescue of people from starvation must be seen as most crucial. The Warsaw ghetto was being supplied with only 15 per cent of the amount of calories required for human subsistence, with the result that 10 per cent of the ghetto population died of starvation in 1941.[44] Anyone who has read about the beggars and the starving corpses in the streets, or seen the terrible pictures of hunger that emerge from diaries from that period, or read Yitzhak Katzenelson's 'poems of hunger' written in the ghetto in May 1941, knows that the consequences of this were beyond description. Later, Emmanuel Ringelblum, witnessing the deportation of some 300,000 Jews from the Warsaw ghetto to the death camp at Treblinka, reminds us that it was hunger that made many of them *volunteer* to be deported.[45]

Between these two phases – the perception in the summer of 1941 that death would come from starvation in the ghetto and the realisation, by the spring of 1942, of the realities of the 'Final Solution' – there was another phase, epitomised in Nathan Eck's postcard of April 1942. Eck sent his postcard to Silberschein, based on news about Chelmno, Ponari and especially the liquidation of the Lublin ghetto in the *Generalgouvernement*. Now, as it was becoming clear that Germany had targeted the Jews for total destruction, the pressing question being asked was whether enough had been done to rescue them until then. Eck's postcard documents one of the earliest moments of realisation of the enormity of the extermination. It is written in a sort of code, Eck using Hebrew words transliterated in his Polish text, to bypass censorship:

> My dear, I am healthy and doing well as usual. I no longer receive food parcels. *Expellees* are apparently transferred to the *earth* [the grave] and *thousands* and *tens of thousands* to *annihilation*. Their aunt *world* [the Jewish world] is not helping them at all. In fact, it does not now have the ability it once had. But had it expressed an interest in so doing, perhaps it would not now be so necessary to be sent to such God-forsaken places as *earth* and *annihilation*.[46]

## IV

There is no doubt that the awareness of total extermination blurs everything that preceded it both inside and outside the ghettos. The history of the second half of the war, the displaced persons' camps, the refugees and, perhaps above all, the establishment of the State of Israel – all these obscure the events which took place at the beginning of the war. The activity of the emissaries in Geneva was integrated in very abridged form in the glorious story the Jewish organisations made up about their rescue efforts at the end of the war. Mentioning them enabled these organisations to demonstrate that Jewish leadership in the free world had been continually active on behalf of European Jewry even in 1941–42, despite the actual severance from them. Thus, for instance, Silberschein's food dispatches appear in one paragraph under the heading 'In the Struggle Against Starvation' – a six-page section of the World Jewish Congress report on activity during the war.[47] Of course, immediately after the war, everyone sacrificed their experiences for a unified 'we' story. But during the past two decades, this 'we' story has collapsed into a collage of different memories and the 'bystander' issue has begun to take a central position in the historiography. One might expect the handful of emissaries in Geneva to find their proper place in the pantheon of Jewish bystanders. Yet Silberschein, who was one of those who had actually listened to Polish Jewry, died an 'unknown soldier',[48] and this is how his memory has remained to this very day.

In conclusion, it may be argued that it is not inexplicable that the place of these people was withheld from the collective memory. The history of *Jewish* bystanders presents no exception to the history of bystanders in general. The Jews were part of the outside world, shared its problems in the face of the Nazi 'Final Solution' (lack of information, the interpretation of information, the political agenda in war-time) and depended on its power and capacity to destroy Nazi Europe. In consequence, the historiography of Jewish 'bystanders' focused, as noted above, on the second half of 1943. The activities of Silberschein are outshone by the War Refugee Board initiated by Roosevelt in January 1944 and by the activities of Yishuv representatives in Geneva – Lichtheim, Schwalb and members of the youth movements – 'the Yishuv mission in Istanbul'. Apart from Riegner (who really only became known because of his telegram), the Geneva emissaries were relegated to the margins of the history of world Jewish activity during the war. In a letter to a friend, who complained that some had turned Saly Mayer into a hero of the rescue operations, Silberschein anticipated the historical revision of that issue. He himself, he wrote in 1950, had neither the energy nor the desire to fight for the truth:

> History will remain distorted, and not only because of Saly Mayer. The distortion begins with the technical trick that all written, printed and oral reports on the war period start (more or less) in the year 1943, at the time when Hitler's defeat was certain. The preceding years, when the meaning of these events truly comes to light, are, for the most part, ignored. Hence, the reports are all the same, whether they be by the Joint, the World Jewish Congress, the Agudah or any other organisation.[49]

Silberschein was right. Yet the main reason seems to be connected to the common meaning of 'rescue' in the historiography of the 'bystanders' – an understanding that examines the response of the free world to its various wings, given the knowledge of the annihilation, after it had already happened. It thus focuses on a small number of rescue operations, many of which failed due to the obstacles the Allies, the Vatican, the Red Cross and other bodies placed in the way of Jewish leaders and anyone who attempted to act in 1943 and particularly in 1944. In this light, the special actions of the representatives in Geneva stand out.

What characterised the Jewish emissaries in Geneva was the consistency of their activity for the benefit of the Jews in occupied Europe, not in an abstract manner but by providing concrete and direct assistance to individuals – many individuals – who were struggling to survive. And despite the fact that they knew that their help was nothing more than a 'drop in the ocean', as they used to say, they persisted. They did whatever they could to assist in the *present* – not after the war – not because they thought there would be no 'after', but because they did not want to disappoint those who looked to them in hope – not to them personally, but to them as symbols of the free Jewish world. Therefore, these 'bystanders' do not share in the guilt of the other 'bystanders' in the post-Auschwitz era who are haunted by the terrible knowledge that 'it is too late now, and it always will be too late'. Rather, theirs is the knowledge that they did all they could do to assist and rescue their brethren.

The marginal place in the historiography accorded to their activity stems not only from the fear that their story would shatter the fragile image of the past that the Jewish organisations had constructed for themselves, as Silberschein hinted in his letter, but also because these emissaries represented the 'world of yesterday', in the sense that they represented the small number of 'bystanders' who did not let down those who were 'drowning'.

Had they survived, many victims would today be able to recount that during that terrible period, these few 'bystanders' in Geneva were 'in their eyes' the address of the Jewish world, and in fact, the address of the free world. And, as another eulogised, 'had Silberschein ... lived in America or in Israel, there would clearly be entire books telling of his life's work and glorifying his name by now'.[50] However, he and his colleagues worked for 'the Jewish people who were killed', and therefore, there is no one left to glorify his name.

## NOTES

1. Gisi Fleischmann, Slovakia, to Saly Mayer, 27 Aug. 1942, Yad Vashem Archives (Jerusalem), M20/93.
2. Jacques Picard, *Die Schweiz auf der "Zuschauerbank" der Geschichte? Ueber die "Neutralitaet" in einem Zeitalter globaler Krisen und genozidaler Kriege* (Uppsala University). See also his contribution to this volume.
3. Albert Camus, *La Chute* (Paris: Gallimard, 1956).
4. See, for example, Yisrael Gutman and Livia Rothkirchen (eds.), *The Holocaust: Background and Implications* (Hebrew) (Jerusalem: Yad Vashem, 1973), especially Yehuda Bauer, 'The Holocaust Today – An Attempt at a New Evaluation', pp.462–6.
5. Ruth Firer, *Agents of a Lesson* (Hebrew) (Tel Aviv: Hakibutz Hameuchad, 1989), pp.76–89; Yael Zerubavel, *Recovered Roots, Collective Memory and the Making of Israeli National Tradition* (Chicago and London: University of Chicago Press, 1995), esp. part 3.
6. Yisrael Gutman (ed.), *Rescue Attempts during the Holocaust* (Hebrew) (Jerusalem: Yad Vashem, 1976). See esp. introduction and table of contents.
7. Ibid.
8. Arthur D. Morse, *While Six Million Died* (New York: Random House, 1968); S. Bet-Zvi, *Post-Ugandan Zionism on Trial: A Study of the Factors that Caused the Mistakes Made by the Zionist Movement during the Holocaust*, 2 Vols. (Tel Aviv: private publication, 1991).

9. Dan Diner, *Zivilisazionsbruch, Denken Nach Auschwitz* (Frankfurt a/Main: Fischer Taschenbuch Verlag, 1988).
10. Yehuda Bauer, 'When Did They Know?', *Midstream*, Vol.XIV, No. 4 (April 1968), pp.51–8.
11. Martin Gilbert, *Auschwitz and the Allies* (New York: Hamlyn Paperback, 1981); Deborah Lipstadt, *Beyond Belief: The American Press and the Coming of the Holocaust 1933–1945* (New York: Free Press, 1986); Walter Laqueur, *The Terrible Secret: An Investigation into the Suppression of Information About Hitler's Final Solution* (Boston: Little Brown, 1980); and, most recently, Richard Breitman, *Official Secrets: What the Nazis Planned, What the British and Americans Knew* (London: Penguin Books, 1999).
12. Leni Yahil, *The Holocaust* (New York: Oxford University Press, 1990), Chapter 20.
13. Raul Hilberg, *Perpetrators, Victims, Bystanders* (New York: Harper Collins, 1992).
14. Michael R. Marrus, *The Holocaust in History* (London: Penguin Books, 1989), p.156.
15. See, for instance, Yehuda Bauer, *Jews for Sale? Nazi–Jewish Negotiations, 1936–1945* (New Haven and London: Yale University Press, 1994).
16. Camus, *La Chute*, p.123.
17. Primo Levi, *The Drowned and the Saved* (New York: Vintage, 1989).
18. Raya Cohen, 'Confronting the Reality of the Holocaust: Richard Lichtheim, 1939–1942', *Yad Vashem Studies*, Vol. XXIII (Jerusalem, 1993), pp.335–68.
19. Raya Cohen, *Between 'There' and 'Here': Stories of Witness to Destruction, Jewish Emissaries in Switzerland 1939–1942* (Tel Aviv: Am Oved, 1999), pp.149–51.
20. Emmanuel Ringelblum, *Diary and Notes from the Warsaw Ghetto* (Hebrew) (Jerusalem: Yad Vashem, 1992), 8 May 1942, pp.357–8.
21. H. Vierbuecher, *Was die Kaiserliche Regierung den deutschen Undtertaten verschwiegen hat: Armenien 1915. Die Abschlachtung eines Kulturvolkes durch die Tuerken* (Hamburg: Berger, 1930).
22. Franz Werfel, *Die Vierzig Tage des Musa Dagh* (Berlin/Vienna/Leipzig: Paul Zsolnay Verlag, 1933), Vol.II, p.203.
23. V. Dadrian, *Histoire du Genocide armenien* (Paris: Stock, 1966), pp.628–35.
24. Raya Cohen, 'History as an Allegory: Franz Werfel and the "Armenian Destiny" during the Holocaust' (Hebrew), *Zion*, Vol.62, No.4 (1997), pp.369–85.
25. Diary entry of 6 June 1942, cited in J. Kermish (ed.), *To Live with Honor and Die with Honor* (Jerusalem: Yad Vashem, 1986), p.34.
26. June 1942, Ringelblum, pp.386–9.
27. Cohen, *Between 'Here' and 'There'*, pp.147, 154. See also Jan Karski, *The Story of a Secret State* (Boston: Houghton Mifflin, 1944).
28. Walter Laqueur and Richard Breitman, *Breaking the Silence* (New York: Simon & Schuster, 1986).
29. Raya Cohen, 'The Riegner Telegram: Text, Context and Subtext', *Tel-Aviver Jahrbuch fuer deutsche Geschichte*, Vol.XXIII (1994), pp.301–24.
30. Cohen, *Between 'Here' and 'There'*, p.95.
31. Schwalb to Lubetkin, 10 Dec. 1941, Melech Neustat (Noy) Files, HaAvoda Archives (Machon Lavon), IV, 104/42.
32. Cohen, *Between 'Here' and 'There'*, p.90.
33. 'You cut us out of your memory, and what of *us*? Shall we not admit that you cannot draw water from a poisoned well?', wrote Tussia Altman to the Hashomer Hatzair leadership in Palestine. See Bracha Habas (ed.), *Letters from the Ghettos* (Hebrew) (Tel Aviv: Am Oved, 1963), pp.41–2.
34. Cohen, *Between 'Here' and 'There'*, p.194.
35. Ibid., p.193.
36. Ibid., p.168.

37. Hava Eshkoli (Wagman), *Silence, Mapai and the Holocaust,1939–1942* (Jerusalem: Shazar, 1994).
38. Cohen, 'Confronting the Reality of the Holocaust', p.339.
39. See Cohen, *Between 'Here' and 'There'*, p.133; *Unity in Dispersion: A History of the World Jewish Congress* (New York: World Jewish Congress, 1945), pp.174–8.
40. Emphasis in original. Wise to Perlzweig, 9 May 1941, American Jewish Historical Society Archives (Waltham, MA: Brandeis University), SSW Papers, box 91.
41. Cohen, *Between 'Here' and 'There'*, p.128.
42. Ibid., pp.173-7.
43. Ibid., pp.161-7.
44. A very concise and harsh description appears in Shmuel Ma'ayan, *Yosef Kaplan*, Part II (Hebrew) (Kibbutz Ma'anit: author's publication, 1993).
45. Ringelblum, p.394; and cf. ibid., p.338, for instance.
46. Nathan Eck (Warsaw) to Silberschein, 5 April 1942, HaAvoda Archives (Machon Lavon, Tel Aviv), IV, 104/42, III 37A/60; Cohen, *Between 'Here' and 'There'*, pp.103–4.
47. 'Abraham Silberschein did not allow himself to be deterred from his duty. With the assistance of the Congress office in Lisbon, he was dispatching food to the Polish Ghettos in 1941 at the rate of 1,500 parcels a week', *Unity in Dispersion*, p.175.
48. Israel Coen and Dov Sdan (eds.), *Chapters in Galician History: In Memory of Dr Avraham Silbershein* (Hebrew) (Tel Aviv: Am Oved, 1957), p.12.
49. Silberschein to Hellman, WJC, Buenos Aires, Yad Vashem Archives, M-20/24, 15 Feb. 1950.
50. Article by Nathan Eck in *Chapters in Galician History*, pp.20, 21.

# 'The War is Over – Now You Can Go Home!' Jewish Refugees and the Swedish Labour Market in the Shadow of the Holocaust[1]

## SVEN NORDLUND

### I

By the end of the 1990s the Holocaust had become an important and heated issue in Sweden. Why is it that attitudes and reactions in Sweden during the 1930s and 1940s to the persecution of the Jews created a debate only in the 1990s and not before? One reason might be the events of the last decade which have made us painfully aware of our role as bystanders during the Holocaust. The horrors of the Holocaust did not, as we imagined they might, disappear once and for all when Nazi Germany was defeated. As long as similar horrors happened outside Europe, in less 'developed and advanced' countries, it was possible to ignore them. For instance, the genocides in Cambodia, Rwanda and other parts of Africa were demonstrable examples of bystander attitudes. Events in Bosnia and elsewhere in former Yugoslavia show that genocidal horrors are still part of contemporary European society.

I will begin with some comments regarding the concept of 'bystander'. One can talk about two different categories of 'bystanders'. In the first place are the bystanders who lived in countries under Nazi rule; in second place are those Jonathan Glover has called 'free bystanders', or those who lived in countries outside the Nazi empire. Those in the latter category had opportunities to rescue victims of Nazism.[2] Swedes belonged to this category. Accordingly, the recent debate about the significance of the

Holocaust has centred on such questions as: Why, as a 'free bystander', did Sweden respond as it did and not help to rescue more Jews in the late 1930s or the 1940s?

Yet some Swedes, such as the famed Raoul Wallenberg and the virtually unknown Valdemar Langlet, did not look away but tried to rescue Jews, often risking their own lives.[3] As in Switzerland, the current debate in Sweden calls into question not only the 'bystander reaction' to the Holocaust, but also general policy towards Nazi Germany.[4] In fact, much of the public debate is a denunciation of the way in which official Sweden succeeded for many years in hiding the true character of its relations with Nazi Germany. People today ask why post-war history books have avoided discussing Swedish collaboration, concessions and compromises with Nazi demands? Why did Swedish officials keep quiet about the Holocaust during the war? And why, since the war, has it taken so long for Swedes to face up to their attitudes and responses to the Holocaust and Nazi Germany?

In early 1998 the Swedish government launched an information campaign about the Holocaust, including the publication of a book explaining the history of the event intended for parents' use in discussions with their children.[5] Prior to that, as in the Swiss case, a national commission was appointed to investigate what had happened to Jewish property that might have entered Sweden in connection with the persecution of Jews in Nazi-controlled countries before and during the Second World War.[6]

Among 'free' bystanders such as Great Britain, Sweden, Switzerland and the United States, the Holocaust was long regarded as an event for which Germany and its collaborators in Nazi-occupied countries were solely responsible. The official reaction was one of unbelieving shock, even though these governments and their peoples were rather well informed of what was happening to Jews in Nazi-controlled areas.[7]

Like Switzerland, Sweden succeeded in escaping the horrors of war – a unique case compared with that of other democratic, western European countries. Thus Swedes, like the Swiss, were not only 'free' bystanders but also 'neutral bystanders'.[8] Although

Sweden admitted victims of Nazi persecution before the outbreak of the Second World War, it did so reluctantly, as Hans Lindberg and Steven Koblik demonstrated in studies they published in 1973 and 1987 respectively.[9] However, their findings failed to make the Holocaust an issue of public morality. An interesting question in this connection is whether this reaction was connected to the achievements of Raoul Wallenberg and Count Folke Bernadotte and the 'White Buses'. Is it possible that these humanitarian efforts in the final stages of the war laid the ground for a post-war image of Sweden as a rescuer of Holocaust victims? If this is so, it can be argued that the image of Sweden as a 'rescuer nation' helped to maintain a clear national conscience. If such an interpretation is valid, then this image may have long made it possible for Swedes to forget, or repress, a more accurate and true picture of Swedish policy and attitudes as a bystander during most of the Nazi era. Did this 'rescuer image' render public opinion immune to the morally disturbing facts presented by Lindberg and Koblik?

The recent interest in the Holocaust may also be seen as a consequence of Sweden's changing economy and its new international relations. As long as Sweden's and the world's economies grew, events linked to the war could be forgotten or concealed. However, since the end of the 1970s Sweden's relative economic and social decline, along with structural changes in the international economy, have changed matters. Growing unemployment and social insecurity have created discontent, and long-standing feelings of social and international solidarity have declined. Immigrants and 'new Swedes' have often been scapegoats or targets of social discontent as manifested in increasing xenophobia, racism and, during the 1990s, frequent episodes of neo-Nazi violence. In Sweden, as in other liberal western democracies, factors such as structural economic problems, increasing numbers of refugees, multiculturalism and ethnic conflicts seemed to generate a growing interest in the bystander phenomenon. Tony Kushner argues that these factors have increased a general desire to explain the bystander and bystander attitudes, making this a central area of inquiry for Holocaust studies internationally.[10]

One might also argue that Sweden's increased interest in the Holocaust is a consequence of conflicting views concerning the country's membership of the European Community and European Union. Interest in Sweden's experience in the Second World War grew as a result of these debates. Was its experience during the war unique? Was that time the beginning of a Swedish *Sonderweg*, compared to the rest of western Europe? Or did Sweden, despite its status as a neutral bystander, actually respond as part of a common western European development and heritage? Finally, the growing preoccupation with the bystander issue and the Holocaust may also be understood as a consequence of the collapse of communism and the Soviet empire. For many Swedes, this increasing interest may be a way of dealing, consciously or not, with earlier bystander attitudes and reactions to the atrocities of communism.

Tony Kushner has pointed out that most research on bystanders and bystander attitudes has had a 'tendency to condemn the contemporaries, rather than to explain', and that these studies have often been oriented towards politics and diplomacy. In doing so, they usually neglected social and cultural aspects of history, and they have not treated the labour movements in the countries concerned. According to Kushner, this has led to the assumption that in the 'free' bystander countries the Nazi persecution of the Jews had no impact on the lives of ordinary people.[11] As a result, we know comparatively little about the socio-economic conditions of Jewish refugees or how they coped with their reception and native attitudes in their host countries. In what follows, I will treat Swedish attitudes and responses to the Holocaust with special reference to Jewish refugees and their circumstances in the Swedish labour market between 1933 and 1945.

During the 1930s refugees from Nazi Germany sought safety in Sweden as they did in other democracies. Their presence and fear of their arrival aroused strong and divided reactions in both the *Riksdag*, Sweden's parliament, and in Swedish society. Yet by 1939 some members of parliament maintained that Sweden, considering its economic and political possibilities, was doing too little to rescue Jewish refugees, while others argued the opposite.[12] The latter group maintained that the country was threatened with an invasion of refugees from Germany, by which they meant Jewish refugees.[13] By describing the arrival of some Jewish refugees as 'an invasion', this group hoped to prevent more Jews from entering the country. An examination of the numbers of Jewish refugees admitted to Sweden during the 1930s will enable us to see if the metaphor 'invasion' was in any way justified.

In the 1930s, for the first time since the 1850s, Sweden experienced a net immigration. The numbers, however, were quite modest. By the autumn of 1933 only some 300–400 German Jewish refugees were in Sweden. By February 1939 there were 2,800 refugees in Sweden, of whom 2,000 were Jews from Germany.[14] Yet in that year 20,000 foreign citizens lived in the country.[15] As a matter of fact, compared with other western European countries during the 1930s, Sweden accepted very few Jewish refugees. For instance, fascist Portugal was more generous towards Jewish refugees than democratic Sweden.[16] There is no question that Jewish immigration to Sweden in the 1930s was strongly resisted. But what explains this negative reaction, and how did it affect those Jews admitted to Sweden?

This question can at least be partly answered by looking at the most important meeting place between immigrants, refugees and the native population – the labour market. Here they met eye to eye and worked side by side. It was also on the labour market and in the workplace that competition, acceptance or dissociation became apparent in both daily practice and social attitudes.

I will start by discussing some aspects of the labour market relevant to the period between 1933 and 1945. Then I will examine the parliamentary debate about the Jewish refugees and the labour market in the late 1930s. What were the official attitudes, reactions and conditions?

Does the presence of antisemitism explain the various reactions, or was the general struggle for vacant jobs decisive in shaping attitudes? What kind of jobs were available? Was there any room for victims of Nazi persecution? Which attitudes and what social climate did the refugees encounter in various trades and workplaces?

In seeking to answer these questions, I will look in detail at musicians, entrepreneurs and the self-employed.

## II

Swedish immigration and refugee policies during the inter-war period were characterised by protectionism and economic nationalism. 'Buy Swedish products!' and 'Play Swedish music!' were mottos reflective of the economic and political climate of the 1930s. The Aliens Act of 1927 sought to create an immigration policy which would protect the labour market by creating an inner protective wall made up of labour and residence permits which blocked access to the job market for foreigners. It also contained rules regarding the expulsion and control of foreigners.[17] When prolongation of this protectionist act was discussed in 1932 the *Socialstyrelsen* (National Board of Health and Welfare) expressed its approval, noting that it had prevented 'the large armies of European unemployed from coming into our country'.[18]

Like all other European countries during the 1930s, Sweden suffered from high unemployment. In 1933 the average proportion of unemployed was 23 per cent, and at the end of the decade it remained as high as 8–9 per cent. And the unemployed were not only industrial workers but included people formerly employed in trades and offices, musicians and those in certain academic professions. Unemployment remained especially high among young people.[19]

When in 1936 work began on passing the new Aliens Act, *Socialstyrelsen* reasoned that it was important to be prepared for an increased period of immigration. In fact, fear of an increasing number of Jewish refugees lay behind this reasoning, for it was understood that the Jews represented occupational groups which might compete with corresponding Swedish groups. Accordingly, the government used labour permits to direct refugees to fields where there was no serious competition.[20] Although it was considered important that refugees receive the same wages as Swedes, this ambition should not be interpreted as a desire to create equal conditions between refugees and Swedes.[21] Rather, it was a fear of 'unfair' competition, especially from Jewish refugees, which influenced the government's policy in this matter.

In the second half of the 1930s Swedish labour-market policy was increasingly influenced by Keynesian ideas. Political measures were enacted not only to finance public works which would reduce unemployment, but also to create employment in order to stimulate the entire economy.[22] The general idea guiding official labour-market policy in the 1930s was the so-called *arbetslinjen*, or 'line of work'. This meant that it was most favourable for the economy as well as for the unemployed if the latter could provide for themselves by having 'productive' jobs, with the government unwilling to take any political or economic responsibility for Jewish refugees.[23] They were expected to find jobs on their own. This circumstance created a conflict between public Swedish labour-market policies and the efforts of some individuals and groups, such *as Stockholms Central Kommitté för flyktinghjälp* (Stockholm's Central Committee for Aid to Refugees) and *Mosaiska Församlingens Hjälpkommitté* (The Aid Committee of the Jewish Community), to help Jewish refugees to find means of support.[24] The authorities sought to limit the influx of Jewish refugees into Sweden to the lowest possible level. Accordingly, in 1938 *Socialstyrelsen* officials questioned whether Swedish citizens who 'invited "non-Aryans" as guests were in fact acting disloyally to their country'.[25]

The basic idea was that the refugees should have labour permits in their possession when they arrived in Sweden. Yet for a Jewish refugee, obtaining such a permit was a genuine 'Catch-22' situation, with unclear and contradictory rules. For instance, refugees would be granted permits if they had an educational or professional background which made it likely that they would later re-emigrate. Thus, because agricultural education and training was thought to encourage subsequent emigration to Palestine, the so-called '*chaluzim* quota' was supported, with the number of permits allotted to this group the subject of discussions between the government and representatives of Stockholm's Jewish congregation.[26] On the other hand, those who managed to enter before visas were required for

German citizens (a measure instituted in autumn 1938), were not given permits. They were considered 'transit refugees' with a greater likelihood that they would re-emigrate, regardless of whether this was true or not. Finally, another group of Jewish refugees was refused residence permits, yet the government considered it unlikely that they could leave the country. They were supposed to make it on their own, or survive on relief. A 'Catch-22' situation indeed![27]

The war years brought changes to the labour situation for Jewish refugees. Beginning in September 1939, the government gradually assumed responsibility for the relief of refugees. Now, the Jews were one group among other refugees, and the focus on them lessened.[28] On the other hand, their private and working lives were placed under increased scrutiny by police and security authorities. This was particularly true for the period between 1940 and 1942, when Nazi Germany's power and influence were at their height. Frequent personal reports to the police authorities regarding social contacts and restrictions relating to residence, travel and checking of personal correspondence were elements of this increased control, which affected not only Jews but also other refugees.

Before the war, a labour-market policy directed exclusively at refugees did not exist. However, the outbreak of the war brought with it a reorganisation of the labour-market, as well as a change in the government's perception of refugees and the labour market. Whereas previously refugees had been regarded as a drain on the economy, now they were increasingly seen as a resource to be exploited. This change affected all refugees. During these years, particularly from 1942 onwards, the Swedish economy suffered from labour shortages.[29] Accordingly, all refugees – Jews included – were regarded as an important feature of labour-market policy. Particularly for sectors such as agriculture, fuel production and domestic services, refugees were seen as a manpower reserve. The question remains however: to what extent, and how, did Jewish refugees manage to take advantage of the new realities prevailing in the labour market?

The other pillar of Sweden's restrictive immigration policy was based on the idea of maintaining the 'purity' of the 'Nordic race'.

The 1927 Act stated that 'this purity had a value which can hardly be exaggerated', and it was considered very important to control the immigration of people 'not suited to become a part of Sweden's population'.[30] Legislators primarily feared immigration by Jews, Gypsies and others from eastern European countries, although fear of increased Jewish immigration from Germany lay behind the renewed Act of 1937, which, however, gave economic and racial reasons as its justification. This legislation stated that Jews fleeing for 'racial reasons' were to be regarded as political refugees, yet government authorities evaded that aspect of the legislation by classifying Jewish 'racial refugees' as economic immigrants, saying that they had to obtain labour permits before entering Sweden. It is uncertain if this antisemitic policy prevailed primarily in the years after 1936 or if it was evident one way or another for the entire period after 1933.[31] What is certain is that to a large degree Sweden refrained from offering protection to Jewish refugees.[32]

What explains Swedish exclusionary and antisemitic attitudes in the 1930s? The historian Alf W. Johansson suggests that they were manifestations of a social democratic, nationalistic policy which sought to defend national economic interests and avoid confrontation with, or damage to, trade relations with Germany[33] Koblik maintains that the basis for negative attitudes towards Jewish refugees can be found not only in a general xenophobia but also within the organised labour movement.[34] In fact, precisely how prevalent antisemitism was in Sweden during the 1930s and the war remains uncertain, yet there is no doubt that it existed within important political sectors. One result was a Swedish anti-Jewish immigration policy.

According to the historian Paul A. Levine, the extremely restrictive policy of the 1930s was supported by pro-German groups and a more or less latent antisemitism within both the Foreign Office and the so-called 'educated upper class'.[35] Yet these attitudes within the Foreign Office changed after 1942, and leading officials tried to rescue Jews from the Holocaust. This change, Levine maintains, had less to do with humanitarian motives than with pragmatic considerations.[36] However, when and if this shift in the government's response was disclosed and/or accepted outside the foreign service remains unknown. Did it affect general opinion, or perhaps the attitudes of domestic authorities such as county administrative boards? Do we see, after the government's shift in late 1942, a similar change in the behaviour and attitudes of the police towards Jews and their presence on the labour market? Or did suspicions and antisemitism perhaps not yield until the last year of the war, or even later? There are no completely satisfactory answers to these questions. It seems, however, that the flight of the Danish Jews from that country to Sweden which began in early October 1943 must be understood as an important turning point. For these Jews were the first refugees, Jewish or otherwise, who were officially received with open arms by Swedish society.[37]

## III

There seems little doubt that before the war xenophobia was widespread within the Swedish middle and working classes.[38] A survey of the country's trades union press confirms this picture, yet as seen in these journals, this sentiment was not necessarily synonymous with antisemitism.[39] Except in the case of *Musikern*, the magazine of the musicians' union, virtually no articles or commentary mentioned Jewish refugees. Does the absence of obvious antisemitic remarks allow us to conclude that within the Swedish labour movement xenophobia can be differentiated from antisemitism? It is, of course, possible that the situation in Sweden was similar to that in Great Britain's labour movement. There, according to Kushner, trade unions avoided stressing the prominence of Jews among political refugees because they believed it would create undesirable antisemitic reactions.[40]

Jewish refugees entering the Swedish job market laboured under three handicaps: they were strangers, Jews and refugees. To be a foreigner was to be a stranger, which meant being an outsider. The stranger had not been there from the beginning and therefore had different characteristics. Strangers came and went and were therefore unreliable, yet at the same time it was this quality that made it possible to tolerate strangers temporarily on the labour market.[41] When the strangers were refugees, their status as outsiders was more obvious and problematic. According to Georg Simmel, the problem regarding refugees, and especially Jewish refugees, was that they could be expected not to come and go but to stay.[42]

It is evident that such considerations influenced anti-refugee opinion both in the *Riksdag* and in the press. In a February 1939 parliamentary debate on the presence of Jewish refugees, fears of continuing unemployment and other strong negative reactions were much in evidence. The question was raised as to whether it was wise for the state to contribute to vocational training for refugees.[43] Some parliamentarians seemed to imply that providing such training would make the Jews less inclined to re-emigrate.[44] And fear of unemployment was used to stir up antisemitism. An oft-heard argument was: 'Sweden does not have a Jewish problem, but if the state contributes to the vocational training of refugees, of whom the great majority are Jews, we may get such a problem.'[45]

As noted before, some opinion-makers argued that Sweden should welcome more refugees. How strong was support for such opinions in the late 1930s, or can these be understood mainly as expressions of exaggerated optimism, humanitarian considerations or a guilty conscience among certain groups in society? Some intellectuals who were well off seemed not to see Jewish refugees as competitors on the labour market.

Sweden's economy recovered relatively more quickly than those of many other European countries during the 1930s, and this upward economic trend, combined with a declining population, created a demand for labour in certain trades. Therefore, limited import of foreign labour was considered necessary. Among the enthusiasts of this idea were the social scientists and economists Alva and Gunnar Myrdal.[46] For instance, in agriculture there was a need for labour, but the government wished to remedy this not with Jewish refugees from Germany but with labour from the Nordic countries.[47] Yet as early as 1934 the Myrdals saw Jewish refugees and their human capital as an important resource for the economy.[48]

To some extent the discussion about whether the labour market could absorb more Jewish refugees or not was between economic nationalists and supporters of a free-trade policy. The economist and liberal Bertil Ohlin, using free-trade arguments, energetically questioned the restrictive policy towards the Jewish refugees. Such opinions as Ohlin's and like-minded thinkers were controversial because they maintained that the immigration of Jewish refugees was economically positive for the country. Furthermore, they stressed the importance of the human capital represented by the Jewish refugees. They maintained that their knowledge and experience were especially attractive as, if properly used, they could generate entrepreneurial activities and employment.[49] Interestingly, a similar discussion took place within the British labour movement at about the same time. The leading figure in this debate, the economist Roy Harrod, was unable to convince labour leaders that they should support the entry of Jewish refugees 'not merely on moral grounds but because of its actual benefit to the country as a whole'.[50] Harrod's Swedish colleagues thought similarly, and the idea of using Jewish refugee labour was not unknown to the Swedish government. This is clear from plans discussed between Sweden and Denmark to exchange refugee labour in order to cover shortages in certain trades.[51]

## IV

In Sweden certain groups and trades articulated xenophobic and anti-Jewish views more than others. In many cases such negative attitudes had to do with the fact that these groups and trades had been severely hit or felt especially vulnerable because of high unemployment and the structural changes in industry and commerce which took place nationally and internationally in the inter-war period. Some of these professional groups saw themselves as victims of the ongoing struggle between old and new products, technology, production, organisational and marketing conditions, lifestyles and ideologies.

The Swedish musicians' union was one group deeply affected by the constant tension between the old and the new and accordingly its members suffered dramatically from these changes.

Technological development and its economic and cultural consequences radically changed both the professional environment and conditions of life for Swedish musicians. Radio and the mass production of gramophone records broke through in the inter-war period, resulting in a drastically reduced demand for live music. The loudspeaker and sound in film made bar, café and cinema musicians redundant. Another disquieting sign for many musicians was the arrival of American jazz music and its demands for new rhythms and stage performances. All of this was connected to the even greater threat to employment for traditional professional musicians posed by growing competition from amateur musicians.

In 1937 unemployment among unionised musicians was as high as 20 per cent.[52] New influences and innovations came from abroad and were most often introduced into Sweden by foreign musicians. It is therefore not at all surprising that discontent with the new trends and their social consequences among professional musicians was often expressed in pronounced negative attitudes towards immigration in general and foreign musicians. The xenophobic reaction to the immigration of Jewish refugees who were musicians was evident as early as 1933–35. During this period one often finds in *Musikern* much talk of an 'invasion' of Jewish refugee musicians from Germany. The union was convinced that competition and unemployment would increase if these musicians were admitted.

In a 1933 letter to the government, the musicians' union, joined by others such as the union of Swedish composers, demanded that Jewish refugees should not be allowed to enter the country. A few years later the union asked the government not to give any foreign musician, Jewish or otherwise, labour permits.[53]

It was this situation which brought 800 musicians belonging to the Stockholm section of the union into the street on 17 October 1937 demonstrating with slogans such as 'Don't give foreign musicians labour permits!'[54] When in late 1938, after *Kristallnacht* and the annexation of the Sudeten region of Czechoslovakia, the numbers of Jewish refugees to Sweden increased, the musicians again argued that the government should not grant the new refugees labour permits. However, one interesting change at this time is that the musicians had nothing against new Jewish refugees being allowed to enter and stay in the country, as long as they were not allowed to work.[55]

## V

Jewish refugees to Sweden were often well educated with an intellectual or academic background. Others had a commercial or business background. During the 1930s the traditional labour market was in many ways closed to Jewish refugees, with limited possibilities of finding employment in their old trades or occupations. Though this changed somewhat during the war, very few refugees had experience of industrial or physically trying manual labour. This meant that even during the war many Jewish refugees could not compete with domestic labour.[56]

What possibilities existed for those who could not find a job or were unable to take the jobs available? Some survived on contributions from Sweden's native Jewish population, occasional work or various aid organisations. Others, like refugees in Sweden today, attempted self-employment or started small businesses. Historically in Sweden, as well as internationally, this strategy has often been the only possible alternative for marginalised groups such as refugees and Jewish immigrants.[57]

But for a Jew in Sweden in the 1930s attempting self-employment in certain trades or starting a new business was like entering the proverbial lion's den. Throughout the period in question small businessmen and tradesmen often expressed antisemitic sentiments.[58] Several organisations of small businessmen viewed the Jews not as refugees but as economic immigrants. Like the musicians, small tradesmen and salesmen were severely hit by the economy's structural changes and crises.[59] Accordingly, Jewish refugees were seen as potential competitors who, as soon as they were in the country, would establish businesses, engaging, it was believed, in unfair competition by offering lower salaries and prices. Giving them a chance to come to Sweden, it was argued from an economic and other points of view, was 'disgusting'.[60]

The Swedish economy was heavily dependent on the German economy and many Swedish firms had close ties to the German market. This circumstance led some refugees to believe they could earn a living by starting import firms and agencies in Sweden or finding employment in these trades. However, the readiness of many in the Swedish economy to accommodate their practices to Nazi Germany's policies of aryanisation often dashed these hopes. This Swedish aryanisation process created an atmosphere of discrimination and racism which made it extremely difficult for Jewish refugees to find employment. Indeed, the ready accommodation to German demands is one of the most depressing and little-known aspects of both Swedish attitudes and the country's adjustment to Nazi Germany.

Sweden's aryanisation process had two basic elements. One concerns decisions taken in Germany considering trade relations, ownership, management and employees of German firms operating in Sweden.[61] The other is the voluntary aryanisation of trades and firms carried out by Swedes for reasons of political opportunism, racism, fear or economic advantage. Many Swedish entrepreneurs and businesses severed relations with Swedish Jewish businesses and other Swedish enterprises that had contact with Jewish interests.

Sweden's voluntary aryanisation process depended on a system of informers who delivered information to Nazi Germany concerning 'non-Aryan' firms and other Swedish firms which maintained ties with Jewish economic interests. The goal was to eliminate these Swedish entrepreneurs and their firms. For instance, in September 1941 an entrepreneur in Borås sent a letter to Germany telling the Wuppertal firm of Langschner Bergman, Spitzenfabrik which customers in Sweden were 'Aryans'. In the same year the Stockholm firm Lundberg and Co. told the German firm Gebhardt and Müller of Schönheide that they were going to send a list containing information about which of their customers were 'non-Aryans' or 'Aryans'. Some Swedish firms moved to accomodate Nazi Germany's racial policies by declaring themselves 'Aryan'.[62]

Some Swedish firms even denounced their German commercial connections to Nazi authorities in Germany for having relations with Swedish Jewish firms using dummy companies. Dummies or front companies in these cases meant that the real owners, Swedish Jewish interests or German Jewish refugee interests, were hidden. They did this either by adopting new firm names or having boards consisting only of 'Aryan Swedes'. In such cases, the aim of the Swedish antisemites was to eliminate competition. In August 1941, for example, a Swedish merchant tried to eliminate a competitor by reporting to German authorities that the latter was  a 'non-Aryan' who had contact with an 'Aryan' firm in Germany.[63]

The Swedish aryanisation process, which began in the late 1930s and culminated between 1940 and 1942, forced some Swedish Jews, both employees and partners, to quit their jobs or leave their firms.[64] One significant example is the case of Turitz and Co., the large department store in Gothenburg. Long owned by Swedish Jews, in 1941 the company informed the German Chamber of Commerce that H. G. Turitz, the founder of the firm, had left the board and the company. In another report, German authorities were informed that the goal of the aryanisation process was to dismiss all Swedish Jews still employed.[65]

In general, we do not know how far the aryanisation process went in Sweden. A 1941 Swedish report on Swedish–German trade relations pointed out that many Swedish firms 'carried out a certain aryanization'. In some firms, however, the Swedish Jewish owners or interests 'kept themselves out of the way and let others take charge of representing their firms'.[66]

Following the occupation of Denmark and Norway in April 1940, the aryanisation process in Sweden intensified, with Swedish firms even more dependent on the German market than before, and it is against this background that one has to view the Swedish process. On 15 November 1940, in a confidential note from the *Reichsstelle für den Aussenhandel* in Berlin to the German Chamber of Commerce in Stockholm, instructions were issued calling for more energetic actions against Jewish refugees as well as Swedish Jewish importers of German goods. The idea was to try to break all German cooperation with Jewish and 'anti-German' firms, which were defined here as Swedish firms that maintained relations with

Swedish Jewish customers, had international Jewish commercial relations or had Jewish employees. By accommodating the demands of aryanisation they were sensitive to German racial policies and sought advantages over Swedish Jewish or anti-German firms. And they were also seriously worried about losing the sources of their livelihood, that is their markets in Germany.[67]

There were, however, some interesting exceptions regarding the German efforts to aryanise the Swedish economy. The Nazis were hesitant to break commercial relations with Swedish Jewish firms important for Germany. This might be explained by the clash of interests between the aims of the *Reichsstelle für den Aussenhandel* and the *Reichswirtschaftsministeriums* in Berlin, that is between German racial and commercial interests. Indeed, the process in Sweden was in some cases contradictory to German commercial aims. One example of this is the case of *Nordiska Kompaniet*, the large department store in Stockholm, which included Jewish interests. Because the store sold large quantities of German wares, had a solid reputation in Sweden and was in 1941 to stage an exhibition that was important for the German furniture industry, the German Chamber of Commerce asked the authorities in Berlin to make an exception regarding trade with these Swedish Jewish interests.[68]

The examples given above raise a number of questions about the character and consequences of both the German and the voluntary Swedish aryanisation process. How far-reaching was it? How did it affect the Swedish Jewish commercial community and the anti-German firms? Was it principally small Swedish Jewish and anti-German firms that were affected? Or was the target of the aryanisation process the large Jewish entrepreneurs? Were Jewish employees or Jewish owners hit hard? Did Jews manage to retain their property by keeping 'out of the way'? Equally, we do not know what happened to those who were victims of aryanisation in Sweden. Many of these questions would profit from a comparison regarding aryanisation in other bystander countries.

The legal aspects raise important questions. Why did the courts, when the process was a clear violation of basic Swedish legal practice, accept confiscations and their subsequent human consequences? According to one report concerning the liquidation of property owned by Nazi Germany and restitution of Jewish victims of the Holocaust, the reasons are clear. The passivity of Swedish courts was due entirely to their understanding of the difficulties disapproval of confiscations would create for trade relations between Sweden and Nazi Germany.[69] There seems little doubt that this response must have encouraged both individuals and firms who saw a chance of profiting from the aryanisation process. Indeed, the entire process in Sweden is an interesting example not only of the strength of anti-Jewish opinion, but also of the bystander mentality of the Swedish government and public opinion. There were few, if any, reactions or comments from either government officials or the press about these actions and their human and economic consequences.

Furthermore, the antisemitic climate created by this process made it extremely difficult for Jewish refugees to obtain employment. In a letter to Argentina from a German Jewish refugee we see a measure of the desperation that many of them felt. The letter-writer complained bitterly that it was impossible to enter the Swedish labour market.[70] With these circumstances in mind, it might be thought that all efforts to start a business were totally in vain. However, even in spite of the difficulties, some refugees managed to establish firms of their own.

But to start a business, foreigners had to obtain a permit from the government, which was often an uncertain, even humiliating and lengthy process involving severe scrutiny on the part of various authorities.[71] This was particularly true for Jewish applicants. Applications from foreign Jews were investigated more thoroughly than those of any other group of applicants, and their applications were declined more often during the inter-war period than those of any other group. Jews constituted a large part of the applications from immigrants from Germany, eastern and central European countries and which were rejected by the Swedish authorities in the period 1920–45. In the period 1920–29, 85 per cent of the rejected eastern European applications were Jewish, while the corresponding share among central European and German applicants was 21 per cent. During the war the share of Jews submitting rejected applications among eastern European nationalities was 75 per cent, while among Germans and central Europeans it was 76 per cent.[72] Indeed, these applications are extremely interesting and constitute one of the most valuable sources for examining the reactions, attitudes, mentalities and prevailing conditions regarding the Swedes and Jews as well as other refugees and immigrants.

One interesting aspect of this material is the view it gives us of the administrative offices to which Jewish refugee applications were submitted when requesting permission to conduct business. These bodies represented different trades, small business and industrial organisations, and regional chambers of commerce. Replies from these bureaux and groups were often characterised by openly antisemitic attitudes. This is especially true for the 1930s and the first years of the war. The applications sometimes included interviews with neighbours and landlords. Interestingly, the latter groups seldom displayed antisemitic sentiments but rather indifferent, non-committal attitudes towards the Jewish refugees. But the chambers of commerce, small business and industrial organisations often expressed extremely negative attitudes towards applications by Jews, although in the later war years such expressions became more nuanced and sophisticated. They were now seldom overtly antisemitic, referring instead to the employment situation. And if that argument was not strong enough, they would contend that the refugees did not have sufficient qualifications or represented unsound ethics – by which they meant business practices.[73]

It can hardly be argued that granting these applications represented any real threat to Sweden's small-business community. Very few refugees began material production or employed others. Most were small, unimportant businesses which in most cases were one-man operations. There were, however some exceptions. Some agencies and small manufacturing firms in Stockholm were engaged in the knitwear and clothing industry.[74] Some of these represented their aryanised firms in Germany. This might have been possible due to the clash of interests referred to above between racial and commercial authorities in Berlin. As we know, the first five years of the Hitler regime's Aryanisation policies were not as restrictive and discriminatory as afterwards. During the earlier period the Nazis merely wanted the Jews out of Germany while in some cases trade representatives wanted to make use of the Jews now in Sweden to keep their markets there. However, antisemitic opinion in Sweden described the activities of the above-mentioned category of refugee entrepreneurs as an attempt by Jewish capital to control the entire textile industry in Stockholm.[75] Following *Kristallnacht*, the possibility for Jews to represent German firms in Sweden disappeared due to stricter rules on aryanisation in Germany.[76]

There is no doubt that the response to the applications by Jews to start businesses were influenced by prevailing antisemitic attitudes within the government and trades and small businesses. On the other hand, there are many examples of positive government decisions for self-employment among the refugees. Such decisions fit into the *arbetslinjen* (work line) of the government, giving the refugees a chance to manage on their own, and – not incidentally – lowering costs for Swedish society.[77]

## VI

There is no question that throughout the 1930s and in the first years of the war, regarding both immigration and labour market policies, Sweden's government and business sector engaged in antisemitic practices. This was expressed in political adjustments to Germany, economic considerations and the voluntary aryanisation process conducted by some sectors of the Swedish business community. Overt antisemitism, combined with a fear of competition and unemployment, adjustments to the demands of the German market, and the passivity of the government and public opinion, made it extremely difficult for Jewish refugees to find employment on the open market.

Again, as in Great Britain under the new Labour government, when the war ended Jewish refugees were not supposed to stay in Sweden and compete in the labour market.[78] For example, one refugee, Gerhard Herzog, applied in May 1945 for a permit to start a small business in the small city of Nyköping. Herzog declared that he could not contemplate returning to Germany, for when he applied, news of the concentration camps was widespread in Sweden. In their reply to the application, Nyköping administrators wrote that they were of the opinion that it was undesirable for political refugees to establish businesses in Sweden; rather, they should return to Germany, where normal conditions now prevailed.[79]

Even later there was an ambivalent and hesitant attitude to Holocaust survivors in Sweden. According to a law passed by the Allies in 1947, those who had lost their property in Nazi Germany because of race should be regarded as victims of Nazism. Those who had lost their property as a consequence of the first Nuremberg laws had lost it by coercion, that the burden of proof of coercion rested not on the individual victim but on the authorities.[80] In connection with the 1946 Washington Agreement, Sweden agreed to liquidate German assets in the country and provide restitution to Jewish victims of Nazi persecution. The restitution referred to Jewish victims, either still living or relatives of those who had been murdered, living in Sweden or those who lived abroad but had assets or demands on assets connected to Sweden.

While liquidation and sales of German assets were taken care of effectively, Swedish authorities were somewhat passive in handling the restitution and rehabilitation of Jewish victims. The authorities paid little attention to the guiding principles for these matters indicated by the Allies, maintaining, for instance, that the burden of proof lay with the victim.[81] The victims themselves were highly dissatisfied with the restitution process. In 1947 some German refugee organisations and Stockholm's Jewish community complained to the government, claiming that with regard to restitution the authorities were behaving as if the Nazi regime still existed.[82]

A striking feature of the administrative process is the lack of ethical considerations. There are very few instances in which Swedish officials and lawyers handling Jewish cases of restitution discussed them in terms of justice, guilt and redress.[83] At the beginning of the 1950s Håkan Nial, one of Sweden's leading authorities in international law, went so far as to comment that 'Sweden should not continue to maintain the results of Nazi Germany's racial persecutions.'[84]

With these circumstances in mind, it would be easy to conclude that, even after the war, antisemitic attitudes were prominent among certain groups and individuals inside Sweden's establishment. Here we can refer to Tony Kushner's remark regarding attitudes in the liberal democracies to Germany's persecution of Jews before 1938. They did not arouse 'much discomfort, and rarely supplied support for the Nazis antisemitic policies'.[85] It seems that the same was true also for Sweden. It may seem astonishing that in spite of awareness of the atrocities of the Holocaust and the Washington agreement, in the administrative processes regarding restitution, attitudes of indifference continued after the war. Were such attitudes present in larger groups in Swedish society after the war, or were they mainly present in the bureaucracies, the result of the well-known fact that bureaucracies tend to maintain former attitudes and habits longer than other institutions?

Although it is obvious that antisemitic attitudes existed among such professional groups as business entrepreneurs, merchants, sales representatives and musicians, we must be careful not to exaggerate the influence of these attitudes when explaining why the labour market was closed to Jewish refugees during the 1930s. As we have seen, the behaviour of the union of musicians in the late 1930s shows that xenophobia was not always synonymous with antisemitism. Union representatives were not opposed to allowing Jewish refugees to enter the country, yet argued that work permits should not be granted. Nonetheless, the antisemitic attitudes we find regarding the labour market during this period could not have had such an impact without the passive support of local authorities, a majority of members of the *Riksdag*, unions, the government and, perhaps most importantly, the broad if passive support of Swedish public opinion. It would, however, be wrong to interpret the authorities' passivity and public opinion regarding the daily life and employment situation of Jewish refugees as primarily an expression of latent antisemitism. While such negative attitudes were certainly true for certain individuals and groups – particularly those involved in what I have labelled Sweden's aryanisation process – it is quite possible that most people were indifferent to both the fate and employment possibilities for Jewish refugees. This indifference could have something to do with the fact that many considered themselves victims of the economic crisis of the 1930s, and thus refrained from involving themselves with the work circumstances of the refugees. Moreover, the particularities of Sweden's aryanisation process in Sweden demonstrates that Swedish–German trade relations in general fostered bystander attitudes on the part of the authorities vis-à-vis the refugees' employment situation.

Finally, we can see some interesting similarities between the situation of Jewish refugees then and the situation of refugees in Sweden today. For instance, most Swedes still do not want the refugees to stay and compete for jobs. The government still seems to think that self-employment is one of the few possibilities for refugees. We are still not interested in exploiting the human capital brought to Sweden by refugees. Indeed, Sweden's current problems – one might call it a racialisation of Swedish society, of which neo-Nazism is the most extreme expression – brings to mind another interesting parallel to the situation before and during the Second World War and today. We know, then and now, that antisemitism and racism are not necessarily connected to the number of refugees or foreigners. By late 1938 only 797 refugees had received labour permits, of whom the great majority were Jews.[86] Bearing in mind this number, plus the small total number of Jewish refugees in Sweden, it is difficult today to accept arguments that they could in any way be regarded as an economic threat to domestic labour. In the 1930s Sweden and its 'Middle Way' of social egalitarianism and democracy was seen internationally as a progressive society. Yet the arrival of a few thousand Jewish refugees was enough to stimulate in the behaviour of many Swedes and their professional groups a striking level of antisemitism, protectionism, economic pragmatism and egoism – all reflected in the immigration and labour policies of the government.

NOTES

1. This is a revised and extended version of an article which appeared in Swedish in *Historisk Tidskrift*, No.1 (1999).
2. Jonathan Glover, *Humanity: A Moral History of the Twentieth Century* (London: Jonathan Cape, 1999), p.391.
3. Björn Runberg, *Valdemar Langlet: räddare i faran* (Bromma, 2000).
4. Maria-Pia Boethius, *Heder och samvete: Sverige och andra världskriget,* (Stockholm: Norstedts, 1991).
5. Stéphane Bruchfeld and Paul A. Levine, *Om detta må ni berätta: En bok om Förintelsen i Europa 1933–1945* (Stockholm: Regeringskansliet Levande Historia, 1998).
6. The Commision published the following reports: *SOU 1998:96, Naziguldet och Riksbanken* (Stockholm: Fritze, 1998) *SOU 1999:20; Sverige och Judarnas tillgångar, Slutrapport and Bilaga till slutrapport från Kommissionen om judiska tillgångar i Sverige vid tiden för andra världskriget* (Stockholm: Fakta Info Direkt, 1999). The Swedish response to the Holocaust was influenced by the Swiss experience. See, for instance, *Die Schweiz und die Goldtransaktionen im Zweiten Weltkrieg: Zwischenbercht* (Bern: Unabhängige Expertenkommission Schweiz-Zweiter Weltkrieg, 1998).
7. Tony Kushner, *The Holocaust and the Liberal Imagination: A Social and Cultural History* (Oxford: Blackwell, 1994), pp.5, 272.
8. See, for instance, Andreas Suter, 'Neutralität, Prinzip, Praxis und Geschichts-bewusstsein', in Manfred Hettling et al., *Eine kleine Geschichte der Schweiz: Der Bundestaat und seine Traditionen* (Frankfurt a. M: Suhrkamp, 1998); Jacques Picard, *Die Schweiz und die Juden 1933–1945* (Zürich: Chronos, 1994); Rudolf L Bindschedler et al. (eds.), *Schwedische und schweizerische Neutralität im Zweiten Weltkrieg* (Basel: Helbing & Lichtenhahn, 1985).
9. Hans Lindberg, *Svensk flyktingpolitik under internationellt tryck 1936–1941* (Uddevalla: Allmänna Förlaget, 1973); Steven Koblik, *Om vi teg skulle stenarna ropa: Om Sverige och judeproblemet 1933–1945* (Stockholm: Nordstedt, 1987).
10. Kushner, *The Holocaust and the Liberal Imagination*, pp.16, 273.
11. Ibid., p.17.
12. Riksdagens Protokoll AK 1939:12, p.37.
13. Ibid. See also Utrikesdepartementets arkiv. UD:s tidningsklipp serie 3, Vol. 64, 400. *Riksarkivet (RA)* (National Archive), Stockholm. Among the newspapers which maintained a manifestly negative attitude towards Jewish immigration, often describing it in terms of an invasion or a flood, were *Hallands Nyheter, Aftonbladet, Norrköpings Tidningar, Nya Dagligt Allehanda, Stockholms Dagblad, Stockholmstidningen, Skanska Dagbladet, Sydsvenska Dagbladet* and *Östgöta Correspondenten.*
14. Lindberg, *Svensk flyktingpolitik under internationellt tryck*, p.217. Most were from Germany and Austria, a few from Czechoslovakia. According to a 1941 German report, there were 5,889 Jewish refugees in Scandinavia, of whom 2,134 had gone to Sweden (1,329 Germans, 725 Austrians and 80 former Czech citizens). See Dokumentationsarchiv des österreishischen Widerstands.Nr 2773. Berichte der Israellitischen Kultusgemeinde Wien an die Reichsvereinigung der Juden in Deutschland. Berichte der beiden Stellen an das RSHA vom 14. November 1941. Auswandering der Juden.II Gliederung der Europa-Wanderung nach ländern. This was one of the statistical reports used at the Wannsee conference.
15. SOU 1946:36, p.32; Another source is Sven Skogh, *Arbetets Marknad* (Stockholm: Almqvist & Wicksell, 1963), p.94. He writes that at the outbreak of the Second World War, there were 24,000 foreign citizens, of whom approximately half had received labour and residence permits.
16. Michael M. Marrus, *The Unwanted: European Refugees in the 20th Century* (New York:

Oxford University Press, 1985), pp.263–5.

17. Tomas Hammar, *Sverige åt svenskarna. Invandringspolitik, utlänningskontroll och asylrätt 1900-1932* (Stockholm: 1964), pp.210–16. To ensure that all economic immigrants were furnished with labour permits when they arrived in the country, they were ordered to report to the police authorities. The Aliens Act also contained rules concerning refusals of entry to aliens, expulsion and deportation.

18. Ibid., p.226.

19. Skogh, *Arbetets Marknad*, p.35.

20. Hammar, *Sverige åt svenskarna*, p.333.

21. 'Förslag till revision av främlingslagen', *Sociala Meddelanden* (1937), pp.3–14, 224–5.

22. Jonas Olofsson and Rolf Ohlsson, 'Labour Market Policies in the Inter-war Years: Passive and Active Actions', *Lund papers in Economic History*, No.22 (1993).

23. Roger Axelsson, Karl Gustav Löfgren and Lars-Gunnar Nilsson, *Den svenska arbetsmarknadspolitiken under 1900-talet* (Stockholm: Prisma 1983), p.47.

24. Kerstin Berggren, *De landsflyktiga efter världskriget* (Stockholm: Albert Bonniers Förlag, 1939), pp.68–9. She also mentions other groups of people and aid committees such as the Internationella Foyern and Lunds lokala kommitté för landsflyktiga. One often finds these groups or committees negotiating with employers, unions and authorities concerning employment opportunities for the Jewish refugees. This was the case regarding applications for permission to become self-employed or to start a business. See *Handelsdepartementets konseljhandlingar, Ansökningar om utlänningars rätt att idka handel eller annan näring 1933–1945* and applications for Swedish citizenship, *Justitiedepartementets konseljhandlingar, Ansökningar om svenskt medborgarskap 1940–1945.*

25. *Sociala Meddelanden* (1938), pp.758–9.

26. Socialstyrelsens arkiv. *RA.* Utlänningsbyrån Ser. EIIb Vol. 1. Skrivelser till och från ämbetsverk och myndigheter 1938–1940. Vördsam promemoria rörande eventuell omflyttning av vissa härvarande judiska jordbrukselever. Stockholm, 16 May 1940. Of the 489 *chaluzim* refugees, 109 went to Palestine. In 1941 237 *chaluzim* remained in Sweden.

27. Socialstyrelsens arkiv. RA. Utlänningsbyrån 1938–1940. Ser. E Iib:1. Skrivelser till och från ämbetsverk och myndigheter 1938–1940, Skrivelse från utlänningsbyrån till Centralpasskontoret i Oslo 29 September 1939.

28. Jewish refugees who came to Sweden from Denmark and Norway after 9 April 1940 (the date of the German invasion of those two countries) did not attract much attention. See Statens arbetsmarknadskommissions arkiv. Utlänningssektionen. EVI:b. Inkomna skrivelser från statens utlänningskommission. See also Statens arbetsmarknadskommissions arkiv 1940–1947. Utlänningssektionen FI:5. VPM till Hans Excellens Herr Ministern för Utrikes ärenden.

29. Statens arbetsmarknadskommissions arkiv. Arbetsförmedlingsbyrån. PM ang arbetskraftsproblemet inom industrin 12 January 1943, PM ang arbetsmarkanden 1942–1944.

30. KM:t proposition 1927:198, p.32.

31. Sociala Meddelanden 1936, pp.396, 402; SFS 1937:344, pp.912–16. See also Ingrid Lomfors, *Förlorad barndom återvunnet liv. de judiska flyktingbarnen från Nazityskland* (Göteborg: Historiska Institutionen, 1996), p.19. Lomfors questions whether between 1933 and 1939 the Swedish authorities ever regarded Jews who left Germany for 'racial reasons' as political refugees.

32. See Lindberg, *Svensk flyktingpolitik under internationellt tryck.*, pp.132–51; Koblik, p.63, and Paul A. Levine, *From Indifference to Activism: Swedish Diplomacy and the Holocaust, 1938–1944* (Uppsala: Studia Historica Upsaliensis, 1996), p.107.

33. Alf W. Johansson, 'Den svenska socialdemokratin och fascismen på trettiotalet. Några reflexioner', in *Utrikespolitik och Historia: Studier tillägnade Wilhelm M Carlgren den 6 maj*

*1987* (Stockholm: Militärhistoriska Förlaget, 1987), pp. 93, 98.
34. Koblik, *Om vi teg skulle stenarna ropa*, p.64.
35. Levine, *From Indifference to Activism*, pp.64, 92–9. See also Levine, 'Anti-semitism in Sweden's Foreign Office: How Important Was It?', *Historisk Tidskrift*, No.1 (1996).
36. Levine, *From Indifference to Activism*, p.64.
37. H. Friedländer, 'Exil-deportation-räddning', *Judisk Tidskrift*, No.24 (1946), p.384.
38. See T. Hammar and Björn Horgby, *Dom där. Främlingsfientligheten och arbetarkulturen i Norrköping 1890–1960* (Stockholm: Carlsson, 1996).
39. The following trade unions publications were examined for the period 1930–45: *Skogsarbetaren* (1940–45), *Mål och Medel*, *Beklädnadsarbetaren*, *Metallarbetaren*, *Fackföreningsrörelsen*, *Lantarbetaren*, *Musikern*.
40. Kushner, *The Holocaust and the Liberal Imagination*, p.79.
41. J. Painter and C. Philo, 'Spaces of Citizenship: An Introduction', *Political Geography*, No.2 (1995), pp.112–13.
42. Georg Simmel, *Hur är samhället möjligt? och andra essäer* (Göteborg: Korpen, 1981), p.198.
43. Riksdagens Protokoll FK 1939:12, p.34. Vocational training for refugees began in 1933.
44. Riksdagens Protokoll AK 1939:12, p.19.
45. Riksdagens Protokoll FK 1939:12, p.21.
46. A. and G. Myrdal, *Kris i befolkningsfrågan* (Stockholm: Bonniers, 1934), p.106.
47. Riksdagens Protokoll. Motion FK 1938:55; Andra lagutskottets utlåtande 1938:39.
48. A. and G. Myrdal, *Kris i befolkningsfrågan*, p.110.
49. Riksdagens Protokoll. FK 1939:12, p.38; AK 1939:12, p.28.
50. Kushner, *The Holocaust and the Liberal Imagination*, pp.74–5, 87–8.
51. Hans Uwe Petersen, 'De nordiske lande og Hitler-flygtningene. Internordiskt samarbejde i flygtningesorgsmålet 1933–1939', in Rune Johansson and Hans Åke Persson (eds.), *Nordisk flyktingpolitik i världskrigens epok* (Lund: Lund UP, 1989), p.43.
52. *Musikern*, November 1937.
53. Musikerförbundets arkiv. Avgående och ankommande skrivelser 1934. Berättelse över Svenska Musikerförbundets verksamhet under år 1933: *Musikern*, 1 April 1935.
54. *Musikern*, 1 Nov. 1937.
55. Ibid., 16 Nov. 1938.
56. Statens Utrymningskommissions arkiv. Flyktinghjälpen 1940–1941, FII:4 Ang. tyska flyktingar; Statens arbetsmarknadskommissions arkiv. Utlänningssektionen 1940–1942, FI:1 Sammanställning över förmedlade arbeten 1 March 1941–30 April 1941, Utlänningssektionen FI, Flyktinghandlingar från krigsåren. PM ang. flyktingarnas arbetsförhållanden i olika delar av landet daterat den 29 January 1945.
57. See Simmel, *Hur är samhället möjligt?* p.150, and for Sweden, *Hammar Sverige åt svenskama 1964* and Hugo Valentin, *Judarna i Sverige* (Stockholm: Bonniers, 1964).
58. See: Hammar, *Sverige åt svenskama 1964*; Lena Berggren, *Nationell upplysning. Drag i den svenska antisemitismens idéhistoria* (Stockholm: Carlsson, 1999). Mattias Tydén, *Svensk antisemitism 1880–1930* (Uppsala: Centre for Multhi-Ethnic Research, 1986); Koblik (1987); Bengt Österman, '785 judar. Sveriges fränaste invandrardebatt för 175 år sedan', *Judisk Krönika*, No.4 (1991).
59. See Erik Dahmén, *Svensk industriell företagarverksamhet, Kausalanalys av den industriella utvecklingen 1919–1939* (Stockholm: Industrins Utredningsinstitut, 1950).
60. Handelsdepartementets konseljhandlingar 1933. RA. Skrivelse till socialdepartementet från Svenska Handelsagenters Förening 21 October 1933; Kommerskollegium Stora Dossierserien Huvudarkivet. RA. F1aa, Vol.952. Similar views can be found in such periodicals as *Industritjänstemannen* (1935, 1938); *Manufakturisterna Tidskrift* (1937–40); *Svenske Småföretagaren* (1939); *Svenskt Affärsliv* (1938–39); *Tidskrift för Handelstjänstemannaförbundet* (1938–39); *Den aktive handelsresanden* (1935, 1939); *Grafisk*

*Faktor Tidning* (1938); *Handelsresanden* (1933–37); and such newspapers as *Aftonbladet*, *Nya Dagligt Allehanda* and *Stockholms Dagblad*.

61. I am referring here to firms which formally were Swedish but in reality were subsidiaries controlled and owned by German interests and capital.

62. Flyktkapitalbyråns arkiv.(FKB) RA. Hemliga arkivet, Vol.7. Utländskt intresse för och inflytande på svenskt näringsliv (Erfarenhet från postgranskningen) Rudberg Agentur, Borås 9 September 1941; Lundberg and Co., 9 September 1941; Mattfabrikernas lager, Göteborg 13 August 1941 till Teppich-und Textilwerke, Adolf in Vogtl.

63. Flyktkapitalbyråns arkiv.(FKB) RA. Hemliga arkivet, Vol.7. Utländskt intresse för och inflytande på svenskt näringsliv, Erfarenhet från postgranskningen, C.B.,22 August 1941, till F:a Edvard Schriever, Dresden.

64. Flyktkapitalbyråns arkiv.(FKB) RA. Hemliga arkivet, Vol.7. Utländskt intresse för och inflytande på svenskt näringsliv; Tyska försök till kontroll av svenska företag som står under judiskt inflytande; PM om iakttagelser vid censurväsendet 15–30 October 1941. See also Flyktkapitalbyråns arkiv, Vol. 376.

65. Flyktkapitalbyråns arkiv.(FKB) RA. Hemliga arkivet, Vol.7. Utländskt intresse för och inflytande på svenskt näringsliv (Erfarenhet från postgranskningen), Deutsche Handelskammer in Schweden, Göteborg, till Berliner Börsenzeitung, Handelsredaktion, Berlin, 11 July 1941; Berg och Nycander till Firma Westmark, Herscheid, 16 June 1941.

66. Flyktkapitalbyråns arkiv.(FKB) RA. Hemliga arkivet, Vol.7. Tyska strävanden i samband med de svensk-tyska handelsrelationerna under 1941. En sammanställning baserad på handelsrapporterna under 1941 samt Informationsavdelningens handelsarkiv.

67. Ibid.

68. Ibid; Flyktkapitalbyråns arkiv.(FKB) RA. Hemliga arkivet, Vol.7. Utländskt intresse för och inflytande på svenskt näringsliv, Erfarenhet från postgranskningen, Wirtschaftsgruppe Holzverarbeitende Industrie to Die Reichsstelle für den Aussenhandel, Berlin 17 June 1941, Bilaga till brev till tyske handelsattachen Behrens, Stockholm.

69. Flyktkapitalbyråns arkiv, Vols.484, 192.

70. Flyktkapitalbyråns arkiv (FKB) RA. Hemliga arkivet, Vol.7, PM över iakttagelser vid censurväsendet gjorda huvudsakligen under tiden 1–15 January 1942.

71. According to the Swedish Ordinance of Freedom of Trade of 1864, which was still valid in the 1930s, every foreign citizen who wished to start a business or to be self-employed was obliged to apply to the government for a permit. The Ministry of Trade and Commerce was in charge of the administrative process for these applications during the inter-war and war years.

72. Handelsdepartementets konseljhandlingar och statsrådsprotokoll 1920–1945, RA, Ansökningar om utlänningars rätt att idka handel eller annan näring i Sverige. Eastern Europeans are equivalent to immigrants coming from Russia, the Baltic states, Poland, Rumania and Bulgaria. Central Europeans are referred to as Czechs, Hungarians and Austrians.

73. Handelsdepartementets konseljhandlingar. RA. Ansökningar om utlänningars rätt att idka handel eller annan näring, 29 January 1943; 28 May 1943; 8 January 1944; 13 July 1945; 7 September 1945.

74. Dahmén, pp.153–5, 273–9.

75. *Nya dagligt Allehanda*, *Stockholms Dagblad*, *Stockholmstidningen*, 20 October 1935.

76. Flyktkapitalbyråns arkiv. RA. Hemliga arkivet, Vol.7. Tyska strävanden i samband med de svensk-tyska handelsrelationerna under 1941.

77. Handelsdepartementets konseljhandlingar. RA. Ansökningar om utlänningars rätt att idka handel eller annan näring, 12 February 1937; 29 April 1938; 9 October 1942; 29 January 1943; 8 January 1944; 23 March 1945, 13 July 1945; 7 September 1945; 19 October 1945.

78. Kushner, *The Holocaust and the Liberal Imagination*, p.233.
79. Handelsdepartementets konseljhandlingar. RA. Ansökningar om utlänningars rätt att idka handel eller annan näring, 25 May 1945.
80. Flyktkapitalbyråns arkiv, Vol.523. See also *Svensk Juristtidning* (1948) pp.469–72.
81. Flyktkapitalbyråns arkiv, Vol.239;
82. Kommitténummer 1073, RA.Vol.3, handlingar ang anmälningar av krav samt olika fordringar. The refugee organisations consisted mainly of German, Czech and Austrian socialist refugees, Jewish and non-Jewish, and those which were still active in Sweden at that time.
83. Sven Nordlund, 'Rapport angående gottgörelse av ariserade företag, patent och varumärken', *SOU 1999:20 Sverige och judarnas tillgångar. Bilaga till slutrapport från Kommissionen om judiska tillgångar i Sverige vid tiden för andra världskriget* (Stockholm: Fakta Info Direkt, 1999)
84. Flyktkapitalbyråns arkiv, Vol.192.
85. Kushner, *The Holocaust and the Liberal Imagination*, p.43.
86. Riksdagens Protokoll 1939:12, p.40.

# A Study of Antisemitic Attitudes within Sweden's Wartime *Utlänningsbyrån*

## KARIN KVIST

### I

One of the many things which create interest in an epoch of history may be the silence which surrounds it. It is easy to be suspicious about such a silence, particularly if one suspects that some sort of silent agreement exists between interested parties. Individual or institutional attitudes about past events might also explain an apparent lack of curiosity in something which appears significant. The silence which sparked my interest concerned some questions raised when considering Sweden's connection with and response to the Holocaust. Of course, some episodes and individuals are well known, such as Raoul Wallenberg's heroic actions in Budapest and the 'White Buses' of the Swedish Red Cross led by Count Folke Bernadotte. Discussions of Swedish neutrality are plentiful but scholarly studies of Sweden and the Holocaust remain limited. What explains this silence among Swedish historians?

One aspect of Sweden's response was its reception and handling of those few refugees allowed into the country before and during the Second World War. This essay will explore some aspects of Sweden's refugee policy by looking at the activities of the *Utlänningsbyrån* (Foreigners' Bureau). This Bureau was one of the primary governmental decision-making bodies regarding the granting and/or refusal of visas and residence permits for refugees. And, while looking at this governmental authority, one central question to be asked is to what degree, if any, the Bureau's decisions were influenced by antisemitism, and – to return to my initial question – whether some continuation of these attitudes has contributed to the silence which has shrouded this aspect of Sweden's response to the Holocaust.[1]

Though the Bureau itself has not been subjected to scholarly investigation, Swedish refugee policy has been examined by a handful of scholars, with two basic interpretations prevailing. Because of its importance in determining Sweden's response to Jews seeking refuge, a closer examination of attitudes prevailing within the *Utlänningsbyrån* should help to answer the question of how important antisemitic attitudes were in determining the nation's response both to the 'refugee crises' of the late 1930s and to information about the increasing persecution and subsequent mass murder of Jews in Germany and elsewhere in Nazi-occupied Europe.

The first relevant study is *Svensk flyktingpolitik under internationellt tryck, 1936–1941* (Swedish Refugee Policy under International Pressure, 1936–1941), Hans Lindberg's doctoral thesis published in 1973. Lindberg argued that Sweden's highly restrictive policy towards Jews fleeing the Third Reich was the result more of fears about the country's labour market, including increased unemployment, than a manifestation of antisemitism.[2] He concluded that expressions of Swedish antisemitism and xenophobia were the consequence of the unemployment of the early 1930s, and that not only Jews but all foreigners were seen as a threat to the labour market.[3] Yet this conclusion was surely influenced by the fact that Lindberg's study ends in 1941. Studies by Steven Koblik, Paul A. Levine and Ingrid Lomfors dispute Lindberg's findings, arguing that antisemitic attitudes were more important than reasoning based on the protection of labour markets.[4] Koblik writes that if protecting the labour market was the primary motive for the construction of the restrictive refugee policy, the debate would have been very different.[5] Levine and Lomfors go even further, arguing that at least until 1942 antisemitism was fundamental to the country's refugee policy.[6]

Lindberg rightly noted that decision-making regarding the admission of refugees was divided between the Foreign Office

(*Utrikesdepartementet*, hereafter *UD*), spread throughout that institution's legations, consulates, domestic passport offices and *Länsstyrelser* (local governing boards). Domestically, the *Utlänningsbyrån*, which administratively remained within the powerful *Socialstyrelsen* (Social Welfare Board), had the primary responsibility for decisions regarding entry visas and work permits – both of which were, of course, decisive for individual refugees and their families. It is these cases – decisions regarding the granting of work and residence permits handled by the *Utlänningsbyrån* – which form the basis of the current study. Additionally, in some special cases even the Parliament (*Riksdagen)* became involved in the decision-making.

Formed in January 1938 as a special division within the *Socialstyrelsen*, which combined elements of the former's *Första byrå* (First Bureau, which handled the activities of foreigners in the country) and the *Statens polisbyrå* (State Police Bureau), the *Utlänningsbyrån* became the highest domestic authority for granting permission to remain in the country. It could also issue refusals for entry (*avvisningar*) and order the expulsion of persons already in the country (*förpassningar)*, which would then be implemented by the police. With the beginning of the war in September 1939, the Bureau's tasks increased considerably. While retaining its original brief, it became responsible for such duties as surveillance, granting residence and work permits, and issuing alien passports and identification certificates. It was also responsible for taking foreigners into custody, sometimes placing them in sealed, cordoned-off areas.

## II

As with all other countries compelled to respond to the 'refugee crises' created by Germany's anti-Jewish policies, Sweden's response passed through several phases. From 1933 to 1938 the number of Jews seeking entry for either residence or transit was limited. As elsewhere in 1938, after the *Anschluss* and *Kristallnacht*, the number of Jews appealing for refuge or transit increased dramatically. As analysed elsewhere, Sweden's general response to the plight of the Jews changed only in the autumn of 1942, when the 'Final Solution' struck Norway.[7] It is in the period between 1938 and 1942, when Jews could still flee and when the need was greatest, that the *Utlänningsbyrån* had its greatest bureaucratic influence.

The government's response during these years was, it seems, based on a number of different, even ambivalent factors. There seems little doubt that throughout the 1930s antisemitic attitudes informed the decisions of some officials. Documentation makes clear that immediately before the *Anschluss*, the *Byrå* based its reasoning on the necessity of 'protecting the country against an abnormal increase [of pressure] against the labour market'.[8] This reasoning resulted in a restrictive policy towards Jewish refugees, yet the prospect of workers from neighbouring Nordic countries supplanting Swedish workers – a sort of limited population movement that was traditionally part of the region's social and diplomatic relations – raised no such concern. Scandinavian workers were thought acceptable to the Swedish population; potential Jewish workers were deemed the opposite. For example, Stockholm's Central Committee for Aid to Refugee proposed to the government that quotas, or groups of refugees (*kontingent*), be granted asylum in Sweden. As seen in the *Socialstyrelsen*'s written response, Sweden had a right to refuse asylum rather than the contrary, that refugees had a right to asylum. In fact, rather than granting admission on the basis of previously agreed quotas, which officials feared would lead to an influx of refugees which might threaten the country's ability to feed itself, they preferred a slow trickle of refugees to 'a torrent' of ever larger groups. This attitude was supported not only by labour groups seeking to protect jobs, but also by the country's Jewish community, which feared that admitting more Jews into the country would result in increased antisemitism.[9]

In Sweden, policy is often implemented at the end of a bureaucratic procedure in which potential or recommended policy (*Remiss*) is passed on by the initiating authority to various departments, governing offices and other authorities, which are then given the chance to comment. Comments, complaints and concurrences (*remissvar*) often play a key role in the formulation of government policy. Importantly, the issue of refugee quotas called for by the above-mentioned Central Committee was returned just days before *Kristallnacht,* and *Utlänningsbyrån* officials raised several objections to the quota idea. Even though *Byrå* officials were well informed of the daily persecution of the Reich's Jewish population, they maintained that Jews were not being compelled to leave and thus could not be classified as 'political refugees'. Reference must be made, they noted, to refugee policy adopted by other countries, to humanitarian considerations, and to the expected pressure of increased requests for entry. The desired restrictive policy towards Jews fleeing Nazi Germany would be harder to maintain if they were labelled 'political refugees' because of previous rulings that 'political refugees' were to be allowed in. In other words, Jews labelled 'political refugees' could not be turned away. On the other hand, Jews persecuted on the basis of their ethnic background were not eligible for the more favourable classification. The *Byrå*'s reasoning was the following:

> Sweden would in practice be a door through which Germany's so-called 'non-Aryans' would seek to flee. But when some states are even less inclined than Sweden to accept German refugees, who have already succeeded in entering another country, the consequence would be that our country would be forced to accept and keep not only those refugees who for different reasons have some connection here, or for other reasons sought to come to our country, but also those looking to use Sweden as a passage to other countries. Such a development would scarcely favour the refugees themselves.[10]

This reasoning reveals several attitudes. Among the most important of these is support for a restrictive policy which the *Socialstyrelsen* sought by referring to the equally restrictive policies of other countries – thus lending credibility to the restrictions. According to this argument, not even those Jews (who in some cases were Zionist pioneers in transit to Palestine) would be helped by temporary refugee. Actually, the *Byrå* feared that even those in transit would stay, defeating their efforts to maintain a restrictive policy. More evidence of the prevailing restrictive policy can be seen in the following months, even after the outrages of *Kristallnacht*, which as elsewhere resulted in increased pressure on Sweden's restrictive policy.[11]

Even for those admitted to Sweden, things were not made easy. The number of refugees in the country began for the first time to be carefully counted, an element of control which was increased with the authorities observing virtually every step taken by the newcomers.[12]

## III

Lindberg argues that the primary reason for Sweden's restrictive refugee policy was a culturally traditional and more general xenophobia rather than specific antisemitism. In fact, the documents of the *Utlänningsbyrån* provide a different picture, and in them we can see the attitudes which underlay the very restrictive refugee policy which characterised Sweden's response to the plight of persecuted Jews in 1938–42.

In an official *Byrå* letter to the government in December 1938, it was asserted that it was now necessary to count foreigners 'for practical reasons' and because of 'strong political worries in the world', by which of course was meant the prevailing tensions in Europe. Although some form of counting had taken place before, race now played a prominent role: 'Ultimately, the foreigner must state if he is of Jewish birth (if both or one of the parents is Jewish) and, if not, if he sees himself as a political refugee.'[13] Now it was important to be able to define Jews by 'race' in order to stop them from entering Sweden, rather than defining them as political refugees, which would increase their chances of admission.

Here we begin to see, whether it was unconscious or not, the adoption by Swedish officials of Nazi terminology and categories. We see evidence of this in the document already referred to regarding *kontingenterna* (quotas or groups). Where before potential refugees were referred to as 'Jews', later in the same document they are labelled 'non-Aryans', terminology borrowed directly from Nazi authorities.[14] The document indicates a clear understanding of the general situation in Germany and Austria. Distinctions made in the Nuremburg Laws of September 1935 are noted and it seems clear that the aim of the German racial laws is to rid the Third Reich of all its Jews.

A further example of this strengthening of antisemitic attitudes can be seen in an undated memo, probably from late 1938 or 1939, in which the *Byrå* argues against a proposed law which seeks to liberalise the definition of a political refugee. Noting that on account of Sweden's geographic location and other circumstances, Swedes are unused to numerous foreigners in their midst and are inclined to be disturbed by them (although hardly those from other Nordic countries), the *Byrå* argues against the proposed liberalisation. The document concludes that 'concerning Jews and other so-called non-Aryans, refugee status does not arise on grounds only of economic difficulties in the country of origin or because of the Nuremburg Laws'.[15]

Thus, in 1938–39, during the months when the need for refuge was greatest, the *Byrå* tightened its definitions of those eligible for political asylum, trying ever harder to keep Jews out while allowing others in. Even in its public reports, the *Byrå* produced statistics showing how few Jews were actually in the country – numbers which hardly constituted the fear 'epidemic'.

## IV

Interestingly, within the *Byrå* during the period from 1938 to 1942 there remained a somewhat uncertain, ambiguous attitude towards allowing more Jews to enter the country, something which might be called a 'third attitude'. There is no evidence of a shift in policy during this period, but rather in the practical handling of the increasing numbers of applications for work and residence permits. The increase in the workload handled by individual officials led to a certain laxness in the application of regulations. The practical outcome of this situation was a certain easing of bureaucratic demands that applicants needed to meet. For instance, whereas previously all applicants had to submit their passports when applying for work and/or residence permits, some officials now wondered if this stipulation might be eased. This was a clear advantage for refugees who did not have passports. It is impossible from the documentation to know which officials sought this easing, but it is clear that their primary motive was to make their own jobs easier.[16]

That the entry door to Sweden might become a little more ajar during this period as a result of the ambivalence within the *Byrå* can be seen in two versions of a bulletin which the *Byrå* sent to the country's most important information outlet, the *Tidningarnas TelegramByrån* (*TT*), and state radio announcing the requirement for all refugees to register for the desired 'foreigners' census'. Surprisingly, an earlier draft contained not only a more precise explanation justifying the need for this census, explaining that the requested count was not, as might be feared by some, a foreshadowing of anti-Jewish laws (none of which existed in Sweden at the time or after for that matter), but for the first time mentioned Swedish Jews in the same context as foreign refugees. This is of particular interest because Swedish Jews (many of them citizens for decades) ostensibly had nothing to fear from the state. However, in the second draft sent to *TT* and the radio, this vague guarantee is replaced by the wording 'meanwhile it should be noted that the raising of this question [the foreigners' census] in these circumstances does not imply that the government will abandon the fundamental principles which have to date been followed regarding policy towards foreigners.'[17] The difference in the drafts indicates not only a discussion within the *Byrå* about the desirability of tightening restrictions both for entry and for work and residence permits, but, as noted, brings for the first time Swedish Jews into a discussion which before dealt only with foreign Jews. The actual significance of this remains unclear, but its mere presence perhaps indicates among some officials a shift in attitudes towards Jews perceptible in several countries in Europe in the years before the war. Thus, immediately prior to the outbreak of the war, there were those within the *Byrå* who sought an easing of restrictions due to the increased work load, while some officials seemed to move towards even greater restrictions, possibly even upon native Swedish Jews.

With regard to his review of Swedish policy during the pre-war period, it seems less likely to be the case that Lindberg's interpretation that restrictions were the result only of a wish 'to protect the Nordic Race and the Swedish labour market'. Rather, I believe that Koblik's argument that antisemitism influenced refugee policy is justified. There seems little doubt that antisemitic attitudes characterised *Utlänningsbyrån* policy and practice. Lomfors goes so far as to argue that refugee policy was influenced directly by Nazi racial policy:

> Swedish refugee policy was antisemitic because it differentiated Jews, generally in a disadvantageous manner; Jewish refugees were refused political asylum, their passports were marked with the 'J' stamp, they were halted at the border, they were allowed in only in limited quotas and their 'racial' background was registered by Swedish authorities on several occasions.[18]

The evidence points to some ambivalence within the *Byrå*, yet in cooperation with refugee policy adopted by the *UD*, the overall direction of Sweden's response to the increasingly difficult situation of the Jews is clear. Refugees in general, and especially Jewish ones, were to be kept out of Sweden. Sweden's doors were to remain closed.

# V

As Koblik and Levine have demonstrated, Sweden's response to Nazi Germany's anti-Jewish policies took a dramatic turn in the autumn of 1942. With the onset of the 'Final Solution' in neighbouring Norway, Sweden could no longer remain indifferent to the plight of the Jews and keep its borders hermetically sealed. The Germans struck in Norway at the end of November, deporting some 800 Norwegian and stateless Jews to their deaths in the gas chambers of Auschwitz–Birkenau. But then and in the following months, approximately 1,000 Jews managed to flee to Sweden.

Significantly, their presence in Sweden – an almost 50 per cent increase in the number of Jewish refugees in Sweden – is scarcely noted in the Byrå's archive. This relative silence is hard to explain since, as we know, the *Byrå*'s tasks were directly connected to the presence of refugees. Perhaps this is because the Jews came in small groups, or perhaps because they were Scandinavians. Yet the reason for the virtual absence of documentation concerning the Jewish refugees from Norway is unknown. Records regarding individual cases exist, but there is no evidence of a general policy within the *Byrå* towards this relatively large group of refugees.[19] The few records remaining which do contain evidence of the prevailing general policy do not specifically mention Jews. For instance, because so many men were serving in the military, there was a shortage of agricultural labourers. The *Byrå* asked the Justice Ministry to waive the requirement that foreign labourers obtain permission to work in bringing in the year's harvest, but there is no specific reference to Jews being an issue.

In general, after the Norwegian episode the *Byrå* seems to have worked for an easing of internal restrictions both to lessen the burden on itself – by seeking to extend the length of time visas were valid – and to make it easier for refugees to work in agriculture and other labour-intensive industries such as timber.[20]

Nonetheless, there were those within the *Byrå* who maintained their suspicions of foreigners. This is apparent in a document dated from August 1943 in which *Byrå* officials commented on a proposed reform of the law regulating the facilities in which some foreigners were detained. The Justice Ministry proposal implied a strengthening of legal protections granted to refugees. *Byrå* officials responded with almost petty suspicion, writing that foreigners had no need to be informed of why they were housed in certain facilities and should not be permitted to have radios, because 'it was even more probable that foreigners would argue, more than Swedes would, about the channel listened to. This would cause quarrels between the internees.'²¹ It is clear that in some cases the presence of foreigners in Sweden still troubled *Byrå* officials.

The *Byrå*'s reaction to the rescue of Denmark's Jews in Sweden in October 1943 is less ambiguous. After that date, Jewish and stateless refugees are no longer differentiated in *Byrå* documents and arguments are no longer made as to *whether* refugees should be rescued and aided but rather *how* they could be helped. Indeed, for the first time *Byrå* officials acknowledge the specific persecution of Jews. In the wake of the arrival of almost 8,000 new refugees, proposals are again made to ease the 'red tape' imposed on refugees – making life easier both for the *Byrå* and the new arrivals.²²

## VI

Interestingly, the increased work load which accompanied the much larger numbers of refugees – Jewish and others – and the change in the manner in which their presence was perceived led to the dissolution of the *Utlänningsbyrån*. At the beginning of July 1944 the *Byrå* ceased to exist and was replaced by the *Utlänningskommissionen* (Foreigners' Commission) which was, importantly, no longer part of the *Socialstyrelsen* but an independent commission which answered directly to Parliament.²³ The reasons given for this apparent change was, according to the newly appointed head of the *Utlänningskommissionen*, Ernst Bexelius, the ever-increasing number of cases which required attention and the change in the nature of the cases. No longer did they deal with issues connected with the labour market but more with domestic security matters involving the police.²⁴

It is clear that by 1944 attitudes towards the reception and treatment of Jews had changed for the better. Swedish officials recognised the special dangers faced by Jews in German-occupied territories. In fact, about six months before the *Byrå* was dissolved, officials commented on a proposed law forbidding what in Swedish is called *rashets*, or incitement to ethnic or racial hatred. This document indicates a genuine shift in attitudes, one which unfortunately was not always mirrored in the *Byrå*'s own policy and actions:

> The proposed legislation in the first case should make it possible to act against antisemitic propaganda. In our country such propaganda has not reached the same intensity and scope as in certain other parts of the world. Yet such virulent tendencies are neither unknown nor missing [in our society]. We have been faced by an international epidemic of a threatening character ... It would have been better if a law of this kind had been proposed several years ago ... antisemitism is a phenomena with a long history which has sometimes been latent and has sometimes flared up. One cannot ignore the fact that a particular attitude towards a certain group of people ... has unfortunately appeared rather natural for some social groups even in our country. A law against racial hatred should be an eye-opener for many, who do not believe themselves evil but have adapted their behaviour and speech on the basis of negative role models.[25]

Remarkably, this document even calls for legal protection for other threatened peoples such as *Zigenare och tattare* (Roma and 'vagrants' or 'travellers'). Yet, as this essay has shown, in the years under consideration the *Byrå* often did not take its own advice, and often dealt with Jews in a manner characterised by xenophobia and antisemitism. Unfortunately, knowledge of widespread persecution did not change their attitudes. For Swedish officials in the *Utlänningsbyrån*, it took evidence of genocide to change their attitudes.

NOTES

1. This essay is based on the author's Master of Arts thesis, 'Svensk flyktingpolitik under andra världskriget: En undersökning av Utlänningsbyråns respons på Förintelsen', *1938–1944* (Swedish Refugee Policy during the Second World War: A Study of the Response of the 'Foreigners' Bureau' to the Holocaust, 1938–1944), unpublished MA thesis (Stockholm University: Department of History, 1999).

2. H. Lindberg, *Svensk flyktingpolitik under internationellt tryck, 1936–1941* (Stockholm, 1973).
3. Ibid., pp.199–201.
4. See the studies by S. Koblik, *The Stones Cry Out: Sweden's Response to the Persecution of the Jews, 1933–1945* (New York, Holocaust Library, 1988), P. A. Levine, *From Indifference to Activism: Swedish Diplomacy and the Holocaust, 1938–1944*, 2nd revised edition (Uppsala: Studia Historica Upsaliensia 178, 1998), and I. Lomfors, *Förlorad barndom – återvunnit liv: De judiska flyktingbarnen från Nazityskland* (Uddevalla: Göteborgs universitet, 1996).
5. Koblik, *The Stones Cry Out*, pp.53–6.
6. Levine, *From Indifference to Activism*, p.92; Lomfors, *Förlorad barndom*, pp.48,77.
7. For a detailed study of the switch in Swedish policy, see Levine, *From Indifference to Activism*, esp. chaps.7 and 8.
8. Socialstyrelsen till Riksdagens först kammares första tillfälliga utskott, Ärende VI: 99, 9 March 1938, *Riksarkivet (RA)*, *Socialstyrelsens arkiv (Socstyr.)*, *Utlänningsbyrån (Utl.byr.)*, B 1:1.
9. Socialstyrelsen till Statsrådet och chefen för Socialdepartementet, VI:274, 28 June 1938, *RA*, *SocStyr.*, *Utl.byr.*, B1:1.
10. *SocStyr.* to Minister of Social Department, VI: 398, 7 Nov. 1938, *RA*, *Socstyr.*, *Utl.byr.*, B 1:1.
11. See, for example, *SocStyr.* to Kungl.Maj:t (Riksdagen), VI:429, 8 Dec. 1938, B 1:1.
12. Letter from *SocStyr.* to Ministry of Defence, VI:417, 3 Dec. 1938, *RA*, *Socstyr.*, *Utl.byr.*, B 1:1.
13. *SocStyr.* to Kungl.Maj:t (Riksdagen), Ibid.
14. See note 10.
15. Internal memorandum, undated, *RA*, *SocStyr.*, *Utl.byr.*, B 2:1.
16. *SocStyr.*, to Kungl.Maj:t, VI:332, 7 Sept. 1938, *RA*, *SocStyr.*, *Utl.byr.*, B 1:1.
17. Kommuniké till TT och radio, 10 Jan. 1939, *RA*, *SocStyr.*, *Utl.byr.*, B 2:1.
18. Lomfors, *Förlorad barndom*, p.77.
19. The number of individual case records in the *Byrå's* archive is approximately 250 for the whole of 1943. But these deal exclusively with such mundane matters as applications for various permissions such as buying property, student issues or requests for exceptions to various rules and laws.
20. *SocStyr.* to Ministry of Justice, VI: 182, 12 March 1943, *RA*, *SocStyr.*, *Utl.byr.* B 1:2.
21. *SocStyr.* to Ministry of Justice, VI: 575 1/2, 31 Aug. 1943, *RA*, *SocStr.*, *Utl.byr.*, B 1:2.
22. Internal minutes, *SocStyr*, 18 Oct. 1943, *RA*, *SocStyr.*, *Utl.byr.*, B 2:1.
23. Sociala meddelanden, #6, 1944, p.487.
24. Ibid., p.557,
25. *SocStyr.* to Ministry of Justice, 15 Dec. 1943, *RA*, *SocStyr.*, *Utl.byr.*, B 1:2.

# Attitudes and Action: Comparing the Responses of Mid-level Bureaucrats to the Holocaust

## PAUL A. LEVINE

## I

It seems safe to say that the less one knows about the Holocaust, the more one praises the United States and United Kingdom (the leading democratic bystanders) for their efforts to defeat Nazi Germany. Conversely, the more one understands the details of Holocaust history, the more one is inclined to severely criticise both nations, and their leaders, for what they did and did not do either to hinder Germany's persecution and murder of the Jews or aid those surviving in occupied Europe. In Sweden, on the other hand, the limited scholarly research which exists about that country's response to the Holocaust has had little impact on issues arising from the nation's far more extensively researched and debated 'neutrality' during the Second World War. And in all three cases, ironically it seems in light of the unprecedented attention paid to the Holocaust during the last decade or so, there remains a persistent and troubling gap between what historians understand about the nature of the event – its almost endless nuances and details – and what even the literate public appears to understand. This gap between history and memory seems especially wide regarding the bystander in Holocaust history.[1]

Moreover, in spite of the dramatic increase during the last two decades of scholarly histories of the 'bystander' during the Holocaust, the judgements and evaluations offered by an earlier generation of historians about the Allies and neutrals still dominate the broader understanding of these issues. For instance, in the latest edition of the widely used but (unfortunately) increasingly outdated text by Michael Marrus, *The Holocaust in History*, the student still reads: 'Writing on bystanders to the Holocaust conveys a persistent and depressing theme – disbelief in reports of mass murder, widespread indifference, and unwillingness to break established patterns to help the Jews – there is a strong tendency in historical writing on bystanders to the Holocaust to condemn, rather than explain.'[2] Such judgements were evident in 1983 when Monty Penkower wrote that '[T]his volume seeks to fathom how and why the nations outside of Hitler's Fortress Europe abdicated moral responsibility and thus became accomplices to history's most monstrous crime.'[3] In 1989 one analyst of Great Britain's response was equally harsh: 'Next to the Germans', wrote William Perl, 'who as the designers of the Final Solution and its executioners are in a category of their own, the British carry the heaviest guilt for that abomination, that collapse of human morality, the Holocaust.'[4] And in Sweden a decade ago, one commentator concluded that 'Sweden was the first country which obtained knowledge about the extermination of the Jews in German concentration camps. But Sweden chose to remain silent ... If Sweden, which was widely known not to have wanted to clash with the Germans, had written the truth about the extermination camps, this information would have gained increased credibility.'[5]

It is germane to point out that while discussions of the other two basic categories of Holocaust historiography – perpetrator and victim– generate direct outrage or feelings of helplessness and pity, discussions of the 'bystander' seem characterised more by ambiguity, controversy and charges of political and moral failure. Discussion of this category of historical actor, by historians and the general public, is usually more about what should have been done than about what *was* done – an obviously problematic situation for the historian. What underlies the controversies surrounding the bystanders? The actions (or lack thereof) of individuals, a structural failure of western civilisation, with the specific failure of democracy in the 1930s and 1940s to respond more forcefully to racist fascism, or, as Tony Kushner has argued so persuasively, is it ultimately a failure of the liberal imagination which causes such controversy?[6] Whatever the final answer may be, accusations of moral failure directed against the democracies, even complicity in the genocide, are, it seems, made even more painful – then and now – because their own citizens – then and now – expected more of their leaders and themselves.

The purpose of this essay is to outline the response to the genocide of the Jews by one 'bystander' nation, Sweden, and briefly compare this response to those of two others: the USA and the UK. This will be done by shedding light on the attitudes and actions of some key individuals. By doing so I hope to gain insight into why and when certain choices were made by some influential 'bystanders' to the Holocaust – choices which sometimes led to lives being saved but more often to innocent lives being lost.

The key question is: why did some officials in Sweden change their attitudes and take different actions that might appear surprising, based on previous attitudes and actions displayed regarding the 'Jewish question' – particularly when others in similar positions in the USA and UK seemed incapable of making a similar shift from established positions? What accounts for what until 1942 was a remarkably similar response to the same set of issues but which became two, even three, different responses to what remained essentially the same problem? A brief answer to this admittedly much larger and more complicated problem may be found by looking at the change in the attitudes and actions of several important officials in the three governments.

Because the two western Allies were fighting Nazi Germany while Sweden was ostensibly neutral during the entire war (in fact non-belligerency more accurately describes its status), such a comparison might appear unjustified. This, however, is not the case. Importantly for our concerns, historians of the Holocaust continue to place them within the same category (although elsewhere I have argued that this is incorrect).[7] Even apart from this factor, the basis for comparison is sufficient. First and foremost, all three were democracies with lengthy and socially valued traditions of either providing shelter for political refugees and/or giving timely humanitarian aid to those exposed to danger and privation. None of them had unblemished records on these issues before the Second World War, but most citizens of these nations considered themselves generous and willing to help others. Although by the late 1930s Sweden was still quite a young democracy, its leaders and population had long considered themselves a democratic, liberal people as did those in the other two states.[8] But perhaps most interesting for the proposed comparison is that until mid-1942 the responses of these three democracies to Germany's anti-Jewish policies remained essentially as it had been since 1933. Their responses were remarkably similar, and worthy of the type of condemnatory judgements cited above. The fate of the Jews remained a matter of indifference to all three governments and any help given was of a highly restrictive, even reluctant nature.

Yet by the end of 1942 these similarities ended. From that point on, the attitude of the government and people of Sweden towards the aid and rescue of some Jews shifted almost 180 degrees in a process I have described as 'from indifference to activism'. For the governments of the USA and UK, another 12 months would pass before their actions diverged. The US established the War Refugee Board, which was committed to the rescue and relief of Europe's remaining Jewish population, while Britain's policies would remain cynically consistent with its earlier (in)actions. Indeed, as the latest study of Britain's response to the Holocaust concludes, 'Since the [British] government did not regard rescue as a British problem, it tried to prevent it from becoming one.'[9]

My basic premise, which is hardly an original one, is that the attitudes of influential officials constitute an important, if not exclusive, element guiding the choices and actions of their governments regarding the murder of Europe's Jews. I believe that locating and discerning attitudes – on both a collective and individual level – is a useful tool in helping us to understand the past. Even given the often sparse nature of the documentation, locating, analysing and understanding with some precision the attitudes of a particular individual at a particular time remains one of the historian's most crucial tasks.[10] As the historian Geoffrey Roberts put it, such an approach 'emphasizes the freedom of individuals to act, the importance of reconstructing what happened from the actor's point of view ... The idea that people do things for a reason, that their individual and collective actions are the stuff of history and that it is possible to construct an evidence-based account of why past actors acted as they did is, for most of us, plain common sense.'[11]

Moreover, in a democracy attitudes can be, and often are, shaped by the diverse types of information available to individual actors, who in turn are also influenced by their own social, ideological and even institutional background and allegiance. Indeed, it is this connection between information and attitudes within a democratic polity which lies at the heart of the controversies related to understanding the bystander in Holocaust history and historiography. Furthermore, because research has demonstrated that the three governments served populations which had access to most if not all of the relevant information, the attitudes and responses of the literate and voting public tell us something about these societies too. Whether or not active members of these societies did or did not pressure officials dealing with issues related to the murder tells us something about such individuals.

## II

Antisemitism is, of course, the primary attitude under consideration, and its impact or absence plays a central role in most discussions on the bystander during the Holocaust. When American, British or Swedish officials made decisions unfavourable or even hostile to the plight of the Jews, were they motivated by a distinct antipathy towards them, or perhaps just a vague feeling of apathetic indifference, alienation, or 'otherness'? Did generally existing humanitarian concerns towards some ethnic or national groups narrow or diminish when Jews were involved? As we know, the evidence is not encouraging.

For instance, in the case of Sweden, it seemed to be self-evident that shelter should and could be provided for 70,000 Finnish children during the war's most precarious (for Sweden) period. Yet even a theoretical decision to bring some 20,000 Jewish children from Poland (two years later, after it seemed clear that Germany would eventually lose the war) took months for government officials to discuss – and then it was finally rejected. Why in 1942 was help to the people of Greece – help offered by both Great Britain and Sweden – deemed an acceptable violation of the continental blockade, when at that time and later such aid was deemed dangerous assistance to the enemy when Jews were the intended recipients? And though it is important to keep in mind Tony Kushner's warning that 'attempts to correlate directly levels of antisemitism with help offered to the Jews are fraught with danger … and are among the most controversial in the continuing debate', determining the existence and impact of antisemitism in studies of the bystander remains, however difficult, central to our concerns.[12]

I have argued elsewhere that at the height of the 'refugee crises' created by Nazi Germany's assault on its Jewish population, some key officials in Sweden's Foreign Office (*Utrikesdepartementet*, hereafter *UD*) displayed clear antisemitic attitudes, and that the government's response to the crisis was marked by policy shaped by such attitudes.[13] In agreement with several other scholars I also showed that the key individual in the construction of that policy was *Utrikesråd* (Under-Secretary) Gösta Engzell. Several years later there are no reasons to call these conclusions into question. Much less clear, however, is whether this particular individual can be labelled an antisemite. And it is through looking at him that we will see the crucial interplay between attitudes, information and choices which were not duplicated by American and British officials holding similar positions to Engzell.

Appointed head of the *UD*'s legal division (the division in charge of all visa and immigration issues) in early 1938, Gösta Engzell was a lifelong, almost archetypical Swedish diplomat, by all accounts a mainstream product of the early twentieth-century Swedish Lutheran bourgeoisie. His cultural and social attitudes towards Jews most likely resembled those of most other Swedes at the time. Tolerance had come late to Sweden and not until the latter part of the nineteenth century was the country's small, native Jewish population (approximately 6,000 by the 1930s) moving towards general acceptance and cultural assimilation. Swedes were characterised by a mild if noticeable xenophobia and nativism. Regarding Jews, these tendencies seem to appear early and often. Though antisemitism never became a significant political force in Sweden during the first decades of the twentieth century, as it did in so many other countries in Europe, there is little disagreement among scholars that most Swedes maintained a distinct antipathy towards people and things Jewish. Antisemitic remarks were frequently heard in parliamentary debates, and the country's Lutheran social, political, business and military elites seldom permitted Jews into their ranks. One scholar of the period has concluded that 'there seems little doubt that a widespread, almost intuitive antisemitism existed, especially among well-educated, upper-class Swedes.'[14] Louise London's conclusion that 'moderate indulgence in social anti-Jewish prejudice was so widespread as to be unremarkable' is certainly true for Sweden too.[15] Racial–biological ideas found favour not only within the government, which in 1922 financed Europe's first 'state' institution at Uppsala University to 'research' the subject, but throughout much of society. And though the country's dominant Social Democratic party managed to limit the growth of political Nazism, Sweden did not lack prominent, outspoken admirers of Hitler and German antisemitism. In fact, there is little question that many of the negative attitudes towards Jews which made up Nazism's political programme were shared on a cultural and ideological level by a substantial portion of those in the socio-economic groups from which government officials, policy-makers and other elites were drawn. Gösta Engzell came from this background.

As noted above, Sweden's response to the 'refugee crisis' of the 1930s was similar to that of the US and UK. The bureaucratic barriers raised were formidable and few Jewish refugees were let into or even through the country. Those who did manage to enter faced discrimination and difficulties, and, sadly, Sweden's well established and assimilated Jewish population embraced neither ideas nor efforts to help as many Jews fleeing the Third Reich as they might have. Indeed, even taking into account Sweden's small population (just over 6 million in a sparsely populated country), the presence in 1939 of just some 2,000 Jewish refugees indicates how successful the government was at keeping them out. Even though Sweden was easy to reach for travellers from Germany, and even though the country gave aid to many so-called 'political' refugees fleeing the terror of the Gestapo, by the beginning of the war even tiny Luxembourg had admitted as many Jews as Sweden.[16]

Engzell was central to the formulation of Sweden's response to the refugee crisis, and when we look at the language he used at several important junctures, we find evidence of some if not all of the anti-Jewish prejudices which were common coin in Europe at the time. Engzell spoke for his country at the Evian conference of July 1938. In his speech to the plenum on 10 July, he said that the issues at hand were not only those of the Jews fleeing Nazi Germany, but that 'the problem [is] European Jewish emigration as a whole.'[17] Even though the evidence that the Jews of most other European countries sought to emigrate during those years is scanty, Engzell appears to have anticipated that Europe would have less problems were it emptied of its Jews.

It is not widely known that the infamous large red 'J' stamped into the passports of German and Austrian Jews after the *Anschluss* was the result not only of Swiss diplomatic efforts to keep Jews out. At the same time, Swedish officials lobbied their German counterparts for such a measure, working hard to erect more bureaucratic barriers against the Jews' entry into, or transit through, the country. Officials in Engzell's Legal Division negotiated with Germany's *Auswärtiges Amt* on this issue, even though they knew that such measures violated their own law and traditional humanitarian norms. Like the Swiss, they sought some measure which would, according to Engzell's chief aide, 'open the possibility of controlling Jewish immigration without resorting to a general visa requirement',[18] making it easier either to keep Jews from obtaining an entry visa or to stop them at the border if they made it that far. Instructing Sweden's minister (ambassador) in Berlin, Engzell wrote that 'We imagine a system in which normal, desirable travellers will ... be able to go through border control. "Non-desirables" should in advance obtain a visa, otherwise they risk being turned away.'[19] And since Engzell had already issued instructions making it almost impossible for Jews to obtain a visa while still in Germany, this 'Catch-22' situation virtually ensured that no Jew would find refuge in Sweden. Furthermore, he regarded it as certain that even those who made it to the border would be turned away. He was led to understand that Sweden's border guards were 'quite good at recognizing "non-desirables"'.[20]

Perhaps the most egregious example of Engzell's tendency to 'buy' into antisemitic ideas can be seen in his extensive correspondence with an important Swedish diplomat who clearly was an antisemite, Minister Folke Malmar. In a lengthy exchange of correspondence in late 1938 and early 1939, the minister in Prague sought assurances that Sweden, even when faced by the increasing pressures and tensions of the prevailing political situation, would not open its doors to Jews seeking shelter. Engzell assured Malmar that he was aware of the difficulties officials had in dealing with people who either appealed themselves for help or had representatives do so. There are 'all sorts of people, refugee sympathizers and others, which naturally makes it difficult to take sober decisions on the matter.'[21] Malmar expressed his fears in blatantly antisemitic terms, while Engzell's responses, although not employing the same language, sought to reassure him that 'Naturally [we are] very restrictive concerning Jewish emigrants, and [we are] very conscious about the danger of growing antisemitism and have certainly seen small signs of it already.' At this time, Engzell's attitudes and actions became manifest in a policy which aimed at keeping Jews out of the country – solely because they were Jews. These efforts were successful. The general sentiment was, and Engzell seems not to have believed differently, that Jews not only had nothing positive to offer Sweden, but that their increased presence would only make an increasingly tenuous situation even more difficult. Interestingly enough, Engzell also indicated an awareness that there was a humanitarian problem which needed to be addressed – although at that time he could not see how Sweden might help to solve it, nor, importantly, did he (like most other Swedish officials) see the prevailing situation as particularly problematic for the Jews. It is important to note that while Engzell supported Malmar's anti-Jewish sentiments, he neither repeated them in his correspondence nor added any defamatory comments of his own. His language, while indicating a general distrust of, and unwillingness to help Jews, was neither inflammatory nor exceptional for the time.

Answering the question 'who knew what when?' is central to our concerns, as well as to understanding the role of the bystander in Holocaust history. Recently, Richard Breitman has demonstrated that the British authorities obtained a significant amount of credible information on the Germans' fateful switch from persecution to mass murder during the second half of 1941.[22] There is no evidence that the British shared such sensitive information with the neutral Swedes. Yet while they did not have the cryptographic skills of the British, officials in Stockholm had many other sources – some of them almost as direct. From the beginning of the war until late 1942, Engzell and *UD* were extraordinarily well informed of the Jews' worsening situation in the Third Reich, occupied Poland and throughout much of Europe as Germany swallowed up the Continent and tormented the Jews of one country after another. Space does not permit a full review of the voluminous, accurate and timely information increasingly available to Engzell and other Swedish diplomats in the war's early years, but we may conclude that from September 1939 until the autumn of 1942, few people in Europe or North America were better informed about the terrible details of the Nazis' assault on the Jews than Engzell. Detailed diplomatic reports, newspaper articles by Swedish journalists travelling throughout occupied Europe, and accounts of military attachés, clergy and businessmen all provided accurate and terrifying information on the growing situation of deportation, ghettoisation and murder.

For instance, because of Sweden's role as a protective power for the exiled Dutch government, Engzell received official German accounts of the 'demise' of hundreds of Dutch Jews deported to Mauthausen concentration camp. During this period Swedish diplomats and journalists reported the very first deportations from Berlin and elsewhere in Germany to the ghetto at Łodz and elsewhere in Poland. Deportations from France 'in sealed cattle cars under extraordinarily revolting conditions' were reported to Stockholm by Swedish diplomats.[23] The relatively uncensored Swedish press carried detailed reports of depredations and killings in the Baltic states and the disappearance of Jews from countries such as France and Croatia. Yet perhaps two of the most interesting items of information about the sufferings of the Jews came to Engzell from both private and internal sources – information not available to the public.

The chance meeting in early August 1942 on a night train from Warsaw to Berlin between the SS officer Kurt Gerstein and the Swedish diplomat Göran von Otter is well known. In their almost eight-hour conversation, Gerstein gave the neutral diplomat a detailed account of the murder of hundreds of Jews in gas chambers which he had personally just witnessed at Bełzec extermination camp. For reasons impossible to ascertain, von Otter never wrote a report – as standard procedure dictated he should – about this meeting. Some historians have maintained that this was a deliberate attempt by some Swedish diplomats to prevent information damaging to Germany's reputation from reaching either Stockholm itself or (as Gerstein intended) the Allied governments in London and Washington.[24] Yet while it is true that the information was not passed on to the Allies, there is every reason to believe that on a visit to Stockholm a couple of weeks later, von Otter told Engzell and others of this shocking encounter. There is no reason to conclude that this information did not enter Engzell's framework of information and reference.[25]

Less well known is a meeting Engzell had with a Latvian Jew, one of the few who after September 1939 had managed to enter Sweden and stay there. On 7 September 1942, about a month after the meeting on the train, Hillel Storch visited Engzell in the latter's office. Describing Storch as 'a Jewish businessman here as a refugee from Riga', Engzell was told terrible things which he immediately included in a report he wrote about the visit. Storch had 'learned of the incredible atrocities and suffering to which the Latvian Jews had been exposed. Families which were deported were separated, with men sent in another direction than wives and children ... Storch's mother, in-laws and some others were probably in the ghetto in Riga, and if they were still alive they were enduring very bad conditions.' (Among other things, Storch stated that, according to what he had heard, about 50 Jews had been gassed to death).[26]

What is most important in understanding Engzell's attitudes at this time is the following. Even though for the Swede Storch was surely a somewhat suspicious source, and even though the details of the Gerstein encounter seem never to have been written down, both 'testimonies' added crucial details to the information framework of a man who had other credible sources stating much the same thing. Perhaps most importantly, even though there were political reasons for Engzell to discount the various items of information and sources (such as his contemporaries in Washington and London often did), Engzell seems to have been inclined to believe that what the Germans were doing to the Jews on the Continent was terrible, unprecedented and now, for him, confirmed. Indeed, years later he told two separate interviewers that by the late summer of 1942 he and other *UD* officials were convinced of the Germans' policy of extermination. Critically, in addition to possessing large amounts of credible information (again, as did his counterparts in the American and British governments), Engzell *believed* this information. And, as events were shortly to prove, he was psychologically prepared to allow this information to affect his actions, motivating him to make different choices than he had previously with regard to matters concerning Jews.

This issue of *belief*, the process by which we somehow absorb, internalise and process information so that it becomes part of our thinking, is in some ways key to understanding what officials of the bystander nations did, or did not do. Making a 'leap of imagination' between knowledge and/or information and belief is central to many aspects of our understanding of both the general and specific aspects of Germany's genocidal assault on Europe's Jews – in fact in understanding the scope of its murderous policies throughout much of Europe. Was it possible? Could 'normal' people do such things? Information (then and now) available from a multiplicity of sources hardly seemed (then and now) possible. To know and believe are two different things. Gösta Engzell, the architect of Sweden's pre-war antisemitic refugee policy, seems to have understood the difference, and he allowed his actions to be influenced by the information he received.

## III

Even though substantial information about the Nazis' shift to mass murder after June 1941 was available almost immediately to Engzell, it was not until the Nazi onslaught struck close to home that he reacted. Before news of the 'Final Solution' reached Norway in the autumn of 1942, there is little, if any, evidence of any shift in Engzell's response: the fate of German, Polish, French and Dutch Jews was neither his nor his government's concern. Yet to his profound credit, once he did adopt a new attitude towards the issue of helping Jews, he did not allow Sweden's increasingly positive response to be constrained either geographically or ethnically. With one important exception, from the autumn of 1942 until the end of the war Engzell used his position to effect aid, relief and even the rescue of, eventually, tens of thousands of Jews. Although the actual figure will never been known with precision, it can be credibly estimated that by May 1945 Swedish action on behalf of some Jews throughout Europe – action almost always initiated and/or supported by Engzell and his staff – contributed to the aid and relief of some 30–40,000 Jews.[27] Diplomatic assistance first involved some few individuals, a few families and small groups of Jews. Yet from Oslo to Berlin, in Denmark and Budapest, until the final episode in spring 1945 known as the 'White Buses' of Count Folke Bernadotte, Engzell's new attitude (and that of his institution) eventually made a genuine difference to the lives of thousands. It should, however, be clearly understood that neither Engzell nor *UD* sought, as a matter of policy, to convince the Germans to halt their campaign against Europe's Jewish population. Nor, even if they had sought this, had they any means of doing so. We can now turn to some examples of what Engzell thought and did.

In early October 1942 the first German-inspired action against Jews living in Norway took place with the arrest of all Jews over the age of 14 in Trondheim. When later that month larger-scale round-ups of Jewish men occurred throughout the country, Swedish diplomats in Oslo and Stockholm reacted immediately. Further measures were ordered against the Jews in Norway, measures which reached their tragic culmination on 26 November with the deportation, first by boat to occupied Poland and then to Auschwitz-Birkenau, of 532 men, women and children. Only 21 men from this group survived the war. The deportation was front-page news in most Swedish newspapers, and immediately Swedish diplomats in Oslo and Engzell in Stockholm tried to help those Jews whom the Swedes identified as having familial or other connections with Sweden. *UD* demanded information from Germany regarding the impact of the measures against the few Jews who were Swedes, or who had Swedish relatives who made a claim for them, or some connection with the country, such as business or cultural. They called for the safe return (understood to be almost impossible) or release (more likely) from one of several internment camps that had been set up in Norway. What we see in the following days, weeks and months are efforts by *UD* officials to identify Jews with some connection to Sweden, and to try to help them. Perhaps even more importantly – and in direct contradiction to the policies of restriction and exclusion heretofore practised by Sweden – the government told Germany that Sweden was 'prepared to accept all remaining Jews in Norway should they be subject to removal'.[28]

Why this sudden change in Engzell's attitude – an attitude which, through his instructions to his subordinates in Oslo and soon elsewhere, became policy? Material conditions in Sweden had worsened since the war had begun, yet now – even before the tide of battle in Europe had changed as a result of Stalingrad – the government was opening its doors to more mouths to feed, and those mouths would be Jewish. It must be underscored that this first shift, albeit a major one, in Engzell's attitudes and Sweden's response occurred not in response to news of the tragedy of the infinitely more numerous continental Jewry: it was a response to the tragedy of the tiny population of the fellow Nordic nation Norway. Norwegian Jews were different; they belonged to a *broderfolk* (a fellow people), and were thus part of a common culture and social structure. As such, they had claims on the emotions of Swedish citizens, and therefore claims to whatever help the Swedish government could give, which other European Jews could not have. Importantly, it must also be pointed out that the attempts in Norway to help Jews were not limited to Norwegian citizens. Some German and other 'stateless' Jews who had fled to Norway also received assistance from Swedish diplomats. This trend would continue now that the shift had occurred, for from this point on Sweden's willingness to help Jews would both expand and deepen. And although occasional hesitation about who should be helped is evident in the months to come, Sweden's subsequent response to the destruction of European Jewry would come to be characterised by an increasingly energetic activism.

Soon afterwards a dramatic shift in Engzell's attitudes became manifest. On 22 January 1943 the German Foreign Office notified all Allied, collaborationist and neutral states which had Jewish nationals living outside state boundaries who had been previously exempt from persecution, that such Jews would now be deported eastward if they were not brought back to their country of citizenship. Engzell's response to the German ultimatum, sent to Arvid Richert, Sweden's minister in Berlin, shows how far he had come in responding to the plight of the Jews. Knowing that time was short and that there was no choice but to accept the German ultimatum, Engzell instructed Richert (who was almost always reluctant to help Jews, fearing German anger) that 'we best act while there is time ... We have received word what is meant with regard to Jews. Probably we should count on this meaning at least half-Jews ... *In the meantime, we assume that it is better to save too many rather than too few*'[29] (emphasis added). This remarkable document reflects not only detailed knowledge of some of the bizarre idiosyncrasies of Nazi racial policy (in this instance, the *mischlinge* issue): it clearly reflects a sentiment rare in Europe of the 1930s and 1940s – a willingness to help as many Jews as possible to escape Hitler.

Engzell's role in assisting the rescue of Denmark's Jewish population in October 1943 was swift and positive. About a month before the Gestapo struck in early October, he instructed the legation in Copenhagen to prepare to help Jews, Swedish and others, requesting assistance.[30] Indeed, the radical shift in the attitude of the entire Swedish government can be seen in the text of a radio announcement broadcast to the world on 2 October 1943:

> Several days ago information became available in Sweden that measures were being prepared against Jews in Denmark similar to earlier unlawful actions in Norway and other occupied countries ... Sweden's Minister in Berlin told German officials of the serious consequences such measures will cause in Sweden. Furthermore, the Minister has put forward an invitation from the Swedish government that it is prepared to accept all Danish Jews in Sweden.[31]

For the first time since Hitler had come to power a sovereign state had without reservation offered some persecuted Jews shelter. In fact, beginning with the Norwegian episode, any Jew who made it to the Swedish borders was allowed to enter the country.

Engzell and *UD* were equally active in attempting to assist Hungarian Jews in 1944 – even endorsing some visas for entry into Sweden before Hungary's occupation by its erstwhile German ally in March 1944. Indeed, by this time Jews in Budapest and throughout Europe had heard that neutral Sweden was willing not only to accept Jews who could make it there, but also to provide protective diplomatic documents. And after the occupation (and months before Raoul Wallenberg arrived in the city) it was clear to the Jews in Budapest that possession of papers, of some sort from either Sweden or other neutral governments with representatives in that city had some protective utility. When the country was occupied, and weeks before ghettoisation and deportations began, Engzell did not hesitate to issue instructions to help Jews appealing for Swedish assistance. Immediately after the occupation he instructed Sweden's minister in Budapest, Ivan Danielsson, and First Secretary Per Anger that 'You may in exceptional cases according to your judgement issue provisional passports ... where a close connection to Sweden exists, for example to relatives of Swedish citizens, those who spent much time in Sweden, or some few long-time representatives of Swedish companies.'[32] About a week later he told the legation that 'On request, three-month visas may be issued to all Jews who request assistance through us.'[33] The most sought-after Swedish document was a provisional passport which indicated Swedish citizenship. And although the Swedes were understandably reluctant to issue this document in large numbers, they were fairly liberal in issuing other documents indicating that the bearer had a diplomatic connection to the country and that some protection was assumed. Sometimes these documents helped to protect, sometimes they did not – the individual circumstances of each bearer varied widely. But what they did provide, regardless of their ultimate utility, was a feeling clearly expressed in the following letter to Engzell by a Hungarian Jew living in Sweden, whose parents were trapped in Budapest:

> Allow me to express sincere thanks to *UD* and the Swedish Legation in Budapest for the wholehearted and quick action. One function the protective letter will serve under all circumstances is to lessen worry and provide moral support for my parents. For people who find themselves in such a situation, the feeling of having a European state's support behind them has a significance scarcely less than life itself.[34]

Swedish diplomatic efforts in Budapest (which due to circumstances could not reach into the more immediately threatened countryside) steadily expanded and received an inspirational boost with the arrival on 9 July of Raoul Wallenberg. Instructed and inspired by the precedent set by Engzell, Per Anger and others, Wallenberg strove to help as many Jews as he and his country could. Sometimes they succeeded and sometimes they failed – but at least they tried. It may thus be fairly concluded that since 1938 Engzell and *UD* had shifted their attitude towards helping Jews.

## IV

We have noted that the responses of Sweden, the USA and the UK to the plight of Europe's Jews show striking similarities for some ten years, but, from late 1942 until the end of the war, striking differences. What explains this 'parting of the ways'? Citing the course of the war is insufficient because the British had been at war since September 1939 and the Americans since December 1941, and they fought the same enemy until the conflict was brought to a victorious conclusion. The 'neutral' Swedes might, like the Swiss, have 'played it safe' regarding assistance to the Jews until the outcome of the war was certain. We have seen that they did not, and that the switch in Sweden's response and policy actually came months before the German defeat at Stalingrad.

Leading a nation during the Second World War was of course an enormous undertaking, and there is solid evidence that the leaders of all three nations were never seriously involved in formulating their nation's responses to the Nazis' assault on the Jews. Yet final responsibility for such grave matters exists at executive levels, and the evaluations of the leaders regarding this question are at best ambiguous, at worst highly negative. Some historians have labelled Roosevelt's response to the genocide the 'worse failing of his presidency', while the judgement on Churchill, if somewhat mixed, makes it plain that his involvement was not extensive. Although the documentation makes clear that Swedish Prime Minister Per Albin Hansson was kept closely informed of Engzell's activities (and, of course, had he disapproved, he would have put a stop to them), there is no evidence that the issue, politically or personally, mattered a great deal to him.[35] Historian Richard Breitman has concluded that British Foreign Secretary Anthony Eden carried primary responsibility for the British government's response to the Holocaust, yet notes that the most recent biographical study of Eden sheds little light on his attitudes towards Jews. He also notes that at the top levels of the State Department there were differences over how the USA should respond to the genocide, but we know from several leading studies of the United States and the Holocaust that policy was made at the next level and not at the top.[36]

Why then after 1942 did such mid-level diplomats as Gösta Engzell in Stockholm, Breckinridge Long and R. Borden Reams in the US State Department, and British Foreign Office officials such as Alec W. G. Randall and Richard Law make such varied choices regarding a policy on which there had previously been such convergence? To answer this question fully, clearly requires more space than is available in this article. What is possible here is to look at a couple of key points in time which begin to illuminate these differences (and in fact still some similarities) made by the mid-level bureaucrats who shaped this policy in accordance with their attitudes and to suggest what explains these differences.

It has been argued that the reception of credible information on the expansion of persecution to mass murder of the Jews made the difference for Gösta Engzell. For the Americans and British, the reception of Gerhart Riegner's famous telegram of August 1942 telling of the Nazis' plans had the same function as the Storch interview and the Gerstein encounter had for the Swedes. Engzell, as noted, later said that at about the same time as the telegram reached the West (and there is no evidence that the Swedes were privy to its contents until they were made public in November) he became convinced of the shift in Nazi policy. Importantly, the documentary evidence makes it clear that Engzell chose to pass available information to his diplomatic and political superiors. How did the Allied officials respond to the same basic information? Long and the other responsible American officials made a decidedly different choice on receiving the Riegner telegram – and of course this was not the only information available to them. As the historian David Wyman wrote, 'The recipients, middle level officials in the State Department's Division of European Affairs, dismissed

Riegner's disclosures as totally unbelievable. They were convinced the Jews were being deported for labor purposes. The only disagreement ... was on the question of whether the message should be delivered to Rabbi Wise.'[37] This was not the only attempt by Long and State Department officials to keep information from Wise, knowing of course that he would use it publicly to pressure the government to act on behalf of the Jews.[38] Furthermore, officials in the White House were also reluctant to grant credibility to the telegram and other sources of information, choosing to continue to believe that the deportations were for the purpose of labour in the East and that news of the mass killings had not been confirmed.[39] Finally, Long fought a lengthy bureaucratic battle to keep the information received from being made available to President Roosevelt.[40]

The British of course did not need the Riegner telegram to be made aware of Germany's genocidal policy towards European Jewry. Yet even the possession of considerable and credible information from mid-1941 onwards did not motivate the British government to change its response. At this time, the attitude of the British government was, as Louise London writes, that 'the issue of rescue still hardly figured on the government's agenda. Details of the slaughter of Jews were minuted by officials in the Refugee Department, but did not prompt them to discuss a humanitarian response.' Indeed, according to London, Alec Randall was 'unable or unwilling to acknowledge that the destruction of the Jewish presence in Europe made it necessary to abandon outdated policies.'[41]

Nonetheless, faced with increasing public pressure to do something, the two Allied governments reluctantly decided that, at a minimum, they had to make a public gesture acknowledging awareness of the mass murder and promising punishment of those responsible. And even though both governments were extremely hesitant to be specific about the crimes being committed against the Jews, the evidence was so compelling that they were forced to do so. The now famed declaration of 17 December 1942, read by Foreign Secretary Anthony Eden in the British House of Commons and released simultaneously under the aegis of the nascent United Nations in both Washington and Moscow, does refer specifically to the 'German government's intention to exterminate the Jewish people in Europe' and condemned in unequivocal language 'this bestial policy of cold-blooded extermination'. Ostensibly, the declaration was a turning-point in the democracies' response to the Holocaust. Yet prevailing attitudes were maintained, and little change in policy took place in the wake of the declaration.

One immediate result, however, was the one feared by American and British officials – that they would be confronted by relentless public pressure which would call for them to act on behalf of the Jews. Noted earlier was the reception in Stockholm in January 1943 of the ultimatum regarding the deportation of even Swedish citizens 'eastward'. The Swedish response – Engzell's response – was that it was 'better to save too many than too few'. Moreover, this change occurred in the complete absence of public pressure. The Allies' response in early 1943 to public pressure to help Jews was to agree, with almost predictable reluctance, to convene to discuss the issue. As Richard Law wrote at the time to his American counterparts, 'public opinion in Britain had been rising to such a degree that the British government can no longer remain dead to it.'[42] This pressure led to the infamous 'Bermuda conference', a meeting of mid-level diplomats and experts whose primary goal was, as Alec Randall put it at the time, not to rescue Jews but to deflect growing public pressure for genuine measures to help.[43]

Historians are virtually unanimous in their condemnation of the Bermuda conference, which is not surprising in light of the attitudes of the participants. According to London, the 'consistently negative attitude' prevailing in the Foreign Office's Refugee Department prior to the conference was that 'the rescue of Jews was not a British problem'.[44] Regarding the Americans, David Wyman wrote that 'help for the Jews was not, after all, the objective of the diplomacy at Bermuda. Its purpose was to dampen growing pressures for rescue.'[45] This attitude is made plain by the fact that the State Department official in attendance at the ineffectual but lengthy conference was R. Borden Reams, who in the months before the conference had fought against US participation in the December declaration. Indeed, even though that declaration mentioned the Jews as Germany's primary victim of atrocities, the two delegations agreed in advance that any statement released or action recommended by the conference would not specifically name the Jews.[46] Clearly, such attitudes maintained by the officials who planned and participated in the conference precluded any substantive action to help Jews. The conference was, as Richard Law admitted years later, 'a conflict of self-justification – a façade for inaction. We said the results of the conference were confidential, but in fact there were no results that I can recall.'[47]

In conclusion, we can again ask: what explains the different responses of the three governments? The men responsible for the creation of their countries' policies all had much the same new and shocking information, some earlier than others. Most if not all recognised that the character of the information morally compelled them at least to re-think previously held positions, if not 'to abandon outdated policies'. Yet the Americans and British – who might have been expected to use the information about the mass murder at least for propaganda purposes – continued to resist almost completely any change in their attitudes and actions. The diplomatic situation confronting the Americans and British was, of course, considerably different from that which faced Engzell and the Swedes, but in the final analysis these differences fail to explain *why* the Americans chose to help only very late in the war with the establishment of the War Refugee Board, and *why* the British, who resented that move by the Americans, never made that choice at all.

The answer seems to lie in their attitude towards the people under attack by the Nazis – the Jews of Europe. In a still valid conclusion regarding the Americans, David Wyman argued that 'It was not a lack of workable plans that stood in the way of saving many thousands more European Jews – the real obstacle was the absence of a strong desire to rescue Jews.'[48] In the most recent study of Great Britain's response, Louise London concludes that 'Britain's great contribution to saving the Jews was its part in the defeat of Nazi Germany … [yet] Without lengthening the war, Britain could have attempted more, but not a great deal more, to save lives ... [and] weak though the prospects of saving Jewish lives may have been, the will to pursue such prospects was significantly weaker.'[49]

After mid-1942, Gösta Engzell and other Swedish diplomats *chose* to help Jews when they could because they understood that the nature of the crisis made the maintenance of longstanding prejudices and policies morally untenable. These men, thoroughly normal products of their society and nation, directed Sweden's government towards making more positive choices than they had previously done, and more positive than those made by most others in similar circumstances. The sociologist Rainer Baum has defined the moral indifference displayed by so many during the Holocaust as *the* dominating form of moral evil.[50] If this is true, then so is its opposite. Not to remain indifferent in a crisis is a form of good. The attitudes and actions of these men demonstrate with clarity that moral indifference was not the only option available to the democratic 'bystander' during the murder of the Jews of Europe.

## NOTES

1. This raises the vital and often ignored issue of understanding how long it takes for the results of cutting-edge historiography to affect the general public's understanding of a particular issue, something which belongs to our discussions but lies outside the scope of this essay.
2. M. Marrus, *The Holocaust in History* (London: Penguin, 1993), pp.156–7.
3. M.N. Penkower, *The Jews were Expendable: Free World Diplomacy and the Holocaust* (Detroit: Wayne State University Press, 1988), p.vii.
4. William R. Perl, cited in T. Kushner, *The Holocaust and the Liberal Imagination: A Social and Cultural History* (Oxford: Blackwell, 1994), p.1.
5. M.P. Boëthius, *Heder och Samvete: Sverige och andra världskriget* (Stockholm: Norstedts, 1991), pp.81, 87.
6. Kushner, *The Holocaust and the Liberal Imagination*, passim.
7. Using the parameters of categorisation common in bystander historiography, I argue that because of its activist diplomacy on behalf of some European Jews in the latter half of the war, Sweden cannot be classified as a 'bystander' nation. See my doctoral thesis, *From Indifference to Activism: Swedish Diplomacy and the Holocaust, 1938–1944*, 2nd edition (Uppsala: Studia Historica Uppsaliensia 178, 1998).
8. Sweden did not formally become a parliamentary democracy until the second decade of the twentieth century. Yet from its earliest days as a nation which never developed feudalism, through an early seventeenth-century form of 'party'-based democracy, to its four representative estates which late in the nineteenth century evolved into parliamentary democracy, Sweden has never had an authoritarian political system.

Consensual decision-making within elite structures in contact with the populace was and remains fundamental to the political thinking of Swedes.

9.  L. London, *Whitehall and the Jews, 1933–1948* (London: Cambridge University Press, 2000), p.191.

10. It is useful to remind oneself of the exact definition of what might seem such a self-evident word. One middle-quality desk dictionary defines an attitude as a 'state of mind, behaviour or conduct regarding some matter, as indicating opinion or purpose'.

11. G. Roberts, cited in R.J. Evans, *In Defence of History* (London: Granta, 1997), p.137.

12. T. Kushner, 'Rules of the Game: Britain, American and the Holocaust', *Holocaust and Genocide Studies*, No.4 (1990), pp.383, 395.

13. See, in addition to my above cited dissertation, the article 'Anti-Semitism in Sweden's Foreign Office: How Important Was It?', in *Historisk tidskrift*, Vol.1 (1996), pp.8–27.

14. S. Koblik, *The Stones Cry Out: Sweden's Response to the Persecution of the Jews, 1933–1945* (New York: Holocaust Library, 1988), p.47.

15. London, *Whitehall and the Jews*, p.276.

16. The best study of Sweden's 1930s refugee policy remains Hans Lindberg's 1973 dissertation, *Svensk flyktingpolitik under internationellt tryck 1936–1941* (Stockholm: Stockholms universitet, 1973).

17. A verbatim copy of Engzell's speech on 10 July 1938 to the conference's plenum session is located in the YIVO Archives, New York, Joseph Chamberlain Collection, folder #93.

18. Lindberg, *Svensk flyktingpolitik*, p.142. For an account in English of these negotiations, see my *From Indifference*, pp.104–7.

19. Cited in Lindberg, *Svensk flyktingpolitik*, p.137.

20. Ibid., p.138

21. Ibid., p.166.

22. R. Breitman, *Official Secrets: What the Nazis Planned, What the British and Americans Knew* (New York: Hill & Wang, 1998).

23. For details, see Levine, *From Indifference*, pp.113–30.

24. Of interest also, and somewhat indicative of the disinterest in the subject among Swedish historians, is the fact that Professor Wilhelm Carlgren, *UD*'s chief archivist and dean of Swedish diplomatic historians of the Second World War, dismissed the notion that Gerstein actually provided the Swedes with any new information. In a 1985 letter written in answer to a query received from Sweden's then ambassador to Israel, Carlgren states categorically that since no contemporary document existed to which reference could be made, it was impossible that Gerstein had actually provided Sweden with valuable information. See Carlgren's letter to Ambassador Sven Hirdman, 24 July 1985, *RA UD* Hp 21 I.

25. I have discussed this issue in detail in *From Indifference*, pp.127–30.

26. Memorandum by G. Engzell, 7 September 1942, *Riksarkivet*, *Utrikesdepartementet* Hp 21 1049/XI. Interestingly, the sentence about the gassing was made parenthetical by Engzell himself, perhaps indicating a disinclination to believe that specific item of information. This memo and all others relevant to the issue were seen by Sweden's foreign and prime ministers.

27. The iconic figure of 100,000 lives saved by Swedish diplomat Raoul Wallenberg is a considerable exaggeration. Yet there is no doubt that Wallenberg's heroic actions in Budapest from July 1944 to January 1945 greatly increased the numbers of Jews who were aided in one form or other by Swedish diplomacy in that city. Concerning the distortion of Wallenberg's role, see my article, 'The Myth Has Obscured the Reality of His Heroism', *Washington Post*, 7 Jan. 2001.

28. In a telegram almost surely written by Engzell, Swedish Prime Minister Per Albin Hansson instructed the minister in Berlin, Arvid Richert, to make this sweeping but still

secret offer to the German government: Cabinet to Swedish Legation Berlin, #84, 3 Dec. 1942, *RA UD* Hp 21 An 1070/II.

29. Engzell to Minister in Vichy E. Hennings, #35, 26 Jan. 1943, *RA UD* Hp 21 J 1049/XI. The replication of his instructions to Richert in a letter to Sweden's representative in another important European capital makes it clear that Engzell wished that his attitudes to helping Jews affected by the ultimatum should be be widely known.
30. Engzell to von Dardel, #37, 31 Aug. 1943, *RA UD* Hp 21 Ad 1056/I
31. Official government statement, read on Swedish radio at 18:00, 2 Oct. 1943, *RA UD* Hp 21 Ad 1056/II.
32. Cabinet to Budapest Legation, #28, 24 March 1944, *RA UD* Hp 21 Eu 1094/II.
33. Cabinet to Budapest Legation, #45, 31 March 1944, *RA UD* Hp 21 Eu 1094/II.
34. Dr L. Porzolt to *UD*, 25 May 1944, *RA UD* Hp 21 Eu 1095/IV.
35. The most important study of Hansson is Swedish historian Alf W. Johansson's *Per Albin och kriget* (Stockholm: Tiden, 1984). This study makes clear that the genocide of the Jews was simply never an issue for him, although it is equally clear from my study that he was informed of Gösta Engzell's activities at *UD*.
36. See Breitman, *Official Secrets*, p.229, and the studies of, among others, H. Feingold, *The Politics of Rescue: The Roosevelt Administration and the Holocaust, 1938–1945* (New Brunswick, NJ: Rutgers University Press, 1970), D. Wyman, *The Abandonment of the Jews: America and the Holocaust, 1941–1945* (New York: Pantheon, 1984), Penkower, *The Jews were Expendable*, and R. Breitman and A. Kraut, *American Refugee Policy and European Jewry, 1933–1945* (Bloomington: Indiana University Press, 1987).
37. Wyman, *The Abandonment of the Jews*, p.43. Rabbi Steven Wise was an influential leader of the American Jewish community during the war. Those mid-level officials who were in contact with him were quite certain, and perfectly correct, to assume that he would make the information public.
38. Ibid., pp.45, 73–4.
39. Feingold, *The Politics of Rescue*, p.170.
40. It was, of course, this ploy of his which, when discovered by others in the government, quickly led to the founding of the War Refugee Board by Roosevelt in January 1944.
41. London, *Whitehall and the Jews*, pp.201–2.
42. Cited in Finegold, *The Politics of Rescue*, p.191.
43. London, *Whitehall and the Jews*, p.202.
44. Ibid., p.202.
45. Wyman, *The Abandonment of the Jews*, p.122.
46. Ibid., p.113; London, *Whitehall and the Jews*, p.212.
47. A. Morse, *While Six Million Died: A Chronicle of American Apathy* (New York: Discovery Press, 1968), p.63.
48. Wyman, *The Abandonment of the Jews*, p.339.
49. London, *Whitehall and the Jews*, pp.283–4.
50. R. Baum, 'Holocaust: Moral Indifference as the Form of Modern Evil', in A. Rosenberg and G.E. Myers (eds.), *Echoes From the Holocaust: Philosophical Reflections on a Dark Time* (Philadelphia, 1988).

# Folke Bernadotte and the White Buses

## SUNE PERSSON

### I

The well-known Israeli writer Miriam Akavia has written the following:

> 1945. My friend Renia (Rina Fried) remembers: a wagon, a spectre, crammed with the barely living skeletons of women. She is one of them. She is 16 years old. By a miracle she has passed all the selections, by a miracle she is still alive. This train is taking them to death. The women in the wagons are completely resigned. Suddenly, halt! Someone has stopped the train. The emaciated women know that now the shouts, the beatings with riding crops will come, and right afterwards, death. They are helpless and indifferent.
>
> The sealed doors of the wagons open. But no one attacks them. Nearby, on the sidetracks, stands another train. Normal, clean wagons with seats and windows. Polite, calm people speaking a foreign tongue help them leave the cattle car. They bring food and drink.
>
> 'Vi åker till Sverige.' 'We are going to Sweden', they say to them in their melodious tongue. 'Your enslavement is over' …
>
> At that time I myself was lying on a heap of dying bodies, and beside me my sister Lusia (Lea Shinar). Our mother was also there with us, but she was no longer alive. For her the war ended too late. Englishmen with gas masks on went into that horrible barrack where sickness and death raged. It was a sad liberation.
>
> After a couple of days the German military barracks were converted into a hospital, and disarmed Germans extracted the

living bodies from among the corpses and carried them to the hospital on stretchers. I was as light as a feather. I remember how I regretted that; I wanted so much for it to be hard for them, at least!

Then I wondered: this taking of still-dying people from place to place, is that all they will demand from the Germans now? Why don't they kill them? Meanwhile they worked on meekly like innocent lambs and said that they had known nothing about the genocide and that they themselves were victims of the war. Medical students from Belgium stood over our beds, looked at our deformed bodies, and fright was painted on their faces. British doctors, mainly women in officers' uniforms, distributed medicines and instructions. Representatives of the Swedish Red Cross, headed by Count Folke Bernadotte, collected the weakest, unhealthiest ones and took them into Sweden. We found ourselves with Lusia in Sweden. I was taken on a stretcher and Lusia went on her own power ...

Sweden chose the weakest and sickest. Nothing was demanded of us. They sanitised us ... dressed us, checked us, fed us vitamins and cod liver oil, and sent us to pretty localities, most of us to hospitals. The hospitals were established in former Swedish schools.[1]

The history of Sweden and the Holocaust has been written only recently. The following, very brief, account is based on the only two existing scholarly studies: Steven Koblik's *The Stones Cry Out: Sweden's Response to the Persecution of the Jews, 1933–1945* and Paul A. Levine's *From Indifference to Activism: Swedish Diplomacy and the Holocaust, 1938–44*. Both works are, interestingly, written by Americans, not Swedes. To me, as a Swede and as a political scientist and not a historian, Koblik has a better understanding of Sweden's difficult geopolitical situation during the first years of the Second World War, while Levine's work provides a much more detailed, and thus more incisive, analysis of the decision-making process within the *Utrikesdepartementet* (Swedish Foreign Office, *UD*) in Stockholm.[2]

Sweden's arch-enemy for at least 700 years was Russia, not Germany. No other country, with the exception of Turkey, has fought as many wars against Russia as Sweden. In the sixteenth and seventeenth centuries an aggressive Sweden became the dominant power of northern Europe. That hegemony came to a dramatic end in 1709, when the Swedish army was routed by the Russian army in the battle of Poltava. In a single day, the Swedish army lost more men in fatalities than the combined Allied forces on D-Day in Normandy in 1944. The spectre of 'Poltava' has haunted the Swedes ever since. The Russian threat became even more imminent when, following the Franco–Russian pact of Tilsit in 1807, Russia attacked Sweden. In the long and bloody Russo-Swedish war of 1808–9, the Russian army again decisively defeated the Swedes and forced Sweden to surrender Finland, the eastern part (or roughly one third) of the country. Not surprisingly, the unification and rise of the German Reich in the nineteenth century was seen by most Swedes as a positive development. The aim of Swedish foreign policy from then on was to strive for an overall balance of power between Germans and Russians in eastern Europe, and in particular between the German and Russian fleets in the Baltic. The Bolshevik takeover in Russia in 1917 rendered the Russian/Soviet threat to Sweden even more menacing, especially to her upper and middle classes, who now also feared that Stalinist communism would crush the fledgling democracy in Sweden. The democratic Germany of the Weimar Republic was perceived as the obvious ally to Sweden, not only by anti-Russian conservatives but also by the Liberal and Social Democratic parties that were now dominant in Swedish politics.

Hitler's rise to power in 1933 put Sweden in a terrible dilemma. The hopes for a strong and efficient system of collective security within the League of Nations and/or a determined British–French security counter-weight on the European continent vanished. The Ribbentrop–Molotov pact of 1939, followed by the onset of a new world war, forced Swedes to face the possibility of a new Tilsit agreement between the two, now dominant powers on the Continent, again splitting Europe in half by military force. On 30 November 1939 the Soviet Union attacked Finland. In April 1940 Germany occupied Denmark and Norway. The ropes of the hangmen Hitler and Stalin came ever closer to Sweden, and the decision-makers in Stockholm expected an imminent German attack on Sweden. Militarily, Sweden was very weak in 1939–41. A determined Swedish policy of disarmament since 1925 had been changed in 1936 into a cautious military rearmament, but not until the outbreak of the Second World War did the Swedish government order the intense and continuous rearmament that would make Sweden the military great power of Scandinavia from 1945 up to the 1960s.

Sweden's foreign policy in 1939 was one of neutrality. As is well known, during the early years of the war this neutrality had a decidedly pro-German orientation. Not until the German defeats at El Alamein and Stalingrad in 1942–43 did Swedish policy change into one of evenhandedness, and then develop a strong pro-Western bias in the last years of the war. The Swedish concessions to Germany in 1939–41 have been, and remain, a topic for heated discussions in Sweden. Interestingly, the equally (at least!) obvious concessions to the British and the Americans in 1944–45 are never debated. There are, at least, two obvious reasons for this incongruity. First, the indirect support for the Allied powers in the final years of the war fitted Swedish national interests well *after* the war, with the British and Americans the dominant powers in the Brave New World. Second, there is no doubt that the overwhelming majority of the Swedish people during the Second World War were strongly pro-Western and regarded the policy of neutrality of the early years, with its patent pro-German taint, as probably necessary but also as a dishonour to the country and its people. This fact was perhaps most obvious in my own city, Göteborg, where the most influential daily newspaper, *Göteborgs Handels- och Sjöfarts-Tidning*, waged from 1933 onwards a ferocious campaign against Hitler and Germany. (I well remember how my father and elder brothers hated Nazi Germany and how jubilant they were at the announcement of Hitler's death!)

All this has been said before stating the grim truth about Sweden and the 'Jewish question' before and during the early years of the Second World War: in the vicious struggle for Swedish national survival, the fate of the Jews outside Sweden had a very low priority for Swedish decision-makers. As has been convincingly shown by Koblik and Levine, before 1942 the Swedish authorities were not only indifferent to the fate of European Jewry but sometimes even actively prevented their rescue by, for instance, refusing them entry into Sweden. From 1942 onwards, however, Sweden shifted its line to a determined policy to try to save Jews, *as Jews*, from the Nazi hell. The story of this change of line and of the impressive individuals behind this shift has been told by Koblik and Levine. It is sufficient to point at Sweden's demand in 1942 that all the Jews of Norway should be allowed to cross into Sweden; the Swedish reception, by official government proclamation, of all Jews able to escape from Denmark in 1943; the heroic work by Swedes to save the Jews of Hungary in 1944 as personified by Raoul Wallenberg; and the topic of this paper, the Swedish rescue expedition of 1945: the 'White Buses' operation.

## II

The decision to send a Swedish relief expedition to Germany was formally taken by His Majesty's Government on 2 March 1945.[3] The Swedish government would cover all the costs of the expedition. Formally, it would be a Swedish Red Cross detachment. In reality, it was a Swedish Army Service Corps detachment, with career officers and conscripts who had volunteered for this dangerous task. Since the Swedish army would not be permitted by the Germans to operate on German territory, and since Swedish army personnel were not permitted to work outside Swedish territory, the entire expedition had to operate under the cover of the Swedish Red Cross. The army uniforms were kept, but all military insignia were replaced by Red Cross symbols. All vehicles were painted white (the 'White Buses'), with large Swedish flags and red crosses on the sides and tops so that they should be easily distinguishable, especially from the air, from German military vehicles. Following German protests, the number of personnel was reduced to 250 men and women, divided into five platoons and a headquarters staff. Besides the military units (all men), three male medical doctors and five female nurses were attached to the staff. The expedition had about 75 vehicles at its disposal. The total transport capacity of the detachment was roughly 1,000 persons, for shorter transports (using also trucks) around 1,200 persons. Offers of assistance by the Danish government in the form of vehicles were refused by the Swedes, who officially pointed out that Sweden was already obliged to scale down the capacity of the operation. The leader of the expedition from 1 March to 4 April was Colonel Gottfrid Björck.

The detachment left Sweden on 9–10 March, passed through Denmark, and on 12 March arrived at its base in Germany, Friedrichsruh castle. The castle, owned by the Bismarck family, was near Hamburg and thus close to the German–Danish border. On its way through Denmark, as well as during its subsequent work in Germany, the practical assistance given by the Danish authorities and the Danish Red Cross turned out to be invaluable for the success of the Swedish expedition. Likewise, Norwegians deported to Germany, but under benevolent 'house arrest', and Norwegian priests working in Germany, who had together established a veritable Norwegian intelligence apparatus in that country during the last years of the war, became important sources of information for the Swedes.

The Swedes had been given only one month's leave of absence from military service. Thus, at the beginning of April roughly half of the Swedish detachment had to return to Sweden. Major Sven Frykman became its new leader on 4 April and remained so until 1 May when the last Swedish Red Cross vehicle left Danish territory for Sweden. In the last phases of this Swedish-led expedition, an increasing number of personnel and vehicles were actually Danish and to some extent also belonged to the International Red Cross. On 1 May 1945 Major Frykman was able to report to the Swedish minister in Copenhagen that the relief expedition had fulfilled its instructions from the Swedish government. But during the following months more prisoners were taken out of Germany on Swedish ships and brought directly to Sweden.

The Swedish Red Cross mission was the biggest rescue effort inside Germany during the war.[4] It is not certain exactly how many prisoners from German concentration camps and other types of camps and prisons the Swedish Red Cross expedition was able to rescue between March and May 1945. The standard Swedish National Encyclopedia states, under the heading 'Bernadotte-aktionen', that by the end of the war, the 'White Buses' had carried 21,000 people to Sweden, and, one month later, a further 10,000 survivors. Of these 31,000, roughly 11,000 were Jews. These figures are frequently given. It is difficult, however, to substantiate them on the basis of primary sources. The Swedish Foreign Office files in the Swedish National Archives (*Riksarkivet, RA*) are, as Koblik and Levine have pointed out, difficult to work with. In the archives of the Swedish Red Cross, now transferred to *RA*, there is one summary, randomly found among other very disparate papers, but close to a report dated 11 May by Dr Hans Arnoldsson, the chief doctor during the entire expedition, which gives the total number as 19,839. This figure is corrected to 20,937, and specifies 8,000 Danes and Norwegians, 5,911 Poles, 2,629 French, 1,615 stateless Jews, 1,124 Germans, 632 Belgians, 386 Dutch, 290 Hungarians, 191 Balts, 79 Luxembourgians, 28 Slovaks, 14 British, 9 Americans, 6 Romanians, 5 Finns, 4 Italians, 3 Spaniards, 2 from each of Argentina, China, Serbia and Russia, and 1 from each of Greece, Egypt and Austria. What these numbers represent, however, is not stated on the otherwise blank document. But they are close to the figures given by the Swedish National Encyclopedia and those provided, uncritically, by Koblik.[5]

The white buses transported the liberated prisoners via Danish territory. This might indicate that Danish statistics are more accurate. On the Danish side, Finn Nielsen, Secretary in the Danish Ministry of Social Affairs, was in practical charge of the rescue work. His private papers contain precise figures and the total number of prisoners transported via Denmark to Sweden on 4 May 1945 is given as 17,353, including 530 internees from the Danish concentration camp at Fröslev.[6]

Furthermore, in his memoirs Dr Arnoldsson gives the precise figure of 9,273 'patients' being transferred from Lübeck to Sweden between 23 June and 25 July 1945. He mentions 20 nationalities and 25 stateless persons but gives no specific figures for Jews.[7]

Koblik quotes an estimate by Hillel Storch, the World Jewish Congress (WJC) representative in Stockholm, that the Swedish Red Cross saved approximately 6,500 Jews. He finds this estimate reasonable, accepting a definition that includes only those who were practising Jews or born of two Jewish parents. On 27 May 1945, at a WJC meeting in Stockholm, Storch stated that Sweden had taken in 'at least 5,000 Jews, of whom 4,000 were sick and 1,000 were children.[8] If we accept a wider, Nazi-type, definition of a Jew, and if we add at least a considerable part of those roughly 10,000 prisoners taken in between June and July 1945, we arrive at a total number of Jews rescued by the Swedish Red Cross between April and July 1945 as close to the 10,000–11,000 conventionally given.

## III

In 1945 Count Folke Bernadotte af Wisborg was the Vice-President of the Swedish Red Cross. But its president, Prince Carl (Folke Bernadotte's uncle) was 84 years old, and Folke Bernadotte was very much in actual charge. He was also the Chairman of the Standing Committee of the League of Red Cross Societies, since Sweden was scheduled to host the next International Red Cross Conference in 1942 (in fact, it did not take place until 1948). In that position, he was a leading actor in the International Red Cross Movement. By birth, he had relatives in all the royal houses of Europe. Besides Swedish, he spoke fluent English, French and German. Belonging to the Swedish upper class, he was characterised by a conservative outlook and had many links with Germany. But his principal orientation was towards the Nordic countries and the United States. In 1928 he had married Estelle Manville, the daughter of a wealthy American businessman. Between 1930 and 1931 he had studied banking in New York and Paris. Bernadotte's first public duties on behalf of the Swedish government were all in the United States. During the Second World War, he was mobilised and, as a major in the Swedish army, he was in charge of internees in Sweden as well as the successful exchanges of disabled German, American and British prisoners of war in Göteborg in 1943 and 1944. On visits to the western Allies in February and November 1944 he had met the British Minister of Foreign Affairs, Anthony Eden, as well as the Norwegian government-in-exile, in London, and the Commander-in-Chief of the Allied Expeditionary Forces, General Eisenhower, in Paris. General Eisenhower had expressed gratitude to him for the work he had done on behalf of American internees in Sweden.

In Paris Bernadotte also met Raoul Nordling, the Swedish Consul-General who had been an important mediator between the German occupation authorities and the Allied powers and French patriotic forces. Nordling suggested to Bernadotte that Sweden should send assistance to French internees in Germany, in the first case to the Ravensbrück camp where 20,000 French women were interned. According to Bernadotte's later narrative, Nordling's suggestion was the seed from which Bernadotte's rescue expedition to Germany sprang in 1945.[9]

In Stockholm, another moving force was Niels Christian Ditleff, the Norwegian Minister Plenipotentiary, who had long been working for the rescue of Norwegians from the Nazi concentration camps. Bernadotte and Ditleff were personal friends. On 30 November 1944 Ditleff suggested, in a memorandum to the Swedish government, a Swedish Red Cross rescue expedition to Germany to repatriate Scandinavian prisoners. As a first step, a Swedish Red Cross delegation, headed by Folke Bernadotte, should be sent to Berlin.[10] In further negotiations in Stockholm, the Swedish government and the Swedish Red Cross accepted Ditleff's proposal. On 16 February Bernadotte boarded an aircraft, officially to inspect a small Swedish Red Cross group in Berlin. His real intention was to attempt to open direct negotiations with the Germans in order to intervene on behalf of the Scandinavian prisoners in Germany. His ultimate target was Heinrich Himmler, who was in charge of the vast system of German concentration camps.

In Berlin, Bernadotte met Ernst Kaltenbrunner, the head of the *Reichssicherheitshauptamt* (*RSHA* – Reich Central Security Office),

Walter Schellenberg, the head of the SS Foreign Intelligence Service, and Joachim von Ribbentrop, the Minister of Foreign Affairs. Bernadotte's meeting with Himmler resulted in Himmler's reluctant permission to bring together all Norwegian and Danish camp prisoners in one camp each and to allow Swedish Red Cross personnel into these camps. Himmler flatly refused to allow the Scandinavians to leave Germany for internment in Sweden. But Bernadotte won an important concession: Swedish transport vehicles were now permitted to enter Germany and move within German territory. He met von Ribbentrop and Schellenberg again and was told that Scandinavian prisoners should be transferred to one common camp, Neuengamme, not far from Hamburg and near the Danish border.[11]

Bernadotte visited Germany again between 6 and 20 March and was now able to visit the Swedish headquarters at Friedrichsruh. In the meantime, Kaltenbrunner had tried to sabotage Bernadotte's agreement with Himmler. The man who saved the agreement, according to Bernadotte, was Brigadeführer Schellenberg. On 17 March Bernadotte also visited Felix Kersten, Himmler's personal doctor, at Kersten's estate Hartzwalde and, back in Stockholm, he saw Kersten again on 26 March.[12]

Bernadotte was back in Germany on 28 March. Two days later, on Good Friday, he inspected the Neuengamme camp. He was the first representative of a neutral, humanitarian, organisation to be allowed to inspect a German concentration camp. On 2 April he met Himmler and Schellenberg for four hours. Schellenberg suggested, in Himmler's absence, that Bernadotte discuss with Eisenhower a German surrender on the western front. Bernadotte refused, requesting an initiative from Himmler. Bernadotte again demanded permission for all Danish and Norwegian prisoners to be taken out to Sweden. Himmler again refused. But Himmler now agreed in principle that all Danish and Norwegian women, all sick, and all Danish policemen, some Norwegian civilian internees and some French citizens should be transported to Sweden. Before returning to Sweden on 9 April, Bernadotte again saw Schellenberg, who continued to implore Bernadotte to intervene with Eisenhower for a

German surrender. Now, Schellenberg said, these pleadings were on behalf of Himmler, who himself still felt tied by his loyalty to Hitler.[13]

Finally, in a new shuttle of visits to Germany and Denmark, between 19 and 24 April Bernadotte met Himmler during the late night of 21 April and at the Swedish legation in Lübeck on 24 April. The military situation was now hopeless for the Germans. General Patton had reached Bohemia. The British were approaching Hamburg. The Soviet army had entered the outskirts of Berlin. On 19 April the Germans suddenly ordered the complete evacuation from Neuengamme of all Scandinavian prisoners, who were to be taken at once to Denmark. On 21 April Himmler agreed to allow the transfer of the Scandinavian prisoners, now on their way from Germany to Denmark, to go to Sweden. Likewise, he permitted the Swedish Red Cross to transport all women, of all nationalities, from Ravensbrück. On 24 April Himmler acknowledged that Germany was defeated and that the war must come to an end; if Hitler were not already dead, he would be so in a few days. Himmler declared that he was 'willing to capitulate on the western front in order to enable the western Allies to advance rapidly towards the East. But I am not prepared to capitulate on the eastern front.' Bernadotte agreed, on condition that Denmark and Norway also be included in the surrender. Himmler promised this. Folke Bernadotte – via *UD* – then communicated Himmler's sensational surrender offer to the western Allies. The latter, however, rejected the offer, repeating their demand for an unconditional German surrender on *all* fronts. On 7 May Germany surrendered. The surrender also applied to Germany's entirely intact forces in Denmark and Norway.[14]

## IV

There have been heated debates about Folke Bernadotte and his mission to Germany in 1945, most of them originating from the version he himself presented in his book *Slutet* in June 1945. One controversy concerns the focus on the Swedish aspect of the rescue expedition, downplaying in the first instance the important Danish contribution as well as the Norwegian initiatives and intelligence in Germany. But that is not the topic of this article.

A second, very heated discussion with strong political undercurrents has centred on Felix Kersten. Kersten does not appear in Bernadotte's book. But in his memoirs, which were published in various editions in Swedish, Dutch, German and English, Kersten claimed that from 1943 onwards he, as Himmler's personal doctor, persuaded Himmler to grant numerous concessions to the Nordic countries, beginning with Finland. It was he himself, Kersten maintains, who in 1944–45 pressured Himmler into the concessions the Nazi leader later formally made to Bernadotte. This is not the topic of this article either, but since some of these concessions dealt with the Jews, we will occasionally have to return to Kersten, who is an enigmatic figure in this drama. The remaining part of this article will deal with the contentious issue of Bernadotte's relations with the Jews in 1945, and to what extent he was a 'bystander' to the Holocaust.

In 1948 Folke Bernadotte was appointed United Nations Mediator on Palestine and in that capacity he was assassinated by Jewish terrorists in Jerusalem on 17 September 1948. Well before his assassination, his Jewish opponents began to besmirch him, depicting him as an antisemite. After the assassination, this charge became an important element in the propaganda campaign to vindicate his murder. Bernadotte's assassination was to haunt Israeli governments, in particular the leaders of the organisation responsible for the assassination, the Stern Gang or LEHI (among whom was Yitzhak Shamir).

There has been a softer variant of this criticism, claiming that Bernadotte gave no priority to the rescue of the Jews in 1945, or indeed that he did not wish to rescue any Jews at all. The most important contribution to this line of criticism is the attack by the well-known British historian Hugh Trevor-Roper. In 1947 Trevor-Roper published the international best-seller *The Last Days of Hitler*, parts of which Bernadotte criticised in private letters to the author. In 1953 Trevor-Roper launched a virulent attack on Bernadotte, ascribing to Kersten the entire credit for rescuing the Jews and the

Scandinavians: 'Of Count Bernadotte's activities in these negotiations little needs to be said, for he was simply an agent – "a transport officer, no more," as one of Himmler's associates has since described him.'[15] Trevor-Roper repeated his argument in a foreword to the English version of Kersten's memoirs (1956). Here, he even argued that 'it is important to note that although Bernadotte seems to have been understood by Himmler as using the language of anti-Semitism – which may have been a tactical necessity – there is no reason to suppose that his motive in refusing to take the Jews was anti-Semitic.'[16] Trevor-Roper's article and foreword are remarkable documents since this world-renowned historian uses almost no Swedish sources, has complete confidence in the account given by Kersten (Himmler's personal doctor!), and includes documents which have subsequently been proven to be falsifications, and were most probably fabricated by Kersten himself. But his writings were the reason for the appointment of the Swedish Royal Commission which, in a 'White Book' in 1956, stated that Trevor-Roper's 'presentation is onesidedly pro-Kersten and anti-Bernadotte, that he is often uncritical of his sources and that he not seldom gives wholly incorrect information'.[17]

For a truer picture of these events we must turn to the contemporary, primary sources. But this is not easily done. All Bernadotte's private appointment books, from 1930 to 1948, are in the Folke Bernadotte Private Papers, Vol.1, at *RA*, but those covering the years 1944 and 1945 were for a long time conspicuously missing. They were rediscovered in 1999 in the Swedish Red Cross Archives, locked away but with no key to open them available. There are a further 42 volumes of Bernadotte's papers at *RA*, in the Swedish Red Cross archives, including his private correspondence of 1945. The principal elements of Bernadotte's negotiations with the Germans can also be traced from his own and other reports to the Swedish Foreign Ministry, now in the *UD* Archives at *RA*. But, as Levine has pointed out, the key political actors on the Swedish side during the Second World War have written little or nothing about Swedish strategic reasoning or decision-making. In the prime minister's archive, the Per Albin Hansson Private Papers at *RA*, there is total

silence on the Jewish issue. The foreign minister, Christian Günther, who was in control of the entire White Buses operation, was known as a reluctant writer of position papers. The Christian Günther Private Papers contain nothing on the White Buses episode. The second most important man within *UD*, Under-Secretary Erik Boheman, who had one grandparent who was Jewish, had an enormous library with personal papers, which was burnt to ashes in a fire in 1975.

We know from Koblik's and Levine's research that from 1942 onwards the Swedish foreign ministry was actively working on behalf of the Jews in Europe and that the white buses operation was the culmination of that strategy. And the documentation in the *UD* Archives makes clear that in the first months of 1945 the Swedish foreign ministry was bombarded by pleas for Swedish intervention on behalf of the European Jews, in particular those in the German concentration camps. So was Count Bernadotte, as is evident from his own correspondence. We can therefore take it for granted that Bernadotte, negotiating in 1945 on behalf of the Swedish government, was acutely aware of the desperate situation of the Jews in the concentration camps. Bernadotte also had contacts with leaders of the Jewish community in Stockholm and with Jewish organisations abroad.

When Bernadotte visited London in November 1944 he also met representatives of 'the Jewish Rabbi' and *Aguda Israel* (an organisation of Orthodox Jews). A letter from L. Zelmanovits, the Secretary-General of the WJC's British section, summarised the most important problems discussed with Bernadotte: a) the Protection Passports scheme for Jews introduced by the Swedish government in Hungary which had proved of 'immense value' and should be continued; b) whether the Swedish Red Cross could assist in sending food parcels to Jewish camps in Germany; c) whether the Swedish Red Cross could send a mission to camps for Jewish children in Slovakia; and d) whether the Protection Passports scheme could be extended to Jewish internees in Germany, especially to Theresienstadt with its 30,000–35,000 inmates? In January 1945 Zelmanovits complained that he was still waiting for an answer. On

9 February Bernadotte replied that since his return to Stockholm he had contacted the chief rabbi of Sweden, Marcus Ehrenpreis (also a member of the WJC executive), about the possibility of solving the problems discussed and that he had had a couple of meetings with him. From Bernadotte's diary, one can trace only one meeting with Ehrenpreis (on 28 November) but it is clear that many other appointments have been omitted from the annotations (for instance, Zelmanovits on 8 November).[18] Bernadotte thus shifts the blame for his silence to Ehrenpreis. I do not know how Ehrenpreis handled the proposals from Zelmanovits and Bernadotte.[19]

But Bernadotte was a long-standing friend of Hillel Storch, the World Jewish Congress representative in Stockholm, and relations between Storch and Ehrenpreis were very tense. Significantly, in 1944 Bernadotte gave Storch and the WJC permission to use the Swedish Red Cross as a cover for the sending of food parcels to Jews in Nazi concentration camps. The Swedish Red Cross then put a truck loaded with Red Cross materials (including letters, forms and labels) at the WJC's disposal. According to Storch, 'Bernadotte was very favourably disposed to the cause of the Jews.' Storch, in fact, saw himself as the initiator of the entire Swedish rescue expedition.[20] During these months Bernadotte and Storch met several times.[21]

Thus, on 23 February 1945 Storch forwarded to Bernadotte a telegram from Zelmanovits containing a dramatic appeal from Stephen Wise and Nahum Goldmann:

> In our desperate efforts to save remnants European Jewry directing following appeal to you stop over fife [*sic*] million Jews were killed by Nazis and their satellites during present war stop 50.000 [*sic*] are still under their domination and may die unless in their twelfth hour the world will intervene efficiently stop let Red Cross secure food for Jews in concentration camps and investigate their situation let neutral governments raise strongest protest against German extermination policy let them grant protection to Jews all possible forms and declare willingness to admit Jews from Axis territories in their countries.

Zelmanovits asked Storch to take up the matter immediately with the Swedish authorites and find out what could be done by the Swedish government or the Swedish Red Cross to avert the grave danger to Theresienstadt and other camps.[22] Bernadotte replied immediately, seeing a glimmer of hope for the Jews in German concentration camps in the promised transfer of thousands of Jews to Switzerland. And the Swedish authorities were now also seriously trying to obtain permission to bring 'some' Jews to Sweden. On his previous visit to Berlin, Bernadotte had found the situation going well in this case.[23]

On 13 February the Swedish minister to Germany, Arvid Richert, as instructed by *UD*, had told the German foreign office that Sweden was now prepared to receive Jews interned in Germany, in particular those in Theresienstadt and Bergen-Belsen, explicitly stating that 'this general offer, that I presented, concerned Jews with no restrictions.'[24] But on 12 March *UD* wondered whether Hitler knew about the concessions Himmler had made to Bernadotte and whether, in case Hitler were to hear of it, he would not 'demand compensation as in the case of the Jews'.[25]

By that time, Bernadotte was back in Germany. Before his departure he had seen Storch. The latter now had (unchecked) information that the Germans might be willing to release all remaining Jews and he asked Bernadotte to use his 'extraordinary authority' to advance this cause, as well as to ascertain the fate of the Danish and Norwegian Jews.[26] In Germany, Bernadotte soon noticed that the German figures for the Danes and Norwegians to be transported to Neuengamme were very low, and that the Danish policemen and Norwegian and Danish Jews were omitted. He discussed this with Danish and Norwegian representatives in Germany:

Concerning the Jews, both Norwegians and Danes believed that they [like the Danish policemen] would be very unwilling to be transported to Neuengamme, as they now are treated very well, information that also came as a great surprise to me. In concert with the Danes and the Norwegians it was decided, however, to try to win permission also to have the Jews taken to Neuengamme and in this I have achieved a very positive result. One must predict, however, that the Jews, especially at first, will acquiesce in this arrangement with very little enthusiasm.[27]

On the basis of daily reports from the Swedish legation in Berlin to *UD* we can follow Bernadotte more closely in his negotiations. Now we find the infamous 8 March memorandum of a conversation with Franz Göring, the German SS liaison officer to the Swedish relief expedition, with, among others, Count Bernadotte, Torsten Brandel and Marc Giron, secretaries at the Swedish Berlin legation, present. The first point in the memorandum states: 'Concerning the Jews: most of them have been evacuated from Auschwitz. The Jews should be taken last' ('Judarna böra avhämtas sist'). This memorandum was the focus of a controversial Swedish radio programme by Bosse Lindquist in April 1998 with the self-explanatory title: 'Ta judarna sist!' (Take the Jews last!). It is, however, difficult to ascertain the exact status of this document: is it only a *pro memoriam* with a resumé of the discussions, in this case stating the position of Franz Göring only, or is it a protocol of decisions taken with the Swedes acquiescing in the German demands *vis-à-vis* the Jews? The second interpretation seems far-fetched as it implies that Swedish diplomats (and Bernadotte himself) did accept a high-ranking German SS officer taking part in Swedish decision-making inside a Swedish legation.[28]

But the latter interpretation can be understood in the context of the Danish and Norwegian reservations. On 6 March Bernadotte had met the Danish minister in Berlin, when they also discussed Theresienstadt: 'As the war is now coming closer to Prague, these [people], although they are living particularly well ['ha det särskilt bra'], should also be transferred northwards to Neuengamme. After some discussion, the Danes declared, on direct questioning, that this would be advisable although it would lead to passing discontent. The whole thing ought to be taken up with Kaltenbrunner.'[29] In a meeting with unnamed Norwegian representatives on the following day, it was stated that 371 Jews had been moved from Auschwitz to

Theresienstadt. 'On Bernadotte's direct questioning, the Norwegians expressed their wish that the Jews be brought to Neuengamme. Conditions in Theresienstadt were now not so good as before ['icke längre så bra som tidigare'] and, moreover, were worse for the Norwegians than for the Danes.'[30]

These Swedish reports are corroborated, directly and indirectly, by Danish sources. In the private papers of the two key persons on the Danish side in Germany, Otto Carl Mohr, the Danish minister in Berlin, and Frants Hvass, the head of the Political–Juridical Section of the Danish Ministry for Foreign Affairs, very little is said about the Danish *Jews* in their records of negotiations with Bernadotte and the Germans. On 28 March 1946 Mohr wrote that conditions in Theresienstadt, according to reports by Hvass and Dr Henningsen, were not 'as bad' as rumours had suggested. Theresienstadt, Mohr stated, was not a concentration camp but a village, in which the Jews had a certain freedom of movement and a certain autonomy. In four other relevant Danish documents, little is said about the Danish Jews but a great deal about the Danish policemen.[31]

But on 7 March, over lunch, Kaltenbrunner gave Bernadotte permission to move *all* Scandinavian Jews to Neuengamme.[32] On 20 March, before leaving Germany, Bernadotte gave the Swedish Red Cross detachment the specific order that 'approximately 800 Scandinavian Jews should be transferred to Neuengamme from places that are so far unknown.' In Bernadotte's order of priorities, the Jews did not occupy last place, but second place (next to the Danish policemen) out of five tasks to be accomplished.[33]

More obstacles were to appear. On 24 March an enraged Bernadotte asked the Swedish legation in Berlin to intervene with Schellenberg since no order for the transport of the Scandinavian Jews (or Danish policemen) to Neuengamme had been issued, thus forcing the Swedish detachment to remain idle.[34] Two days later Bernadotte received instructions for his coming negotiations with Himmler. Since this is an important document, I will relate it *in extenso:*

In a meeting yesterday with Under-Secretary Boheman, Count Bernadotte and the undersigned, the following guidelines were drawn up for Count Bernadotte's planned talks with Himmler.

In the first place, permission would once again be asked for the transfer to Sweden of all Danes and Norwegians interned in Germany (Neuengamme). Secondarily, he should: (1) request that Swedish Red Cross personnel be allowed in the whole Neuengamme camp (roughly 50,000 interned); and (2) offer Swedish Red Cross buses for use as transport to the Neuengamme camp, or other suitable camp, of non-Scandinavians interned in Germany. This should chiefly concern 25,000 French women who, in connection with the German retreat from France, were taken to Germany and there placed in a camp.

Today the above has been supplemented with a message to Bernadotte that, provided it should prove appropriate and that *no disadvantage from it could be expected to affect the above assignment, he should ask for the transfer to Sweden of a number of Jews.*[35]

This memorandum is, as far as I know, the sole existing government policy paper on the White Buses operation. Obviously, the leading officers within *UD* and Count Bernadotte agreed on the strategy (on the document it is pencilled 'announced to His Excellency [Günther] who has seen [it]'). The emphasis was still on the rescue of the Scandinavians, but Bernadotte's mandate was extended to non-Scandinavians and to the Jews, although the Jews were the last on the list and their rescue was conditional.

The inclusion of the Jews in the new mandate for Bernadotte was probably attained by the zealous Storch, but also by Kersten. The Swedish minister to Germany on 22 March had sent a message to *UD* that Kersten had received 'the list of [Swedish] Jews' and that he had also been working for other Jews 'with good results, as he believes himself'. Kersten had also sought to convince Himmler to permit the interned Scandinavians to be transferred from Neuengamme to Sweden and found him 'won over to this line of thought whose implementation, however, also required consent from other agencies' – that is, from the Swedish Foreign Ministry and the Swedish Red Cross![36] On 27 March Storch, optimistic as usual, cabled the American Minister of Foreign Affairs, Stettinius, via the World Jewish Congress in New York:

> have 3/3 conferred with Doctor Kersten masseur who Himmler's private doctor 4/3 he departed to Himmler Doctor Kersten has great influence on Himmler stop I am negotiating regarding release and cessation murders and permission better treatment stop 22/3 Kersten returned with letter Himmler and related that Himmler promised consider our desires kindly also prepared release about 10,000 Jews to Sweden or Switzerland I am invited together with Kersten to negotiations with Himmler have been promised free conduct stop Swedish Foreign Office decided permit entrance of the 10,000 Jews also assistance with transport stop Swedish Foreign Office finds my journey important Count Bernadotte who today departed Berlin to negotiate concerning interned 5,000 Danish 3,000 Norwegians will also negotiate regarding our question.[37]

Despite the optimistic forecasts of Storch and Kersten, Bernadotte's long meetings with Himmler and Schellenberg at the beginning of April produced nothing for the Jewish camp inmates. We may surmise that Bernadotte did discuss the 'Jewish question' with Himmler, notwithstanding the complete silence on this topic in his fairly lengthy report. First, the transfer of Jews to Sweden was included in his mandate from *UD*. Second, Kersten had been told by Himmler about 'the talks about the Jewish question, which we have started, [have to] continue with Count Bernadotte, in particular about the Norwegian and Danish Jews.'[38]

## V

In 1942 and 1943 767 Jews were deported to Germany from occupied Norway; the remainder, 925 Jews, escaped to safety in Sweden. Almost all the deported Norwegian Jews were sent to Auschwitz, and most of them were immediately killed. Those who survived Auschwitz were sent on a death march in December 1944 and most of them could not be located by the Swedes and the Norwegians in March–April 1945. Five were traced to Buchenwald and they were placed on the transport list for the white buses, but the SS eliminated these five 'non-Aryans' from the list and they were not taken out. They were sent back to Kleinlager – where they were hidden and saved by fellow German prisoners! Another Norwegian Jew, Robert Savosnick, in Allach camp, hearing over the loudspeaker that all Norwegian prisoners were to report to be taken out by the Swedish expedition, reported to the nearest SS man, was knocked down, carried away unconscious and only later rescued by the Americans. Only 28 Norwegian Jews survived the German concentration camps and of those only three were saved by the white buses.[39]

In an attempt to rescue the Danish and Norwegian Jews, the Swedish relief expedition focused on Theresienstadt. All deported Danish Jews had been brought there, totalling 456 men and women (Levine, p. 229, says that 477 were deported). The white buses, all of them Swedish but with attached Danish ambulances and led by the Swedish Captain Harald Folke, began on 12 April to take out the around 450 Danish and Norwegian Jews reported to be in Theresienstadt. The Allied military fronts were now closing in rapidly and the transport was effected at the very last moment. On 15 April the Swedish and Danish vehicles left Theresienstadt with 423 Jewish passengers. No Norwegian Jews were found. And of the Danish Jews, 5 had earlier been sent back home, while the remaining 28 were dead. On the way back, the buses could still use the Dresden–Berlin autobahn, with a distance to the Soviet front of only 10 to 15 kilometers. At Potsdam the transport column was very close to the western front but on 16 April it reached Lübeck safely, with the loss of only one motorcycle orderly, who was later located.

On 11 April Hillel Storch had asked Bernadotte for information about the fate of the Danish and Norwegian Jews as well as the Jews interned in Bergen-Belsen. He also asked whether Bernadotte had received promises from Himmler about improving the treatment of the Jews and the non-evacuation of Jews from concentration camps close to the fronts. He referred to a letter from Kersten stating that Jews at Bergen-Belsen should not be evacuated. Bernadotte answered on 17 April that 423 Jews, being all the Scandinavian Jews located at Theresienstadt and nearby camps, had been saved and were expected to arrive in Sweden the following day. Also, in his negotiations with Himmler, it had been 'clear' that concentration camps for Jews in Germany should not be evacuated but left intact for the Allied military authorities; this explicitly included Theresienstadt, Bergen-Belsen and Buchenwald. Bernadotte was also able to hand over a letter from Himmler's adjutant Brandt stating that Himmler had appointed 'a special commissar' for Bergen-Belsen, 'who had been given careful guidelines by him [Himmler]'.[40]

The liberation of the Scandinavian Jews from Theresienstadt was a magnificent exploit and, like all such feats, it has many fathers. Franz Göring, the SS liaison officer, gives the primary credit to Schellenberg and the secondary credit to Kersten.[41] In 1984 a Dane, Dr Johannes Holm, published a book, *Sandheden om de hvide busser* (The Truth about the White Buses) in which he gave an account of the Danish contribution to the expedition, which in its last phase was considerable and which, no doubt, had been largely neglected in Sweden. In March 1945 Holm was attached to the Swedish Red Cross expedition as a representative for the Danish foreign ministry. Holm states that Bernadotte, due to resistance from the *Reichssicherheitshauptamt* (under Kaltenbrunner), had promised Schellenberg he would drop the transfer of the Danish Jews from Theresienstadt, since any such attempt might have a negative impact on the chances of transports of other Scandinavian prisoners. But, according to Holm, the Danes insisted on rescuing the Danish Jews and planned a wholly Danish expedition to Theresienstadt. The rescue expedition was then delayed until after the departure of Bernadotte for Stockholm and, with the agreement of Major Frykman, it became Swedish-led under Captain Folke. Furthermore, at the *Reichssicherheitshauptamt* in Berlin it was Holm who by various means obtained the necessary permit to take out the Danish Jews from the Protektorat Böhmen-Mähren.[42]

Holm's book is a plea for recognition of his own claims but also a plea for recognition of the Danish contribution to the operation. It is based, he says in the foreword (p.13), on his reports from February 1945 before leaving for Germany and memoranda he dictated immediately after the war. His attack on Bernadotte is somewhat strange since earlier in the book he stated that Bernadotte had 'communicated that Sweden would willingly take in the Danish Jews' ('gerne tog imod de danske jöder', p.113). Copies of Holm's reports (but not the originals!) are in Finn Nielsen's Private Papers at the Danish National Archives (*Rigsarkivet*) in Copenhagen. However, in Holm's 1945 report none of the accusations against Bernadotte are to be found! On the contrary, Holm states that Mr Hvass raised the question of the Danish Jews with Dr Rennau (a German liaision officer) and Count Bernadotte and 'both made their greatest efforts'.[43]

I surmise that in 1984, Holm, in order to embellish his own (and perhaps the Danish) cause, invented anti-Bernadotte arguments that did not exist in 1945. This conclusion is corroborated by Swedish primary sources on the Theresienstadt expedition. On 7 April (before Bernadotte's departure on 9 April), (the Swedish) Captain Folke reported to Stockholm that most Jews were probably still in Theresienstadt and that 'they should be taken out some time next week.' Then we have a list of planned (Swedish) transports, between 7 and 10 April, including one of 'Jews (420-800) Theresienstadt-Neuengamme resp. Danish Border', scheduled for 9 April. And on that day there is a message from the Swedish legation in Berlin that Göring is travelling to Theresienstadt to collect all the Jews there to be taken out, probably on 12 or 13 April.[44] In the corresponding Danish primary sources, there is not a single mention of Danish plans for a Danish expedition to Theresienstadt.

We also have four memoirs by Swedish officers. Dr Arnoldsson's *Natt och dimma* (Night and Fog) contains no more than a brief reference to Theresienstadt. Lieutenant Åke Svenson, in his *De vita bussarna* (The White Buses), refers to 'the pleasing announcement that everything was now ready for the Danish Jews' and then gives a long account of the Theresienstadt transport. The leader of the

Theresienstadt expedition, Captain Harald Folke, completed his memoirs, *Officer 37*, just before his death in 1999. He wrote that it was Bernadotte himself who conceived the entire plan to remove the Scandinavian Jews from Theresienstadt, that Bernadotte's order was to begin the operation 'at once', but that the German liaision officer, Dr Rennau, delayed the operation from day to day. The commander of the detachment, Major Sven Frykman, in his book, however, tells how the white column roared along Friedrichsruh, where the Swedish minister in Berlin, Richert, was on the telephone with *UD* in Stockholm. While he is informing *UD* that the white buses have just started their journey to Theresienstadt, Richert receives an order to use all his powers to prevent this. His answer is: 'Unfortunately, I can't do that! From my window I can see the column already on its way southwards.'[45] I do not know who tried to stop the Swedish expedition. It is very unlikely that it was Bernadotte since he was not a *UD* official. In fact, on the same day Bernadotte was consoling a Danish woman, who was praying for her husband, deported to Theresienstadt:

> Yesterday evening a transport column from the Swedish Red Cross Detachment in the vicinity of Hamburg left for this camp [Theresienstadt] to take out all Danish and Norwegian internees. I do not know whether the transport column, due to the war events yesterday, actually can leave for Theresienstadt. But if this is not the case, I don't think you should worry for the fate of your husband, because I have been told in Germany that there are good prospects that Theresienstadt will be handed over intact to the Allied Military Authorities.[46]

## VI

As we have seen, the seed of Bernadotte's relief expedition was a suggestion that he provide assistance to the French women in Ravensbrück, the main female concentration camp in Germany. We have also seen that on 27 March *UD* extended Bernadotte's mandate to include the transport of some 25,000 French women, and on 21

April Himmler gave his consent to the Swedish Red Cross to transport women of all nationalities out of Ravensbrück.

The Scandinavian women in Ravensbrück had been moved by the white buses on 8 April and, via Denmark, brought directly to Sweden. Now on 21 April, after an early breakfast with Himmler, Bernadotte ordered the Swedish Red Cross detachment to deliver the women from Ravensbrück. He ordered the transport of primarily all French women, then Polish, Belgian and Dutch women. That was also the prioritisation given in his letter of the same day to the Ravensbrück camp commander.[47]

His order was the beginning of an intensive effort by the Swedish detachment, reinforced by 15 Danish ambulances and 12 trucks on loan from the International Red Cross. Between 22 and 26 April, by dramatic transports, some 3,000 women were brought from Ravensbrück to Denmark and then to safety in Sweden. Ravensbrück was situated some 80 kilometers north of Berlin. The Soviet army had now began its final offensive on the German capital, which was under heavy attack. The Soviet advance could reach Ravensbrück at any time, but their army commanders chose to complete their encirclement of Berlin and the Red Army did not reach Ravensbrück until 29 April. The transports thus succeeded in reaching Denmark through the very narrow corridor between the Soviet front in the East and the British front in the West.

The main threat to the white buses now came from the low-flying Allied aircraft, *Tiefflieger*, which, unhindered, strafed all German roads. And they, especially the British pilots, no longer respected the white buses with their red crosses and Swedish flags. Some of the convoys were attacked. The transports from Ravensbrück to Denmark cost 25 lives, according to Dr Arnoldsson. Most of the casualties were concentration camp prisoners, just liberated from the German camps but now being killed by, most probably, British aircraft. One Swedish driver was killed. The leader of this particular convoy, Lieutenant Hallqvist, still has bullets in his head and has been in continuous pain since 1945.[48]

This was to be the last effort by the white buses. On 26 April Major Frykman announced that further transports were cancelled until the Allies gave safety guarantees. Such guarantees were never given. On 28 April Bernadotte concurred. The last Swedish vehicles were ferried over from Copenhagen, among jubilant Danes, to Sweden on 1 May.

But the Swedes had quickly understood that the use of road transport alone would not suffice to remove all the women from Ravensbrück. And, to his own great surprise, Captain Folke managed to have an entire German train put at his disposal. The train, holding some 4,000 female prisoners crammed into primitive cargo wagons, left Ravensbrück on 25 April. This so-called 'ghost train' disappeared amidst the breakdown of all communications in Germany, but surfaced some three days later in Lübeck. When the frightened Dr Arnoldsson opened the locked doors on the train, he found that only two women had died and that some ten were severely ill. They were all re-loaded on to a Danish train and taken to Sweden.

Later, Count Bernadotte was also criticised for his instructions concerning the Ravensbrück expedition, implying that his order of priorities favoured the liberation of the western European women at Ravensbrück, and that he was negatively inclined to saving the Jewish females. This accusation does not hold water. After the prioritised French women (and this order of priorities was drawn up by the Swedish *UD*), came the Polish women. And Himmler made it perfectly clear that 'Polish' women included Polish Jewesses, although, still in fear of Hitler, he could not explicitly promise this. Indeed, the Red Cross Archives contain a sheet of paper on which Count Bernadotte himself has pencilled in the number of women from 'Ravensbrück and Aussenkommandos from Neuengamme', totalling '946 Poles, 254 French, 51 Belgians, 15 Dutch and 1,607 Jewesses of various nationalities'. It is likely that Bernadotte's calculation includes all 2,873 women transported from Ravensbrück by the White Buses. This figure fits in well with the statement made in 1945 by Norbert Masur, the WJC representative who met Himmler on 21 April, that the Swedish Red Cross saved some 7,000 women from Ravensbrück, roughly half of whom were Jewish.[49]

3. The formal decision (the original), signed by King Gustaf V, is in the Swedish Red Cross Archives (SRCA), 'Överstyrelsen'. For the remaining part of this resumé, unless otherwise stated, I have used the short summary *Svenska Röda Korsets detachement i Tyskland 1945. En sammanställning av Gunnar Henriksson och Lennart Jansson* (Swedish Red Cross Detachment to Germany, 1945: A Summary by G. Henriksson and L. Jansson) (Stockholm: Swedish Red Cross, 1997).

4. Koblik, *The Stones Cry Out*, p.3.

5. The document is in the SRCA, 'Överstyrelsen'. Fla. Vol. 506. Koblik, p.138, labels the figures given 'internees', which is not stated on the document.

6. Original figures in Finn Nielsen Private Papers, Vol.6, *Rigsarkivet*, Copenhagen (Danish National Archives, DRA).

7. H. Arnoldsson, *Natt och dimma* (Night and Fog) (Stockholm, 1945), p.194.

8. 'Rapport über die Arbeit innerhalb des Relief und Rehabilitation Departements', Central Zionist Archives (CZA), Jerusalem, C4/448. In an interview with this author (Stockholm, 27 July 1979), Storch claimed that between 6,500 and 7,000 Jews were evacuated to safety in Sweden before the end of the war.

9. F. Bernadotte, *Slutet: Mina humanitära förhandlingar i Tyskland våren 1945 och deras politiska följder* (The End: My Humanitarian Negotiations in Germany in Spring 1945 and Their Political Implications) (Stockholm: Norstedts, 1945), p.15. Bernadotte's book appeared in June 1945 and was serialised in the British *Daily Telegraph* newspaper. It became an international success and was translated into 18 languages (English ed.: *The Curtain Falls: Last Days of the Third Reich* (New York: Knopf, 1945)). The book made Bernadotte world famous. But it was later to bring about accusations that he had taken the credit for what others, in particular Felix Kersten, had done.

   Nordling's concrete suggestions are not referred to in Bernadotte's *Slutet* but are taken from his handwritten diary, Folke Bernadotte Private Papers, RA, Vol.2. The following 'account of Bernadotte's negotiations in Germany in 1945 is based on his reports to the UD, Folke Bernadotte Private Papers, *RA*, Vol.2: 'Dagboksanteckningar från greve Folke Bernadotte angående sammanträffanden i Berlin under tiden 16.–21. Februari 1945' (original signed in Stockholm, 23 Feb. 1945) and 'Anteckningar över vissa samtal m.m. under Greve Folke Bernadottes vistelse i Tyskland den 29. Mars – 8. April 1945' (original signed in Stockholm, 9 April 1945) and to the Swedish Red Cross, in SRCA/Överstyrelsen: 'Anteckningar över vissa samtal m.m. under Greve Folke Bernadottes vistelse i Tyskland den 17–24 April 1945' (unsigned original, Stockholm, 27 April 1945). There are small differences between Bernadotte's reports and his book.

10. Ditleff, 'Momenter til svensk aksjon for fangehjelp', Stockholm, 30 Nov. 1944 (original), RA HP 1617; *Slutet*, p.18

11. *Slutet*, pp.22–65. Interesting details in Bernadotte's diary (Folke Bernadotte Private Papers, RA, Vol.2) but omitted in *Slutet*, are remarks by Himmler and Ribbentrop concerning the bombings by the western Allies, but not the Russians, of Dresden (corroborated by Swedish eye-witnesses) and Bernadotte's vague hint to Kaltenbrunner regarding Swedish intervention in the war: 'public opinion in Sweden is incensed against Germany and this public opinion may result in Sweden not being able to remain neutral'. In *Slutet*, p.29, this is watered down to 'public opinion in Sweden is highly anti-German.'

12. There is only a brief description of this visit in *Slutet*, pp.70–82. Bernadotte's meetings with Kersten are not reported in *Slutet* but are noted in Bernadotte's private calender.

13. *Slutet*, pp.83–100. Omitted here is an interesting discussion, rendered in Bernadotte's report to *UD* on 9 April, with Himmler on 2 April concerning the military situation, in which Bernadotte asks: 'Would it not be wise to try to concentrate all defence on the eastern front to prevent the Russian offensive, soon to come, and more or less open up the western front to the western Allies?' I pointed out, once again, the meaningless sacrifice

made by thousands of Germans who were dying every day and that, in any case, one could hope that if American and English troops occupied Germany before the end of the war, this would be considerably more to the advantage of the German people than if it were Russian troops. *Himmler said yes to this but made no further comment.'*

14. *Slutet*, pp.101–33. The quotation is from *The Curtain Falls*, pp.110f.
15. H.R Trevor-Roper, 'Kersten, Himmler, and Count Bernadotte', *The Atlantic Monthly*, Vol.191, No.2 (Feb. 1953, pp.43–5), quotation from p.44.
16. F. Kersten, *The Kersten Memoirs 1940–1945* with an introduction by H.R.Trevor-Roper (London: Hutchinson, 1956), quotation from p.16.
17. *1945 års svenska hjälpexpedition till Tyskland. Förspel och förhandlingar* (The Swedish Relief Expedition to Germany in 1945: Prelude and Negotiations) (Stockholm: Aktstycken utgivna av Kungl.Utrikesdepartementet. Ny serie II:8, 1956), quotation from p.38.
18. Diary notes, Folke Bernadotte Private Papers, Vol.2, *RA*; letter from L. Zelmanovits to F. Bernadotte, London, 9 Nov. 1944 and Bernadotte's reply, 9 Feb. 1945, both copies in RA/SRCA/FBA, Vol.9.
19. M. Nathanson, telephone conversation with author, Stockholm, 8 Nov. 2000. The Marcus Ehrenpreis Private Papers at *RA* contain nothing of interest related to this question. His daughter has told me that Marcus Ehrenpreis was a very sick man by 1945, operated on for cancer, with diabetes, almost blind and senile. And in 1945 Ehrenpreis was fighting on two fronts: against the Swedish authorities and against the two chairmen of the Jewish congregation in Stockholm, who were both against increased immigration of Jews to Sweden.
20. Hillel Storch, interview with author, Stockholm, 27 July 1979.
21. Bernadotte's private calendar, SRCA, notes meetings on 25 Nov. 1944, 4 March 1945 and 11 April 1945.
22. Letter from L. Zelmanovits to H. Storch, London 23 Jan. 1945, original in CZA, C4/588.
23. Letter from F. Bernadotte to H. Storch, Stockholm, 26 Feb. 1945, copy in Storch's Private Archives, given to me in 1979.
24. Telegram, A. Richert to *UD*, Alt-Döbern, 13 Feb. 1945, original in *RA*, HP 1050.
25. Letter from E. von Post to A. Richert, Stockholm, 12 March 1945, copy in *RA*, HP 192.
26. Letter from H. Storch to F. Bernadotte, Stockholm, 4 March 1945, copy in Storch's Private Archives, given to me in 1979.
27. Report by F. Bernadotte to Board of Swedish Red Cross, Berlin, 15 March 1945, forwarded to *UD*, original in *RA*, HP 1618.
28. 'P.M. angående samtal med Göring den 8 mars.' M. Giron, Berlin, 10 March 1945, original in *RA*, HP 214.
29. 'P.M. angående samtal Bernadotte-Minister Mohr-avdelningschef Hvass-Brandel-Giron-Hultgren.' T. B[randel], Berlin, 6 March 1945, copy in *RA*, HP 1618.
30. 'P.M. angående greve Bernadottes samtal med de norska representanterna den 7 mars 1945', T. B[randel], Berlin, 7 March 1945, copy in *RA*, HP 1618.
31. C. O. Mohr to *Berlingske Tidende*, 28 March 1946, C. O. Mohr Private Papers, Vol.B2 (copy). Mohr no doubt relied on the infamous report by Dr Henningsen and Hvass on their visit to Theresienstadt on 22 June 1944. There is very little on the Jews in C. O. Mohr's annotations 'efter Anmodning av Christmas Möller, i Berlin', last part of 1945' and his 'Samtaler med Greve Bernadotte om Hjemsendelsen af de danske Politifolk', July 1946, both copies in C. O Mohr Private Papers, Vol.C:1 and B:2; and in Hvass's reports on discussion on 8 March between Count Bernadotte, Minister Mohr and Hvass, Berlin, 10 March 1945, and discussions on 8 March between Minister Mohr, Obergruppenführer Kaltenbrunner, Secretary of State Baron von Steengracht, Under-Secretary of State Hencke, Legation Councillor Steensen-Leth and Hvass, Berlin, 12 March 1945, both copies at Danish Udenrigsministerium 84.G.5, Vol.390a. All these files are at DRA. I

have, unfortunately, found no Danish records of the 6 March 1945 meeting.

32. 'P.M. angående lunchsamtal greve Bernadotte-Kaltenbrunner den 7 mars 1945', T. Brandel, Berlin, 7 March 1945, copy in *RA*, HP 1618.

33. 'Orientering given av Greve Bernadotte den 20/3 rörande detachementets 'fortsatta verksamhet', original at SRCA, Överstyrelsen', Fla. Vol.506.

34. Telegram, F. Bernadotte to Berlin Legation, Stockholm, 24 March 1945, original in *RA* HP 1618.

35. P.M., signed v. Post, Stockholm 27 March 1945, original in *RA* HP 1619 (emphasis added). I have used the English translation in Koblik, *The Stones Cry Out*, p.284, with some modifications closer to the Swedish text. The document was handed over in 1955 to Trevor-Roper who did not understand, or wish to understand, its importance.

36. Letter from A. Richert to E. von Post, Schönhausen, 22 March 1945, copy in *RA* HP 1619; Koblik, *The Stones Cry Out*, p.280f.

37. Cable from H. Storch to Stetinius for Rabbi Weiss Goldmann Tartakower [*sic*], Stockholm, 27 March 1945, copy in *RA* HP 1051, also reproduced by Koblik, 283f. Kersten, in his letter to Storch, Stockholm, 27 March 1945 is, however, more modest: 'die Befreiung von *etwa 5000 Juden* und ihre Freilassung nach Schweden und in die Schweiz zugesichert worden ist; ich glaube jedoch, das es uns bei unserer mündlinchen Verhandlung mit Himmler möglich sein wird, diese Zahl zu verdoppeln' (emphasis added); original in CZA, C4/483. Copies of Himmler's and his adjutant Brandt's letters to Kersten (unsigned), Berlin, 21 and 20 March 1945, containing lists of names, are in *RA* HP 1618, with a pencilled note that these copies were handed over by Kersten to *UD* on 23 March and seen by Günther; also in Koblik, *The Stones Cry Out*, p.279f.

38. Letter from F. Kersten to H. Storch, Stockholm, 29 March 1945, original at CZA, C4/483.

39. K. Ottosen, *I slik en natt. Historien om deportasjonen av jöder fra Norge* (On Such a Night: The Deportation of Jews from Norway) (Oslo: Aschehoug,1994; with list of names) and K. Ottosen, *Redningen. Veien ut av fangenskapet våren 1945* (The Rescue: The Way Out of Imprisonment, Spring 1945) (Oslo: Aschehoug, 1998), pp.241–50, 'Bernadotte and the Jews'.

40. Letter from H. Storch to F. Bernadotte, Stockholm, 11 April 1945; letter from F. Bernadotte to H. Storch, Stockholm, 17 April 1945; letter from R. Brandt to Herr Kersten, Berlin, 8 April 1945 (note the vague wordings in the letter and the fact that it was addressed to Kersten); all copies from Storch's Private Archives, given to me in 1979. In another copy, at CZA, C4/551, Storch has written in pencil in Swedish: 'this letter has been received from Count Bernadotte following the Count's intervention.'

41. F. Göring, 'Auszug aus meinem Tagebuch über die Befreiung von Menschen aus der deutschen Konzentrationsläger', typewritten original at CZA, C4/495, probably written in Sweden, May–June 1945.

42. J. Holm, *Sandheden om de hvide busser* (Copenhagen: Samleren, 1984), pp.112–31, esp. p.114.

43. J. Holm, 'Theresienstadt' (copy), in Finn Nielsen Private Papers, Vol.11, DRA.

44. 'P.M. Telefonmeddelande från kapten Folke den 7 april 1945' and 'P.M. Telefonmeddelande från legationssekreterare Brandel i Berlin den 9 april 1945', both copies in *RA/UDA*, HP 1619; 'TP att utföra', SRCA, 'Överstyrelsen'. F1a. Vol.506.

45. Arnoldsson, p.121; Å. Svenson, *De vita bussarna* (The White Buses) (Stockholm: Bonniers, 1945), p.82; H. Folke, 'Officer 37: Memoirs by Colonel Harald Folke', p.33, unpublished manuscript in English, sent to me in Oct. 1999; S. Frykman, *Rödakorsexpeditionen till Tyskland* (The Red Cross Expedition to Germany) (Stockholm: Bonniers, 1945), p.102.

46. Letter from F. Bernadotte af Wisborg to L. Majin, Stockholm, 12 April 1945, copy in *RA/SRCA/FBA*, Vol.6.

47. Telephone message from F. Bernadotte to *UD*, Stockholm, 21 April 1945, copy in *RA*, HP 1619; letter F. Bernadotte an den Herrn Lagerkommandant des K.L. Ravensbrück,

Schloss Friedrichsruh 21 April 1945, copy in *SRCA*, file 'Folke B[ernadotte] Felix K[ersten] and Trevor-Roper: 'zuerst sämtliche französische Frauen ... nachdem ... die Polinnen, Holländerinnen und Belgierinnen auf gleichem Fusse'.

48. Arnoldsson, p.137. The figures given in other sources differ slightly.
49. Bernadotte's calculation is in *RA/SRCA/FBA*, Vol.2; Masur's is in N. Masur, *En jude talar med Himmler* (A Jew Speaks with Himmler) (Stockholm: Bonniers, 1945), p.34.
50. *UD* White Book 1956, p.27.
51. This passage is not included in Bernadotte's report of 23 Feb, as given in note 9 above. It was obviously added to *Slutet* later and in the wrong context.
52. *UD* White Book, p.30.
53. E. Boheman: 'Bernadotte was as eager as anyone to save Jews', letter to Counsellor Kromnow, *UD*, Washington, 2 March 1953; T. Brandel: 'no discrimination made between Jews and non-Jews', PM, 6 September 1984; L. Nylander: 'not true ... Bernadotte often expressed the hope of extending the relief expedition ... to non-Scandinavians, irrespective of race', *UD* White Book, p.36; H. Arnoldsson: 'absurd thought ... never a question of nation or race', *Aftontidningen*, 26 Jan. 1954; S. Åström: 'a lie', telephone conversation with this author, 25 Jan. 2000; H. Storch: 'the rescue of Danish Jews in 1945 was carried out by Count Bernadotte alone', letter to Chief Rabbi Bent Melchior in Copenhagen, 14 Oct. 1970; H. Cappelan: 'the position of the Jews was the subject of special anxiety for Bernadotte', *Verdens Gang*, 27 Jan. 1953; I.E. Elliot, quoting official Danish memorandum of 22 March 1945: 'Count Bernadotte ... intervened with ... Obergruppenführer Kaltenbrunner and won his agreement that Jews and policemen should be included in the transports', *Svenska Dagbladet*, 9 Feb. 1999.

# Conclusion

## DAVID CESARANI and PAUL A. LEVINE

This volume of essays has attempted to show that the category of 'bystanders' cannot be used in a uniform or unproblematic sense to describe the response of the democratic nations, their citizens, or the agencies which they sponsored and to which they played host during the persecution and mass murder of the Jews between 1933 and 1945. The essays demonstrate that for analytical purposes the governments and peoples of the democracies cannot be lumped together with the Third Reich, its allies, client states, or those of the countries it occupied. Despite the evidence of official complicity in Nazi economics and in some cases shared hostility towards Jewish refugees, the policy-makers in the neutral states operated within a different political and ideological framework and displayed significant shifts as overall relations with Germany changed. Radically different structural conditions, if nothing else, demand a more nuanced analysis.

These essays also demonstrate that the dissection of responses cannot be reduced to the dichotomy of rescue as against indifference or antisemitism versus philo-semitism. As Tony Kushner shows, ambivalence was more prevalent that any simplistic polarity. The example of Gösta Engzell, explored by Paul Levine, shows how one influential figure could move from one position to another on the basis of shifting personal attitudes in combination with larger, objective considerations. Nor can neutrality any longer be treated as a monolithic and static notion. Jacques Picard establishes that in the case of Switzerland it was always a fluid, relational concept in practice if not in theory. Sven Nordlund and Karin Kvist illustrate that in Sweden, also, treatment of both native and refugee Jews was influenced by that country's theory and practice of 'neutrality'.

Each contributor to this book delineates a spectrum of responses to the crisis that befell the European Jews. Such responses were influenced by and calibrated to the extent of information, what action was possible in a democracy at any particular moment, and the general political conditions in peace as well as wartime. Proximity, knowledge, and the will to act were no guarantee of success. Raya Cohen and Meredith Hindley explain that rescue and relief activists could be tragically thwarted in 'neutral' Switzerland as much as in belligerent America. Proof that impediments were not specifically placed in the way of aid for the Jews, although there were important and unique obstacles in this case, comes from the evidence that Jews were not the only victims of the paralysis which modern warfare imposed on the humanitarian conscience.

Personal courage and elusive psychological factors played their part in forging 'rescuers'. David Cesarani describes the particular qualities needed by activists in democratic countries, in many ways quite different from the attributes necessary to be a rescuer in Nazi-occupied Europe. Sune Persson's study of Folke Bernadotte's mission blends the elements of individual bravery and political choice that turned rescue from an idea into a reality. All these cases suggest that it is necessary to look beyond such over-exposed figures as Raoul Wallenberg in order to appreciate the complexity of the democratic rescuer. This is all the more imperative since genocide, the forced displacement of populations, the mass abuse of human rights, and vast refugee movements have all marked the birth of the twenty-first century and show no sign of fading. It is more important than ever to understand how the democratic process, the media, and international agencies assist or frustrate the efforts of individuals and groups who wish to assist the persecuted and the uprooted.

The persistence of analogous situations to those occurring in the 1930s and 1940s and the eruption of controversies based on newly disclosed documentation persuaded the editors of this volume that the reevaluation of the 'bystanders' could not end with the democracies – Britain, America, Switzerland, Sweden, and the Jews. They decided to extend the ambit of the research project to encompass the response of non-democratic countries that were non-belligerent or neutral as well as a variety of international agencies and movements. It was also realised that much more comparative work was required to compare how the democracies responded. Thanks to generous support from the Arts and Humanities Research Board in Britain, the Swedish government and the University of Uppsala Programme for Holocaust and Genocide Studies, and the newly created Danish Centre for Holocaust and Genocide Studies, the project will be extended over the next four years and will embrace Catholic and authoritarian neutral or non-belligerent states, non-democratic states with international connections, and international agencies and movements. It will use a comparative analysis to explain how diverse political cultures respond in the face of massive human-rights abuses and genocide against a minority.

Over the next four years the project will evolve through four successive phases involving further colloquia and publications. The next phase will include research into Spain, Portugal, the Vatican, Mexico, Argentina and other countries in Latin America. It will be followed by work on the Soviet Union, the International Communist movement, Turkey, the Islamic world, China and Japan. Finally, the project intends to stimulate comparative work on the League of Nations, the Intergovernmental Committee on Refugees, the Red Cross, and international responses to the refugee crisis 1933–39. Further information will be posted on the websites of the Parkes Centre for the Study of Jewish/non-Jewish relations and the Uppsala Programme for Holocaust and Genocide Studies. The organisers of this project will welcome contributions and constructive comment from researchers around the world.

# Abstracts

## Mad Dogs and Englishmen: Toward a Taxonomy of Rescuers in a 'Bystander' Country – Britain 1933–45 *by David Cesarani*

In recent years, a variety of studies have begun to discuss those people who attempted to rescue Jews from the Nazis and their accomplices, focusing on the activity of rescuers in Nazi Germany and wartime Europe. Comparatively little notice has been taken of rescuers who operated from so-called 'bystander' countries, geographically removed from the Third Reich. This article considers the difficulties and dilemmas of rescue work carried out in a liberal democracy. It examines 12 leading, non-Jewish refugee activists working in Britain between 1933 and 1945, and attempts to explain their awareness of the Jewish emergency and their motives for acting in response to it. This article concludes, by creating a taxonomy of rescuers, that the only experiences uniting the sample of 12 are their cosmopolitanism and sense of personal responsibility.

## 'Pissing in the Wind'? The Search for Nuance in the Study of Holocaust 'Bystanders' *by Tony Kushner*

After an initial silence which lasted until the 1960s, subsequent historiography on the subject of the liberal democracies/western Allies and the Holocaust has tended to be deeply polarised between apologetic and accusatory camps. This article teases out the ideological and cultural underpinnings of the divided literature and makes a plea for more wide-ranging, contextualised and ultimately more nuanced research on this emotive but important aspect of Holocaust bystander studies.

## Constructing Allied Humanitarian Policy *by Meredith Hindley*

The article explores the question of whether humanitarian intervention was compatible with Allied strategy during the Second

World War by comparing the response of the Allies to the Holocaust and the European hunger crisis. Intervening in both crises required the Allies to take action in Nazi-occupied territories and to aid civilians by either sponsoring or permitting others to operate rescue and relief programmes. This article reconstructs Allied humanitarian policy by examining the conditions that generated Allied policies, their effects, and the ability of public opinion to change policymakers' minds. A comparison of the two crises reveals a fundamental contradiction between strategies developed to pursue victory, specifically economic warfare, and the imperative of humanitarian intervention.

## Switzerland, National Socialist Policy, and the Legacy of History *by Jacques Picard*

This article addresses, on the one hand, the relationship between National Socialism's foreign and economic policies, and on the other, Swiss models of behaviour in dealing with Nazi Germany. It also examines post-war explanations of this period in Swiss memory and historiography. The first part of the article recapitulates some aspects of National Socialist policy and economic ideology, in particular the project of a 'Germanised' Europe and a racial 'Greater Germany'. Antisemitism is an important factor in this context. The second part of the article then considers three features of the Swiss state of affairs in terms of how the National Socialist ideology of *Lebensraum* was perceived: military matters, economic issues and attitudes towards refugees. What emerges is that the state of knowledge concerning these three features varies greatly. Furthermore, after the war, the bearers of responsibility in Switzerland found themselves confronted by the Swiss relationship to National Socialist crimes, the nature of which was a question not only of politics, but also of such values as human rights.

## The Lost Honour of the Bystanders? The Case of Jewish Emissaries in Switzerland *by Raya Cohen*

The prevailing emphasis placed by the historiography of the bystanders to the Holocaust on the cognitive aspect of internalizing an unprecedented truth, and the exclusive emphasis placed on the rescue of life, tends to reflect the point of view of the heirs of both victors and survivors, but not necessarily the point of view of those who were 'drowned'. Through the example of Jewish emissaries stationed in Switzerland I would like to suggest a different view of bystanders, one modelled by those who have engaged themselves to help the Jews of Europe during the war at the time when most of the European Jewry was still alive. Those bystanders, many of whom worked against the orders of their superiors, represent a different model of bystander, rooted in both, the model link then existing between morals and politics and the desperate cries of the victims whom they were willing to hear.

## 'The War is Over – Now You Can Go Home!' Jewish Refugees and the Swedish Labour Market in the Shadow of the Holocaust *by Sven Nordlund*

How many Jewish refugees entered Sweden in the late 1930s and what happened to them? What were their experiences of the Swedish labour market? What kind of reactions did the refugees encounter and provoke in Sweden? How did the Swedish economy and authorities react to the process of 'aryanisation'? These are some of the questions addressed in this article, which also considers why the Swedes have taken so long to begin discussing their bystander role, behaviour and attitudes towards the Jewish refugees from Nazi Germany in the 1930s and the beginning of the Second World War.

## A Study of Antisemitic Attitudes within Sweden's Wartime *Utlänningsbyrån by Karin Kvist*

This article examines antisemitic attitudes within Sweden's wartime *Utlänningsbyrån* (Foreigners' Bureau). The Bureau was important in determining Sweden's response to Jews seeking refuge, and a closer examination of attitudes prevailing within the *Utlänningsbyrån* therefore helps to address the significance of antisemitic attitudes in determining the nation's response to Nazi German policy. In common with all other countries, Sweden's response passed through several phases and, as analysed elsewhere, Sweden's general response to the plight of the Jews changed only in the autumn of 1942, when the 'Final Solution' reached Norway. The *Utlänningsbyrån's* response during these years was influenced by a several different, even ambivalent factors, but there seems little doubt that, throughout the 1930s, antisemitic attitudes informed the decisions of some officials.

## Attitudes and Action: Comparing the Responses of Mid-Level Bureaucrats to the Holocaust *by Paul A. Levine*

This article explores the 'bystander' in Holocaust history by comparing the response to the genocide of the Jews from three countries ordinarily grouped together in that category of Holocaust historiography: the United States, Great Britain and Sweden. The first two were of course warring belligerents while Sweden was *de jure*, if not *de facto*, neutral during the Second World War. The article compares not the top leadership of the three nations, but rather sub-Cabinet level officials serving in the respective foreign ministries. This emphasis is justified, as is the comparative point of departure, because existing scholarship demonstrates that in these countries much of the response to Germany's persecution and extermination of European Jewry was formulated at that level, and then implemented.

Emphasis is placed on detailing Sweden's response because its case is far less well known than that of the other two. Among the questions explored is how, when and why a policy response so similar in those countries through many of the Nazi years then diverged. Both the practical and moral importance of conscious choices made by the officials involved, from what is generally thought to be the 'bystander' position, is also explored.

## Folke Bernadotte and the White Buses *by Sune Persson*

The Swedish Red Cross expedition to the German concentration camps in March-April 1945 was the largest rescue effort inside Germany during World War II. By a conservative estimate, over 17,000 prisoners were transported via Denmark to Sweden up until 4 May 1945. This expedition, though formally a Red Cross detachment led by Count Folke Bernadotte af Wisborg, Vice-President of the Swedish Red Cross, was in reality a Swedish Army detachment whose costs were covered by the Swedish Government. All vehicles were painted white so that they should be easily distinguishable from German vehicles, especially from the air, and so are known as 'the White Buses'.

Count Bernadotte arrived in Berlin on 16 February 1945, for political negotiations that included four meetings with Heinrich Himmler. Bernadotte's original instructions had been to intervene for *Scandinavian* prisoners in Germany, and one controversy about his mission has been his relations *to the Jews*. But on 26 March Bernadotte received new instructions from the Swedish Foreign Office, extending his mandate to non-Scandinavians and to 'the transfer to Sweden of a number of Jews'. On 21 April, Himmler also gave his consent to the Swedish Red Cross to transport *women of all nationalities* out of Ravensbrück camp. Some 3,000 women were brought out from Ravensbrück by the white buses, and, with an entire German train made available, some 4,000 more female prisoners were transported from Ravensbrück to Denmark and onwards to Sweden.

The accusations against Bernadotte to the effect that he refused to save Jews from the concentration camps are obvious lies. *Roughly half of the 7,000 women saved from Ravensbrück seem to have been Jewish.* Hillel Storch, the World Jewish Congress representative in Stockholm, estimated that the *Swedish Red Cross saved at least 5,000 Jews before the end of the war.*

# Notes on Contributors

DAVID CESARANI is professor of modern Jewish history and Director of the AHRB Centre for the Study of Jewish/non-Jewish Relations at the University of Southampton. His publications include *Arthur Koestler: The Homeless Mind* (1998) and, as editor, *Genocide and Rescue: The Holocaust in Hungary 1944* (1997) and *The Final Solution: Origins and Implementation (1994)*.

PAUL A. LEVINE is assistant professor of history at Uppsala University's Programme for Holocaust and Genocide Studies. Author of *From Indifference to Activism: Swedish Diplomacy and the Holocaust, 1938–1944* (Uppsala, 1998), his latest work is the article 'Swedish Neutrality during the Second World War; Tactical Success or Moral Failure?', in *European Neutrals and Non-Belligerents during the Second World War* (Cambridge UP, 2001).

TONY KUSHNER is Marcus Sieff Professor in the Department of History and Head of the Parkes Institute for the Study of Jewish/non-Jewish relations at the University of Southampton. His most recent book, co-authored with Katharine Knox, is *Refugees in an Age of Genocide: Global, National and Local Perspectives During the Twentieth Century* (Frank Cass, 1999).

MEREDITH HINDLEY is a PhD candidate in Modern European History at American University in Washington, DC. She has published articles on the Holocaust and intelligence in the journals *Intelligence and National Security* and *Holocaust and Genocide Studies*.

JACQUES PICARD is professor of Modern Jewish History and Culture at the University of Basel, and currently director of the Institute for Jewish Studies. His most recent work is the article 'Switzerland as a Bystander of History? On Neutrality in a Time of

Global Crisis and in an Age of Genocidal Wars', in *Remembering for the Future; The Holocaust in an Age of Genocide* (London/New York, 2001).

RAYA COHEN is currently Senior Lecturer at the Department of Jewish History, Tel Aviv University. Her most recent publication is *Between 'there' and 'here': Stories of Witness to Destruction; Jewish Emissaries in Switzerland* (Tel Aviv, 1999).

SVEN NORDLUND is Associate Professor at the Department of Economic History, Umeå University. His most recent work is the article 'Independent Markets or Baltic Provinces? Swedish Images and Attitudes to the Baltic States during the Interwar Period' in *Time of Change in the Baltic Countries; Essays in Honour of Aleksander Loit* (Stockholm, 2000).

KARIN KVIST is Master of Arts in History, Stockholm University, where she completed her study *Svensk flyktingpolitik under andra världskriget; En undersökning av Utlänningsbyråns respons på Förintelsen, 1938- 1944* (Swedish Refugee policy during the Second World War; A study of the 'Foreigners Bureau' and its response to the Holocaust, 1938–1944).

SUNE PERSSON is Senior Lecturer and Associate Professor at the Department of Political Science, University of Göteborg. His book *Palestina konflikten* is in its 5th edition, and his most recent work is the forthcoming (in Swedish) *White Buses in the Heart of Darkness*.

# Index

# Books of Related Interest

# In Search of Refuge
*Jews and US Consuls in Nazi Germany 1933–1941*

## Bat-Ami Zucker

US Consuls played a distinctive and crucial role in control of Jewish refugee entry to the United States between 1933-1941. The consuls decided individual cases and in doing so had discretion to grant immigration visas. This extended to interpreting aspects of the immigration laws and regulations which were not fully defined, notably the 'likely to become a public charge' clause.

*In Search of Refuge: Jews and US Consuls in Nazi Germany 1933-1941* examines how the consuls perceived, interpreted and administered immigration policy towards the refugees. The book explores the relationship of consuls with the State Department, giving examples of initiatives by consuls; instances of prejudice and showing methods by which consuls obstructed entry of refugees in ways which went beyond instructions and even defeated the object of instructions. However, it also examines some cases of consular initiatives to offer aid, such as by issuing protective letters.

The book indicates that, overall, American consuls in Germany adopted a restrictive policy in both the interpretation and administration of the laws in order to delay and deny visas – especially visas sought by refugee Jews. Further, *In Search of Refuge* shows that, given the strict US immigration and anti-refugee policy as well as the general anti-alien and anti-Semitic atmosphere in the United States during these years, a large part of the responsibility for these actions was due to consular anti-Semitism, both overt and latent.

248 pages  2001
0 85303 400 1 cloth
*Parkes-Wiener Series on Jewish Studies*
*Vallentine Mitchell*

**FRANK CASS PUBLISHERS**
Crown House, 47 Chase Side, Southgate, London N14 5BP
Tel: +44 (0)20 8920 2100  Fax: +44 (0)20 8447 8548  E-mail: info@frankcass.com
**NORTH AMERICA**
5824 NE Hassalo Street, Portland, OR 97213 3644, USA
Tel: 800 944 6190  Fax: 503 280 8832  E-mail: cass@isbs.com
**Website:** www.frankcass.com

# Switzerland and the Second World War

## Georg Kreis
## With a Foreword by David Cesarani

This wide–ranging collection of essays sheds important light on key aspects of the history of Switzerland during the Second World War, dealing with such important topics as trade, financial relations, gold, refugees, defence and foreign relations. It also touches on official post-war measures to suppress the problematic aspects of Switzerland's involvement in the war. Switzerland and the Second World War is a major scholarly contribution to the debate that has raged since 1996 over the 'dormant accounts' of Holocaust victims still held by Swiss banks. This issue quickly pushed Switzerland to the top of the political agenda and rapidly spread to include questions of fugitive Nazi funds and the gold trade between the Swiss National Bank and the German Reichsbank. As the controversy grew, further questions – concerning art dealing, insurance companies, participation in the 'Aryanisation' of Jewish companies in Germany, slave labour, etc. – began to cast their shadows.
A number of the above questions have long been topics of Swiss historical research; others have been tackled only recently in the wake of current discussion. The present compendium offers insight into the latest scholarly findings and provides an overview of the relevant literature. Each of the 16 contributors is an authority in their field, and together they provide a comprehensive survey of historiographical development over the past five decades, as well as indicating perspectives for future research. Already published in a French/German edition, this is the first academic work in English to tackle these subjects in this manner and it will certainly become a standard reference work.

384 pages 2000
0 7146 5029 3 cloth

**FRANK CASS PUBLISHERS**
Crown House, 47 Chase Side, Southgate, London N14 5BP
Tel: +44 (0)20 8920 2100  Fax: +44 (0)20 8447 8548  E-mail: info@frankcass.com
**NORTH AMERICA**
5824 NE Hassalo Street, Portland, OR 97213 3644, USA
Tel: 800 944 6190  Fax: 503 280 8832  E-mail: cass@isbs.com
**Website:** www.frankcass.com